Wayward Shamans

Wayward Shamans

The Prehistory of an Idea

Silvia Tomášková

UNIVERSITY OF CALIFORNIA PRESS
Berkeley · *Los Angeles* · *London*

University of California Press, one of the most distinguished university presses in the United States, enriches
lives around the world by advancing scholarship in the
humanities, social sciences, and natural sciences. Its
activities are supported by the UC Press Foundation and
by philanthropic contributions from individuals and
institutions. For more information, visit www.ucpress.edu.

University of California Press
Berkeley and Los Angeles, California

University of California Press, Ltd.
London, England

Library of Congress Cataloging-in-Publication Data

Tomášková, Silvia.
   Wayward shamans : the prehistory of an idea / Silvia
Tomášková.
       pages : illustrations, maps ; cm
   Includes bibliographical references.
   ISBN 978-0-520-27531-7 (hardcover : alkaline
paper) — ISBN 978-0-520-27532-4 (paperback :
alkaline paper)
    1. Shamans—Russia (Federation)—Siberia.
2. Shamanism—Russia (Federation)—Siberia.
3. Siberia (Russia)—Religious life and customs.
4. Siberia (Russia)—Civilization.   5. Siberia
(Russia)—Colonization.   I. Title.
  GN475.8.T66 2013
   201'.44—dc23

                                    2012047119

Manufactured in the United States of America
22 21 20 19 18 17 16 15 14 13
10 9 8 7 6 5 4 3 2 1

To my parents, Eva Tomášková and Jaroslav Tomášek (in memoriam), who came to accept this wayward spirit.

Contents

Illustrations

Acknowledgments

The distance between an idea and the final book is always substantial. But the time this project took was much longer than usual as I kept uncovering new layers, new connections, new sources, and new ideas. I followed many of them much farther than anyone else would (or should). I am grateful to many institutions and individuals who provided support along the way. Several foundations and financial sources generously supported the research and writing that helped to complete this project. The Spray-Randleigh fellowship at the University of North Carolina enabled my research in Siberia, France, and Germany in 2004 and 2005. The American Council for Learned Societies awarded me the Ryskamp Fellowship in 2005–2006, the School for Advanced Research in the Human Experience in Santa Fe provided a residential fellowship in 2007–2008, and the Andrew W. Mellon Foundation made my stay in South Africa possible in 2010–2011. Aside from the essential financial resources, these foundations gave me the confidence that my idea was of interest and worth pursuing. Most valuable though were the prolonged periods of uninterrupted time to work on the project.

While I was conducting research in Akademgorodok, outside Novosibirsk, the librarian Tatiana Sergeevna eyed me suspiciously at first, waiting for my departure. Once it became clear that I was not going away, could speak Russian, and would gladly discuss politics, she brought out materials not in the catalogue, dusted off old files, and pointed me to books that turned out to be invaluable. The many cups of tea in between were as kind a gesture as all the materials. The staff at the Bibliothèque at the National Museum of Archaeology in Saint-Germain-en-Laye in France deserves mention as well for facilitating access to all the boxes of personal correspondence between Cartailhac, Breuil, Reinach, and de Mortillet (even if his handwriting was truly illegible). The employees at the Bayerische Staatsbibliothek (Bavarian State Library) in Munich provided me with archival materials and access to specialized copying technology that I did not even know existed. My research in Munich was greatly accelerated by Eva Tomášková's expert translation of old German script. The special collections staff at the American Museum of Natural History in New York generously assisted my foray through photographs and personal correspondence from the Jesup North Pacific Expedition. Kristen Mable and Barbara Mathe in particular arranged for all the proper permissions and access. Andrea Felder at the New York Public Library helped with my requests for images with amazing speed and understanding. Lisa Viezbicke from Morse Library, Beloit College, Wisconsin kindly assisted with images from the Nuremberg Chronicle. Laurie Klein of Beinecke Rare Books and Manuscripts Library at Yale University provided the requested images from their collection; staff at the Houghton Library and the Map Library at Harvard University assisted with my numerous requests for images and reproductions. Kyril Tolpygo, the Slavic collections librarian at the University of Chapel Hill, tracked down, pursued, and obtained the Northern Lights Route map from Tromso University Library when I was ready to give up. His perseverance is greatly appreciated. John Robb at Cambridge University generously offered an image from his own project when I could not locate a particular reproduction. Thank you.

Stan Holwitz of the University of California Press encouraged this project from its inception, seeing in it a story worth pursuing even if it was then just an idea. When Blake Edgar and subsequently Reed Malcolm agreed to take the book over, many years later, it was a leap of faith only a few would make. I truly appreciate the trust.

Meg Conkey has been the most ardent supporter from my first year in graduate school. I will always be grateful for her constant encouragement ever since. Prehistoric art was not a research topic that I intended to pursue, but the intellectual challenge of the history of ideas led me to it despite my initial resistance. I hope that with this book I have made a contribution to the conversation Meg started, as a passionate and determined feminist scholar. Françoise Audouze was the first French archaeologist I ever met, and she set the bar high. Her kindness and mocking observations remained a cherished gift throughout this effort. Michael Bisson has been a steadfast academic mentor and a friend much longer than anyone else, and patiently endured many permutations of this book. While many people engaged my ideas in conversations over the years, the Centennial Class at the School for Advanced Research in Human Experience (SAR) in Santa Fe in 2007–2008 was a group who became family and true intellectual companions. Tutu Alicante, Omri Elisha, Joe Gone, Tiya Miles, Malena Morling, Monica Smith, James Snead, and Angela Steusse contributed to this book in so many intangible and personal ways. James Snead, in particular, shared my passion for the history of archaeology and willingness to pursue every tangential issue. Our group could only come together due to the nurturing atmosphere created by all the people at SAR, ably led by James Brooks and John Kantner, and nourished by Leslie Shipman.

In South Africa, I have benefitted from the support of the Department of Archaeology at the University of Cape Town. Judy Sealy and John Parkington in particular were welcoming and generous with their time. Sven Ouzman offered valuable suggestions and challenged my ideas, thereby helping with clarity when making connections between arguments. Ben Smith invited me to give a talk at the Rock Art Research Institute at Witwatersrand University in Johannesburg. I am grateful to him for the kindness with which he treated someone whom he had never met before. The South African Archaeological Society, and especially Yvonne Viljoen, invited me on a research trip that proved a wonderful introduction to South African rock art. Richard Foden generously gave me all his pictures when my camera failed, not to mention letting me drive his jeep through the snow of the Drakensberg Mountains. I met a number of truly impressive women in South Africa to whom I am grateful just for the acquaintance, their generosity and kindness. Denise Murray turned her house in Cape Town into our temporary home, and Brigitte Hall in Morija, Lesotho provided a few brief but memorable days. Our South African life would have been very different had we not reconnected with Justin Hyland and Margot Winer. What a gift!

The material in this book has been presented in numerous talks, and the response of the various audiences has helped improve the argument and the clarity. I offered a first sketch at a symposium honoring Bruce Trigger at the Society of American Archaeology meetings in Montreal in 2004. Bruce's kind comments and support in subsequent years were a major influence in my interest in the history of ideas in archaeology. My faculty colleagues and students in the Department of Anthropology, and the Department of Women's and Gender Studies at the University of North Carolina at Chapel Hill generously listened to presentations of chapters from the book. I received valuable feedback during talks in the Department of Archaeology at the University of Cape Town, the Rock Art Research Institute at Witwatersrand University, the Archaeology of Gender in Europe meeting in Oslo, Norway, and during the South African Archaeological Society speaker series.

Whenever I was ready to toss in the towel and thought this project has grown insanely complicated, Peter Redfield pulled me through, reminding me of my own main points and English grammar. This book truly would not exist without his support. Zoë Sofia has been my travelling co-spirit for more than sixteen years, a time I have cherished no matter where we found ourselves. Anyone who had anything to say about the manuscript or the ideas within bears no responsibility for the final execution: all statements, controversial or not, are my own.

Introduction

"Why are shamans so popular?" a team of art historians asked recently, in a somewhat exasperated tone. They were attempting to counter the rise of shamanic interpretations in Mesoamerican prehistoric art, part of a common, widespread trend.[1] In offering accounts of the origins of the human capacity for art, religion, and even science, archaeologists regularly cast shamans as the stars of their scenarios. By the early twenty-first century, tales of powerful prehistoric sorcerers have grown familiar to both scholars and popular audiences alike. The term *shaman* appears regularly in reference to ancient and indigenous forms of knowledge to describe a ritual specialist, a categorical figure imbued with wisdom. Shamans now walk through the pages of academic journals, tourist guide-books, and New Age stores. They perform rituals, promise wisdom, and promote products. They also provide a ready answer to the question of who made the first art and what inspired them.

If newly popular, this story itself is hardly new. Rather, shamans have traveled with us for well over three centuries since emerging from Siberia. Over the years, they have played a range of roles, depending on the setting in which they were imagined. Proto-priests, religious leaders, artists, and medicine men, shamans remain ever mysterious, however instinctively familiar. In archaeology, they have primarily appeared as male figures, less by conscious design than unthinking assumption. Yet even after the rise of New Age perspectives in North America and Western

Europe that emphasize feminine spirituality, the shamans projected into prehistory continue to be a largely male crew.

Trained as an archaeological specialist in Paleolithic Europe and teaching partly in women's and gender studies, I had long been wary of the manner in which we casually project gender back into time. How well, I wondered, did this vision of shamans fit the evidence? Given that the material traces of prehistory offered few certain clues about social life, let alone gender, history seemed the obvious place to turn. What was the story behind this anthropological category? Where had the term "shaman" come from, before its popularity in both archaeology and drumming circles? How might it have changed along the way? The answer, I would discover repeatedly, was far more complex than I initially had imagined. Its details provided as many detours as certainties, and suggested as much about the evolving present as they did about the deeper past.

TRAVELERS AND SPIRITS

In many native traditions of Siberia, shamans appeared as travelers guided by spirits, people who could reach other places and other worlds, and so connect the known with the unknown. In this book, I will follow this motif with regard to their conceptual offspring, tracing some of their journeys as they crossed from Asia into Europe, from history into prehistory and back again. This was hardly a nonstop flight. Rather, it involved multiple landings, each of which altered the appearance of these figures and the purpose of their travel. The large and diverse party of Siberian shamans, as reported in sixteenth-, seventeenth-, and eighteenth-century accounts of travelers and explorers, diminished with every stop. But their legacy of attracting attention remained, and even as these sorcerers became increasingly familiar, they continued to signal mysterious distance.

Described in vivid detail by early ethnographers and geographers of the eighteenth and nineteenth centuries, shamans grew abstract as they left their homeland. Soon they became a category: every tribe considered outside civilization could now have at least one of them. As the term came to describe practitioners of traditional rituals, shamans migrated around the planet. Sightings were reported in North and South America, Australia, and Africa. In transforming into a universal trope, shamans suggested power, mystery, madness, and brilliance across a range of different imaginary frontiers. They now not only connected their world to other worlds, but also increasingly linked the primitive and the civilized.

European societies in the nineteenth century were judged too advanced to have shamans of their own, but archaeologists avidly debated when similar healers and religious leaders might have been part of their distant past as well. Some shamans were said to have lived in caves; some appeared reclusive, but others social. But more importantly, they now stood at the very beginning of our collective social existence, to guide us through human history, down the path that led away from them. At the same time, a few still lingered beyond the eastern edge of Europe, where we could discover them yet again at the end of the twentieth century.

Yet this book is *not* strictly speaking about shamans, let alone the peoples of Siberia. Rather it is about the *idea* of a shaman, the imagination that fueled that idea and the history that nourished and encouraged it. I offer an account of those who encountered and imagined shamans, a long story about all sorts of fascinating characters, mostly at the edges of their own maps. Out of these elements I have sought to fashion a historical mosaic, less a singular picture than an assemblage of fragments. At its center lies Siberia: the Siberia imagined as well as encountered, the beliefs about its native peoples, and the multiple appearances they made in European history and eventually prehistory. The surrounding panels sometimes overlap, and sometimes leave large gaps. I examine a few of them closely to fill in the details, while only suggesting a larger whole. To see the shaman involves peering against the light, as if through stained glass. Many layers now stand between us and the distant world of human prehistory, each imparting its own colorful vision. The images we have of shamans, after all, come to us from others, be they travelers, ethnographers, descendants, or archaeologists. To understand the greater assemblage, we must try to see through each broken piece in turn, recognizing its particular hue. Only then can we better evaluate what a general concept might capture, and what it might be missing.

THE LONG ROAD TRAVELED: MEETING THE SHAMANS

My interest in the history of Siberian shamans stemmed from encountering them in archaeological discussions of prehistoric symbolic behavior, and wondering when this explanation had first emerged. My initial task seemed simple and straightforward enough: to trace the concept from its present-day understanding back into the history of Siberia and its indigenous populations. My modest plan was to broaden the horizons of current literature by bringing writings in Russian and German into view alongside well-known ethnographies circulating in English. I anticipated some theoretical differences based on the historical, national, and political contexts of the writers. While tensions of interpretation might appear, I thought, I ultimately expected to find a recognizable conception at the core, the ideal shaman then projected into the past. Hundreds of pages later, I found myself facing a far more daunting project: a history far more complex and knotty than I had imagined, stretching over centuries and across continents. By the end of my research, the "core of a shaman" still remained elusive, and I doubted that any definition could apply cleanly across time and place. However, I began to realize that this was the point, that the fragile instability of categories, their precarious nature, should give us pause when moving any concept across space and time.

My extended journey in search of shamans, real and imagined, started with recent accounts of indigenous groups in the broader region of Siberia. The last decade of socialism and the first years of post-socialism had opened a door for historical and ethnographic research in the former Soviet Union to a degree unprecedented for most of the century. Even if the archives were still centrally controlled and travel was monitored, Western as well as Russian scholars had an unsurpassed moment of opportunity to communicate with members of indigenous groups and decipher the records in historical archives. The resulting ethnographically rich work has revealed the immense diversity of the surviving native groups.[2] Many of these ethnographies also make it clear that the unprecedented resurgence of shamanism in Siberia in the last two decades cannot be understood without recognition of the momentous social, demographic, and political shifts of a collapsing social system. New histories and new identities emerged in the region, reassembled from a mix of ancient, new, and invented traditions.

Marjorie Mandelstam Balzer, one of the early ethnographers in postsocialist Siberia, recounts a particularly telling story of a modern female shaman [who] reputedly used spirit power to fix a broken bus on the way to a meeting with Native American visitors.[3] The anecdote succinctly captures both the bricolage of present-day shamanism and the ever-evolving historical context that surrounds it. Not only does spirit power now engage with modern transportation, but disparate indigenous groups also forge transnational connections. Such unorthodox examples offer cautionary tales about any simple use of ethnographic analogy.

The incident also introduces another dimension of current concern: gender. Contemporary ethnographies commonly mention practicing women shamans. Their presence at the end of the twentieth or early twenty-first century does not appear unusual, or particularly worthy of comment. Nevertheless, a historically minded reader would wonder whether this was always the case. Were women shamans ubiquitous throughout history, or were they the exception? And most importantly for archaeologists, how far back might we push such analogies? This was the thread I started to follow more closely, when turning from ethnographic accounts to historical archives.

MAPPING THE PATH

The chapters in this book are organized only partly chronologically. Rather than attempting a more comprehensive account, which would threaten to tax the reader as well as my own abilities, I have chosen a set of episodes that highlight shifting visions of Siberian shamans. Together they comprise a study in the geography of imagination and the wayward paths that shamans and their spirits took. My ambition is to explore the edges of possibility as they appeared to scholars of different generations, backgrounds, and orientations.

Encounters between explorers and native men and women in any colonial expansion involved a complicated alchemy of fear, curiosity, and aggression as well as a desire for knowledge. Siberia was no exception. Nonetheless, the colonial project in that part of the world possessed particular qualities meriting close attention. The history of Russian colonial expansion into the vast land to the east has not been a common part of the history of European science, nor is it commonly addressed in discussions of European colonial endeavors. Yet the threads of Siberian natives interlace the texts of European anthropology, geography, and botany. As well as traveling the world, then, shamans in this story also serve as guides through different layers of Europe's own sense of place.

In following the itinerant history of Siberian shamans, I also want to retell the history of prehistoric archaeology as it came to be defined at the end of the nineteenth century, suggesting that the search for the origin of civilization led east as well as underground. Europe, we too often forget, is a region bounded not just by coastline but also by a less certain limit on land. The practice of a more "worldly" archaeology is thus not simply a matter of moving beyond such continental confines but also reimagining them. The formation of prehistory involved a complex interplay between religion and science, alternately opposed and intertwined. Amid discussions of origins, empirical evidence met dreams about the past, to the extent that a scientist could not be defined by fieldwork methods alone. The fathers of the discipline translated many layers of evidence and imagination when speaking about the emergence of society, as well as art, science, and magic. Did ancient humans display modern capacities? If so, then when and how did they arise naturally? If not, then how to explain odd traces that remained? Shamans ultimately served to mediate such questions, moving between human and nonhuman forms of life, from animals to spirits.

However, before reaching this early twentieth-century moment in the history of archaeology, we need to travel even farther back and explore the ethnography out of which such shamanic analogies would be drawn. This book, then, is about the places and people who brought us shamans—their motives, histories, and mundane practices. In order to understand the tales of wayward shamans, I argue, we need to find all the characters that carried those tales to us.

Siberia has captivated travelers for centuries, and has been imagined and discovered many times. The first chapter recounts the centuries of descriptions of the region as a vast, frozen, and desolate place. An area covering most of northern Asia, Siberia remains a vast land—"the largest country in the world," as an immodest self-description posted on billboards throughout the region claims—with a climate more varied than often supposed, except for the northern-most quadrants. Nevertheless, from the ancient Greeks on, imagination rather than reality has dominated the visions of the area, and placing shamans into this space long filled with monsters and unbelievable natural phenomena recalls the sense of wonder that once surrounded them. Precisely such a space accommodated the wildest imaginings of European historians and travelers. Distant and hard to reach, Siberia inspired accounts that were only intermittently encumbered by facts. One could imagine a frozen, distant place where boundaries lost any meaning, where the land stretched for days, and rivers and land merged, where humans, animals and vegetation mutated into each other, and one could not tell men from women. Later, scientific and ethnographic wonders replaced the monsters of ancient times, and mammoth bones emerged from the ground, bringing the Ice Age into the present. In this setting, shamans and their magic were no longer the only surprising characters.

Once I began to address Siberian history, I came to realize that uncertainty was nothing new. Like the question of shamans and their "discovery," the landscape they inhabited was built of fact and sentiment: a combination of knowledge gained from travelogues and scientific expeditions, along with feelings of grudging admiration intermingled with fear. Archival and literary records, going as far back as the Greeks, tell tales of Siberia as a distant land beyond the edge of ordinary knowledge. An early boundary of civilization, it suggested the edge of Europe and the beginning of a vast, dramatically different space, a land of both emptiness and infinite possibilities, teeming with creatures that no longer followed the laws of nature, such as the half-plant lamb of Tartary or humans with bodies partially submerged in water. This fantastic place emerged at the eastern edge of the Russian empire through foreign descriptions, the tales of travelers who did not linger while crossing it in haste to reach India and China.

Although Siberia's natural resources, furs, and minerals became of increasing interest to Russian emperors, for a long time they exhibited only a reluctant desire to govern such an immense territory. Did ownership of a seemingly barren, empty, unknown, frozen land make a European empire? The persistent dilemma of size and importance haunted Russian emperors, who wished to join the powers of civilized Europe. Science offered one solution: mapping, surveys, and ethnographic descriptions produced the knowledge necessary to delineate the empire's boundaries and define a civilization that included Russia and separated it from Asia. I therefore devote some time to exploring this space of imagination, as Siberia stands geographically for what shamans do in terms of spirituality—it is a concept ready to be filled with ideas.

Indeed, reading closely the earliest eighteenth-century accounts, I was often struck by the *lack* of surprise in the face of magic. Travelers seemed to expect conjuring, magical tricks, and even transformations of people and objects. Although the details of magical practices in Siberia may have been considered unusual and its practitioners sometimes charlatans, European travelers anticipated the existence of otherworldly powers. Thus, the second chapter examines the longstanding interest of European societies in magic, particularly among the nobility and royal courts. To make sense of these early encounters with shamans, we need to recall that traditions of alchemy and magic constituted serious alternative pursuits amid premodern science, and that Christian sensibilities about the occult reflected the significant influence of Islamic and Jewish traditions as well as the well-established circulation of scholars throughout the continent. Thus, when German ethnographers encountered practices and beliefs in magic in the eastern regions in the eighteenth century, they were neither surprised nor unprepared. To the contrary, despite the overwhelmingly Christian character of European societies, forms of instrumental magic—practical efforts to address challenges of the physical and spiritual worlds—remained intimately recognizable, if alternately desirable and threatening. Shamans were both familiar and foreign characters, whose potential skills might be acknowledged and derided as trickery at the same time.

Chapter 3 sketches the history of exploration and appropriation of Siberia as a place filled with indigenous people. Russian expansion to the east represented a peculiar form of colonialism in its haphazard nature, carried out almost by proxy. Russian rulers desired all the natural resources of Siberia, its furs in particular, but they were reluctant to invest much time or energy in the project. Consequently, the colonial policies and practices of each ruler would vary quite significantly, and were often reacting to Western European colonial expansion overseas. Greater recognition of Russia as a European power was a primary motive, and the size of the Russian empire mattered to its rulers, while simultaneously representing a major challenge, as their knowledge of the land remained quite loose. Thus, in initial descriptions, Siberia appeared as a land teeming with animals, rich in minerals, and relatively devoid of people. Problems of violence, corruption, and unpaid taxes did periodically come to the attention of colonial bureaucrats, who entered the details in official letters and documents. However, during the initial stages of Russian expansion, native people mattered primarily to the extent they either abetted or hindered trade—as fur providers, rather than as potential Christian souls or subjects of the ruler. Like the land of Siberia, its people remained the opposite of civilizing Russia, distinct in appearance, custom, religion, and way of life. Even their gender appeared disturbingly indeterminate; the travelers did not find it easy to distinguish the men and women on sight.

Peter the Great ratcheted up Russian aspirations to be European, and Siberia served him well for that purpose. The eastern lands provided an ideal contrast to "European Russia," and German scientists served as the ideal character witnesses. Chapter 4 describes the early systematic survey and description of the indigenous people, animals, and plants of Siberia. Peter and later Catherine (both aptly and immodestly named "the Great") may have wished for the natural recognition of Russian grandeur and sophistication in its own right, but in practice they turned to Scandinavian and German scientists for such confirmation. The thorough and detailed knowledge that emerged from the subsequent decades of ethnographic labor reflected on both the colonial masters and the native subjects. And despite all their effort and Protestant ethic, the scientists' descriptions of the native groups were filtered through the simultaneous judgment of their Russian hosts, recording the latter's inadequacies, uncivilized ways of being, brutality toward the locals, and gullibility in the face of magic and conjuring.

Invited and paid by the Russian emperors, the German scholars carried out extensive fieldwork, collecting and describing with stoic determination for more than a decade. These natural historians thus laid the foundation for later Siberian ethnography, and it was from this space, geographic and conceptual, that our first pictures and impressions of shamans emerged. Although commonly described as tricksters, the reputed magicians and conjurers also had certain admirable skills that impressed not only the locals but also Russian soldiers and traders. In the exacting work of these scholars invited from the German centers of learning, shamanism appears a matter of things and actions, practiced by a diverse set of people.

Chapter 5 picks up one thread in this story to show the changing nature of encounters and the shifting ways of imaging difference. From the earliest sightings of indigenous people in Siberia, their lack of readily observable sexual characteristics seriously troubled the traveling scientists. Their writings are permeated with anxiety over an inability to tell men and women apart. Not only did the native men sport no beards, but both men and women grew very long hair and were permanently bundled up in the same kind of clothing, making it difficult for the visitors to distinguish gender. So pervasive was this theme that it spilled into the descriptions of everyday activities, routines, and customs, and combined with an active interest in sexual practices. Thus, early on we meet women shamans, some thought to be imposters, others considered very powerful or dangerous, given the female proclivity toward trickery.

The early German understanding of a shaman was very broad and, for the most part, did not intend to evoke admiration or a comparison with priests or artists. Consequently, the travelers at the time readily associated women with the term, as they viewed trickery, deception, fortune telling, and performance as falling within the realm of "typical" comportment for women. We find numerous accounts of both male and female shamans performing all sorts of tasks, some important and crucial, others amusing or deceptive to the eyes of these early ethnographers. We know that the initial historical category of shamans as it appeared in European accounts included women both young and old because in the masculine space of military camps, trading posts, and scientific expeditions, these native women garnered an inordinate and unwelcome amount of attention. They regularly featured in official letters, legal cases, and personal and scientific diaries, enmeshed in relations of desire, lust, loneliness, violence, and distorted power. Later, once the scientific descriptions had stabilized in mapping indigenous groups and their ways of being into a known pattern, this anxiety dissipates—and with it, many traces of diversity. By the time the prehistorians adopted shamans, they no longer imagined gender in all its confusing detail; they were quite certain about the roles that men and women should perform, no matter in which corner of the world.

Nowhere is this shift more apparent than in relation to reports of "changed women"—men who became women in order to perform shamanic duties. Chapter 6 tells the story of this practice and its varying ethnographic visibility. The earliest mention of such a category of people appears in the eighteenth century, amid confusion over the sexual identity of the native Kamchadal in eastern Siberia. In the context of all the local traditions appearing strange, the observers did not find that a man choosing to become a woman was particularly remarkable, which makes the later absence of such descriptions seem far more striking.

Yet this was not a simple vanishing act. In the late nineteenth century, Russian revolutionaries were exiled to the very eastern edge of Kamchatka, where these avid readers of Marx and Engels found themselves amid people who were living proof of the existence of primitive communism. They subsequently became ethnographers and passionate advocates for native difference; they pursued exemplary fieldwork, and dedicated their lives to understanding the indigenous way of life, myths, and customs. For them, these indigenous communities held the potential for envisioning a different future, one where social arrangements could be reconfigured, unlike the dominant exploitative capitalist forms of their day that they fought against. They, too, reported men becoming women when ordered by the spirits; for them, in their search for alternative political regimes, varying bodies or sexual identities did not seem too far-fetched. By then, open to the possibility of radical difference, the Russian revolutionaries themselves had become "changed men."

Picking up the eighteenth-century thread of shamans who traversed bodily boundaries, changed gender, learned to fly, and turned into animals, the Russian ethnographers soberly commented on a slowly vanishing world. Through them, the imagined Siberia of the earliest encounters briefly reemerged—the land of open, boundless possibility. Their accounts of changed women would subsequently intrigue the scholars of psychoanalysis, who viewed them as evidence of formative neuroses and varieties of hysteria. Through this medical lens, shamans now appeared as the potential prototypes for out-of-this-world artists, visionaries, and mystics. As the study of myths and rituals merged with interests in personality, individual psychology, and deviancy, the spirits that had ordered gender or sex changes in earlier times became per-sonal demons, haunting troubled individuals as they teetered toward madness.

Thus, by the early twentieth century, shamans were increasingly less a reminder of a primitive past than they were symbols of a possibility of impermanence of boundaries and categories. The skilled shape-shifters turned into psychological individuals, with personality traits that predisposed them toward certain behaviors. Under the new lens of psychology, sex or gender change among shamans reflected a complex of personality and desire, universal traits subject to professional analysis. Rather than an aspect of folklore or mythical storytelling, shamanic behavior constituted a medical condition. From "arctic hysteria" to later theories of deep neurological sediments undergirding the human psyche, traditional indigenous populations appeared universally human, even amid their most dramatic expressions of difference. The twentieth-century psychological concept of a person stretched worldwide, back through the eastern edges of Siberia. Writing decades later in "The Sorcerer and His Magic," Claude Lévi-Strauss makes a sustained comparison between a psychoanalyst and his patient and a shaman and the sick in his community, clearly working with an accepted and seemingly undisputed category.[4] For Lévi-Strauss, it was the detail of practice and the relationship between magic and the social world that posed a problem to ponder, not the given role itself.

The seventh chapter returns full circle to archaeology, as I describe the late nineteenth- and early twentieth-century institutionalization of the European science of prehistory. French archaeology played a pivotal role in establishing the conceptual parameters of the contemporary discipline, with key figures featuring prominently at this moment of birth. I focus on two well-known "fathers of archaeology," Gabriel de Mortillet and Abbé Henri Breuil. However, I rely on them as representatives of different ways of imagining the past, rather than as individual founders of a discipline. They each stood at opposite ends of an argument about the place of art and religion in the earliest stages of human evolution. De Mortillet receives credit for providing chronological stages for early human culture, though he situated all the events in France. At the same time, as a fervent and active socialist, he defined humanity through technology and labor, not through art and certainly not religion. So strong was his opposition to any notion of religiosity—and consequently, to any signs of nonutilitarian creativity—that it was only after his death that French prehistorians accepted the possibility of prehistoric art. Rather, it was a Catholic priest, Henri Breuil, who drove archaeology to recognize spirituality, expressed through art, as a fundamental aspect of human evolution.

In both cases, I draw attention to the institutions in which they operated as necessary physical places of ideas. Moreover, their collaborators played a crucial role in conveying theoretical building blocks, creating networks of like-minded researchers, keeping opposition at bay, and marshaling evidence to support new interpretations of prehistoric art. Henri Breuil introduced the figure of the sorcerer who painted caves at the dawn of civilization. In his version, it was an unquestioned male religious leader, without a hint of gender ambiguity, let alone sexuality. With the foundation of hunting magic in place, French archaeology held prominent place throughout the twentieth century not only as the location of most of prehistoric art but also as the center of its interpretation.

The conclusion brings the story of shamans into the present by the way of South Africa. When archaeologists in the 1980s rediscovered the shaman as the key creator of prehistoric art, it was only the latest in a long string of permutations for this spirit guide. A renewed tie to a different ethnographic record—this one of the San in southern Africa— would offer a direct historical connection. At the same time, claims about the neurobiological grounding for the earliest forms of human art, religion, and ritual claimed universal truth at a new level of detail. The figure of the shaman redoubled on itself: neurological functions of the brain in a state of trance united varied practitioners across time and the globe. By then, the term and category had traveled quite far from the tents on the eastern Russian frontier, to now identify a general pattern of human behavior, one projected backward onto ritual specialists of the Ice Age. Yet most of its history and rich ethnographic detail had been lost, forgotten, or considered irrelevant. The sense of variation in the persons who might house such a wandering brain grew thin.

WAYWARD SHAMANS

What becomes of a shaman when far from Siberia? What changes in crossing such enormous distances and so many centuries? These questions suggest issues beyond authenticity. Because my search for a historical shaman never sought purity, I can hardly return to some "ur-shaman," put on display as the only true specimen. To the contrary, after pouring through German archives, getting hopelessly lost in Siberia, reading the personal correspondence of Gabriel de Mortillet, Abbé Breuil, Émile Cartailhac, and Salomon Reinach, and eyeing rock shelters and painted caves, I emphasize, more than anything else, the impurity of all categories. The messiness and multiplicity of history rarely allow for simple claims. Shamans are useful guides precisely because they are so unstable, having changed over and over, never standing still long enough to be unquestionably real. Alternately loathed, admired, copied, cleaned up, and reintroduced many times, any claim of their universal transcendence falls flat in the face of their evident impermanence.

Instead, I suggest that shamans offer a mobile mirror for our own shifting curiosity. This is not to say that they have never existed or do not exist still, but simply to recognize that the concepts we use to describe things at the edge of our knowledge are inherently uncertain. Amid the remnants of strange and distant worlds, we project our own assumptions and anxieties alongside the things we take as evidence, the past that we catch as a glimpse of, say, through painted surfaces of rocks. Categories are useful and necessary heuristic devices, in scholarly as well as everyday life. When archaeologists approach representations and beliefs without the benefit of ethnographic records, they necessarily appeal to general concepts and forms drawn by analogy. Yet it is precisely when we do not have access to ethnographic and historical accounts—troubling our generalities with varied and sometimes contradictory detail—that concepts appear the most deceptively pure. Projected into prehistory, shamans assume a firm, convincing, universally understood character.

In a striking photo of a painted rock surface, a lion, a bull, or an eland can easily appear to be transformed shamans doing their magic, performing their art, engaged in a clear ritual. When you visit the site, however, you must climb a steep slope, at times walk through dark, long passages of a cave, and only find the paintings after considerable effort. In person, you now notice little stick figures to the right, bird-like creatures underneath, a dotted line running in and out of a rock, and animals and shapes crowded, drawn over each other. Yes, there may be a lion, a bull, or an eland, but so much else is also going on—and behind you is the sound of wind, and above you a glimpse of open sky. That has become my goal in following my traveling spirits: to point beyond these figures to the ground behind them, to broaden the focus enough to suggest other ghosts and other wondrous paths along the margins of history.

CHAPTER I

Discoveries of an Imaginary Place

No new land, no new place is ever terra incognita. It always
arrives to the eye fully stocked with expectations, fears,
rumors, desires and meanings. And even as discoverers claim
new knowledge from direct and unmediated experience with
nature, history intervenes, filtering and imposing meaning on
their experiences in the natural world.

—Richard White (1992)

Santa Fe, New Mexico, 2008: "I have a Master's degree in shamanic
practice, and am a member of the association of shamanic practitioners." The woman who organized the workshop spoke to us matter-of-
factly, as if describing her accounting credentials. She described her earlier training with a psychologist, whose patients had not been getting
better despite extended sessions. So she went to study with a "real shaman" in Borneo. A short discussion followed as to where exactly Borneo
might be; because the organizer and the lone man in the audience could
not agree, we moved on to another geographical conundrum. "The
original shamans came from Mongolia," the man stated in a friendly but
authoritative tone. "Well, shamans as we know them came from Siberia,"
the organizer replied quickly, trying to regain her momentum without
much success. "That's in Mongolia, Siberia is in Mongolia," the man said
calmly and with impressive certainty. "Sure," the organizer agreed, capit-
ulating geographically for a second time in a row.

I was determined not to take on any role in this conversation, as it
did not ultimately appear to be about facts of geography. Rather, I
wanted to find out how "Every Woman's Shamanism," as the seminar
was titled, had come to this part of the United States in the twenty-
first century, and what connection, if any, it might have to the longer
history I had begun to trace. Where is Siberia for today's shaman practitioners? Indeed, *what* is Siberia if it can just as well be in Mongolia as

in any other equally distant, vaguely connected place in the eastern part of the Russian empire? Clearly, it was not simply an area on the present-day globe, struggling through the aftermath of Soviet industrialization; it also was a conceptual space, a site of difference and spiritual purity.

The participants of this workshop were hardly alone in either their fascination with or their imprecision about Russia's eastern frontier. Western Europeans have long located Siberia in both a real geographic place and an imaginary space. Their narratives describing the people, nature, and physical geography of the region have changed multiple times, depending on who was searching. Siberia, tracked down through this geographical and cultural imagination, acquired an additional dimension of being a place that was "not Europe," while still attached to it physically and historically. It was a strange, mythical land, ever famous for its vast size and forbidding climate. The details about it continued to change, conjured up as possibly true or possibly not real at all.

To survey this imaginary terrain alongside the physical one, we should recall even early associations, such as a child's map of the cardinal compass points. Writing in England in 1926, A. A. Milne, the author of the children's books *Winnie-the-Pooh*, described the "Eastern Pole" as accurately and evocatively as any geographer writing about Siberia over the previous three centuries:

> "There's a South Pole," said Christopher Robin, "and I expect there's an East Pole and a West Pole, though people don't like talking about them."
>
> Pooh was very excited when he heard this, and suggested that they should have an Expotition to discover the East Pole, but Christopher Robin had thought of something else to do with Kanga; so Pooh went out to discover the East Pole by himself. Whether he discovered it or not, I forget; but he was so tired when he got home that, in the very middle of his supper, after he had been eating for little more than half-an-hour, he fell fast asleep in his chair, and slept and slept and slept.
>
> Then suddenly he was dreaming. He was at the East Pole, and it was a very cold pole with the coldest sort of snow and ice all over it. He had found a bee-hive to sleep in, but there wasn't room for his legs, so he had left them outside. And Wild Woozles, such as inhabit the East Pole, came and nibbled all the fur off his legs to make Nests for their Young. And the more they nibbled, the colder his legs got, until suddenly he woke up with an *Ow!*—and there he was, sitting in his chair with his feet in the water, and water all round him!
>
> He splashed to his door and looked out. . . .
>
> "This is Serious," said Pooh. "I must have an Escape."[2]

The cold, the ice, and the strange mythical animals, whether called Wild Woozles or otherwise, were common tropes in describing the eastern expanse of Russia. The Eastern Pole—previously known as Tartary—persists in various renditions to this day. In descriptions alternating between horror and wonder, Siberia has for centuries occupied a space "between heaven and hell."[3] Westerners continue to imagine Siberia through such metaphors—a frozen land at the edge of the world, a place where few have actually gone but which still evokes strong associations. The Russians, on the other hand, have long had a far more complicated relationship with the region, for reasons of greater familiarity, proximity, and centuries of involvement. Wild Woozles have haunted Russia's narratives of Siberia for a very long time.

THE LAND OF WHITE DEATH

> Not all the horrors of the Western front, not the rubble of Arras, nor the hell of Ypres, nor all the mud of Flanders leading to Passchendale, could blot out the memories of that year in the Arctic.[4]

Although Siberia may be synonymous with the Arctic in many people's imagination, geographically speaking large parts of the land are not in the Arctic at all. Moreover, large parts of the Russian Arctic are not a part of the Siberian landmass. Nevertheless, accounts of Siberia circulating through the Western world from at least the sixteenth century on were united by a sense of the place as an elemental challenge, a harsh obstacle that was known beforehand as insurmountable. Defeat by the environment was almost anticipated, felt in the bones upon merely pronouncing the name. It was, in George Kennan's words, "a country where winter reigns supreme throughout almost the entire year, and where simple existence is a constant struggle with an inhospitable climate."[5] The Siberia of these images was bleak and cold, if not permanently frozen, and devoid of even the smallest life-form that could thrive. George Kennan, an American explorer and a telegraph employee who had sought business opportunities in Russia at the end of the nineteenth century, offers a full sense of this perceived desolation in his depiction of the same frozen, bleak land described by every traveler since the sixteenth century:

> At all seasons and under all circumstances this immense borderland of moss tundra is a land of desolation. In summer its covering of water-soaked moss struggles into life, only to be lashed at intervals by pitiless whips of icy rain, until it is again buried in snow; and in winter fierce gales, known to the

Russians as poorgas, sweep across it from the Arctic Ocean, and score its
snowy surface into long, hard, polished grooves, called sastroogee. Throughout the entire winter it presents a picture of inexpressible dreariness and
desolation. Even at noon, when the sea-like expanse of storm-drifted snow is
flushed faintly by the red, gloomy light of the low-hanging sun, it depresses
the spirits and chills the imagination with its suggestions of infinite dreariness and solitude; but at night, when it ceases to be bounded even by the
horizon, because the horizon can no longer be distinguished; when the pale
green streamers of the aurora begin to sweep back and forth over a dark seg-
ment of a circle in the north, lighting up the whole white world with transi-
tory flashes of ghostly radiance, and adding mystery to darkness and solitude, then the Siberian tundra not only becomes inexpressibly lonely and
desolate, but takes on a strange, half terrible unearthliness, which awes and
yet fascinates the imagination.[6]

For many dark months lacking even a horizon on which to rest ones'
eyes, the tundra was thoroughly dreary and desolate. This was nature in
the raw. Yet it also acquired an air of personality—forlorn, filled with
melancholy, possessing a ghostly radiance that was not quite physical,
not of this earth, more a product of one's imagination.

A state of mind or of existence at its most lonely and depressing, "Siberia" named as much an idea as a physical entity, despite the numerous
travel accounts, explorations, and permanent settlements over the centuries. Portraits of silent, white, wind-swept nature at its most still have
for centuries dominated representations of the eastern part of Russia.
For hundreds of years, this outstretched land behind the "Rock"—the
Ural Mountains—represented the emptiness, the frozen state of Europe's
distant past. Even before Europeans began searching for their long-
forgotten ancestors, Siberia represented for them the sort of silent, snow-
covered expanse that they might have left behind. The land, in other
words, was a ready stage for prehistory. Its vast geographic space not
only suggested the Ice Age, the sense of an entire landmass frozen, but
even yielded ancient remains. From time to time mammoths would re-
surface, still standing with all their fur intact in the very place where they
had been trapped for thousands of years.

When the spring thaw comes to the frozen plains of eastern Siberia, huge
curved tusks sometimes appear on the surface of the ground. They are usually found singly, but sometimes as part of a skull or an entire skeleton.
They are the remains of prehistoric animals that lived in these regions, at
the distant time when our ancestors were still chipping stones into tools. . . .
Once in a while, the thaw reveals the entire body of an animal buried for
millennia in the frozen ground, its flesh and bones virtually intact. The Siberian permafrost has preserved the flesh and bones of these animals, extinct

for thousands of years; sometimes the flesh still edible, and the natives occasionally eat it.[7]

When the Siberian permafrost thaws, with just a little rubbing of its glassy surface, we have a window into Ice Age prehistory, including whole, fully preserved prehistoric animals, ready for any ancestors chipping stone into tools.

Like other real but imagined locales, Siberia's strangeness is rooted in its stubborn persistence as a natural place. Yet unlike descriptions of tropical nature such as the Amazonian rainforest or the African jungle, which usually appear as lush and obscenely overflowing with vegetation, animals, and gemstones, Siberia stands out for its stark nakedness. Its desolate emptiness presents an opposite view of life from that of the tropics; rather than lush and vibrant, it is frozen and hibernating. It seems a place to endure, to show one's fortitude and resolve. Settlers and peasants moved east for centuries; missionaries ventured there to gather souls, and trappers to gather pelts; mines and industries with thousands of workers reached deep inside the earth to extract raw wealth. Most fundamentally, numerous groups of peoples inhabited the river valleys, lake shores, plains, steppes, forests, and coasts, their arrival there sufficiently distant and mythical to merit the term "indigenous."

In spite of Siberia's full history, many descriptions either overlooked the human inhabitants or stressed their absence, preferring to focus on the dramatic appearance of strange, extinct, or frightening animals instead. In a landscape devoid of people, the frightening wildlife, peering at the travelers from a distant time, underline the rarity of encounters with any living creatures:

> I have just seen a few more walruses. They often poke their heads out of the water. They are far more repulsive than one might imagine. Their heads and necks form a mass of bloated folds; from their lips and around their muzzles hang long, thick whiskers, which give them a sort of mustache. But strangest of all are their bloodshot eyes and their astonished and threatening—even aggressive—gazes. Their long tusks give them a prehistoric look, which has earned them a reputation of feeding solely on human flesh.[8]

Looking into the bloodshot eyes of the repulsive walruses, Albanov, a Russian navigator and one of only two survivors of the 1912 Northeast Passage, Saint Anna expedition, described his heroic fate in *In the Land of White Death* (1917). He evoked the excruciating pain of hunger, frostbite, loneliness, despair, and fear, and his attempts to overcome the nature surrounding him for hundreds of kilometers—without ever mentioning any native people whom he might, or hoped to, encounter. This was a land of no people, only nature at its most threatening, where walruses eat human flesh in a manner reminiscent of the natives eating thawed mammoths.

The idea of Siberia as devoid of humanity, frozen in time persisted. The land measured time in thousands of miles of empty space, the uncertain boundary between the end of Europe and the beginning of Asia. Time and geography merged to form a space of pure nature, white and terrifying, the prehistoric Ice Age available to any intrepid traveler.

THE END, THE BEGINNING, AND THE CLASSICAL LEGACY OF MONSTERS

The most beautiful regions of the world are the furthest.[9]

Siberia has always lacked clearly defined borders. Currently, geography designates Siberia as the beginning of Asia, starting at the Ural Mountains and extending all the way to the Pacific Ocean. However, the view that the Ural Mountains represent an obvious and natural dividing line between Europe and Asia is a relatively recent historical convention.[10] At the same time, judging everything behind the mountains as "Siberia" asserts a much older conception of the primacy of natural space. Although the land is occupied by diverse nomadic and sedentary groups of people, this assertion of an unpopulated expanse has not changed much since the time of antiquity.

To some degree, views on Siberia have been a reaction to its lack of obvious ethnic or political unity. Siberia is not and has never been a state in either archaeological or modern political terms. As an observable physical feature, the mountain range could serve as the separation of Europe from Asia, if such a separation were needed; indeed, most geographers have for centuries agreed that the western flanks of the Ural Mountains are rich forests, in contrast with the eastern slopes where the grassy steppes start. Yet one should be wary of writing physical geography into cultural history, retroactively conflated as obvious or self-explanatory. Amid Russia's own historically unstable relationship with Europe and its attitude towards Asia, the addition of Siberia into the conversation highlights the ambivalent historical unity, or lack thereof, of Europe as a geographic or cultural space. By analogy, Siberia is an appendix that serves an essential role in the functioning of the body, purifying it but also potentially threatening it with exploding, polluting, or poisoning.

Writing in 450 B.C., Herodotus tells us of a possible but not certain boundary, traced from the Black Sea, the Bosporus, and the Caspian Sea, a boundary between Asia and Europe, mainly understood as the separation from Persia: "But the boundaries of Europe are quite unknown, and there is not a man who can say whether any sea girds it round either on the north or on the east, while in length it undoubtedly extends as far as both the other two continents."[11] The general idea was that Europe, Asia, and Libya formed an island, surrounded by an ocean of unimaginable extent. The Greeks themselves were located somewhere in a space between Europe and Asia, with very little knowledge of the northern limits of the world. However, lack of empirical knowledge hardly prevented them from having extensive discussions about the northern regions, which represented a utopian realm that was worth exploring in the abstract. The North in this world was not a place but a boundary, a liminal region that framed their realm, a frozen wasteland known as *eremoi*—empty uninhabited spaces at the edges of the world.[12]

According to myths and Herodotus's *Histories,* somewhere to the north, past the last *Rhipaean* mountain range (now believed to possibly have been the Ural Mountains), lay the land of the mythical Hyperboreans. Idealized and known barely more than the inhabitants of that other, more western, mythical northern kingdom known as the Land of Thule, the Hyperboreans occupied a magical land beyond the reach of ordinary humans, an enchanted space where noble and horrific events occurred simultaneously, a space that was reputed but not knowable in any empirical sense. Questions about the geographic and historical accuracy and factual veracity of Herodotus have preoccupied classical scholars and geographers for some time, but I do not intend to enter this debate, tempting as the exercise may be. Rather, the imaginary quality and details of his depictions are the pertinent issue for our discussion, as they established an enduring frame: the classical legacy in geography, ethnography, and travel accounts that remains a crucial component of any account of the North.

Greek myths accord the people of the extreme north a status and importance that are equivalent to, or even exceed, their own. According to many legends, Apollo, the god of light and the sun, truth and prophecy, medicine and healing (and much more), spent his winters among the Hyperboreans, who venerated him as greatly as those in Delos and Delphi, the oracle sites he had established. Boreas, the brutal northern

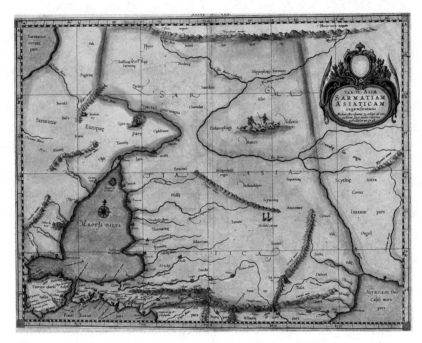

FIGURE 1.1. Asiae Sarmatiam Asiaticam repraesentans. One of the early maps of the region, located in "Sarmatian Asia." A reprint of Gerhard Mercator's (1512–1594) map of Ptolemy's Geography, *Atlas Tabulae geographicae Orbis Terrarum, second century*, from designs ascribed to Agathodaemon of Alexandria. The reproduction was printed in Amsterdam in 1730, suggesting a long-standing belief in the veracity of the myths about northern lands. The Hyperboreans are prominently indicated on the map at the top, with "Terra incognita" adjacent to them to the west. Native peoples of "monstrous races"—Hippophagi Saramate, Pathirophagi—are illustrated tending their flock. The Bohdan & Neonila Krawciw Ucrainica Antique Map Collection. Uk-400. Record no. G7000 1730 .T3. (Reproduced with permission from the Harvard Map Library, Harvard University.)

wind, prevented any "human activity," meaning plowing, growing, and harvesting crops, anywhere to the north of classical Greece. The Hyperboreans lived past that harsh climate, in a utopian land with an ideal environment. They were said to lead happy, unencumbered lives that lasted for a thousand years (which they would end by voluntarily leaping off a cliff) in a land of immense beauty where the sun would rise and set only once a year, with several growing seasons every month. However, this idyllic land was separated from the land of the Greeks by an uninhabitable wasteland that would bring instant death to anyone who tried to cross it.

The fantastic nature of the Hyperborean land and its inhabitants, emphasized by the dangers involved in crossing the cruel North, underlined that one entered a region that was beyond knowing. This was not merely a scholarly discussion of what lay to the north of the ancient civilizations but also a discussion of *ecumene (oikoumene)*—the world inhabited by humans, as opposed to other creatures and mythical beings. The Hyperboreans and the North that kept them apart were a geographically anchored statement on both what was humanly possible and what range of beings inhabited the knowable world. The Greeks and the Hyperboreans were related, linked through Apollo as well as through beauty and bountiful nature. The Hyperboreans represented an extended version of the Greek world, past the worldly limits, which could be imagined but not reached by mortals. Between them lay the harsh, cruel, monstrous expanse of the North, which according to the Greek view could have been populated only by monsters in animal or semi-human form. The classical maps depicting this world, in a trope reproduced for centuries afterward, show vicious sea monsters swimming menacingly in icy waters. The North was not just a place, but also a boundary.

MAPPING THE MONSTROUS

Cartography entails a history of place, space, and knowledge making. All maps embody traces of fantasy within their depiction of reality, as they orient the world around points of local and cultural specificity, firmly rooted in history. The beauty of maps is in their representation of a society's given perceptions about what is important as well as the desire to locate it. But they also engage in a larger work of translation of such knowledge, through circulation, exchange, and frequent appropriation. Maps capture a curious blend of representational imaginary and a practical necessity for accuracy.[13] However, the balance between the two—between fantasy and reality—proves especially interesting when a map illustrates a general idea as much as serving any immediate need for navigation or the practical purpose of a journey.

This is particularly striking in both indigenous map-like representations and pre-Enlightenment maps alike. Classical maps of the world were not only representations of knowledge but also a narrative, an itinerary that had never been traveled but remained a possibility. As Michel de Certeau has noted, narratives and maps in pre-Enlightenment cartography intertwine into a route, a temporal narrative of storytelling connected with a spatial imperative of mapmaking.[14] The boats, sea monsters, wild animals, and half-humans stand witness to the course of a traveler on a spiritual journey at the edges of the world. At the same time, they defined the local by drawing attention back to the center of the known world, contrasted with the dangers of the remote, cruel North.

The classical tradition of mapmaking did not dwell on a practical purpose, so it incorporated little empirical evidence. It is thus important to recognize the remarkably long duration and stubborn persistence of these mapmakers' representations. Despite the fact that after the first century A.D. sailors and travelers ventured north and could easily have disproved the mythical aspects of ancient cartography, the images remain. We find the same depictions of beastly wildlife again in the fifteenth and sixteenth centuries, reproduced not only by scholars from Mediterranean Europe but even by writers from northern latitudes with firsthand knowledge of the region. As Margaret Small notes,

> the peculiarities and the marvels with which the Mediterranean endowed the North spilled over into Northern self-perceptions. In 1539, the Catholic Bishop of Uppsala, Olaus Magnus, produced *Carta Marina* depicting northern lands. . . . Although more or less accurate in outline, in content the map reinforces many classical ideas. It is filled with a plethora of monsters and strange people, which are clearly more than a motif filling up blank spaces on the map.[15]

Magnus accompanied his illustrations with a narrative describing the peoples of the North as victims of the harsh environment, entirely determined by their climate and reduced to a savage existence, hiding in caves or eating their own limbs.[16]

The revival of classical scholarship during the Renaissance eagerly filled in any details that were missing from firsthand accounts. The scholarly classical tales supplied travelers with the appropriate language to describe their encounters with the natives of the edges of the world. Abraham Ortelius illustrated his 1570 *Theatrum Orbis Terrarum*, arguably the first scientific or modern atlas of the world, with over a hundred images and descriptions of northern creatures that haunted the seas.[17]

Sebastian Münster, a professor of Hebrew at the University of Basel, published the *Kosmographie: Beschreibung Aller Länder* (1561), providing not only those same illustrations but also a whole lexicon of sea monsters. His major contribution though was the expansion of the vocabulary on the variety of fiends of foreign lands, to which he added the "monstrous races." Münster classified all peoples into forty nations, depending on their external appearance and personal disposition. These

FIGURE 1.2. Cynocephalus from the *Nuremberg Chronicle*, 1493. Cynocephalus in Latin, derived from Greek, means "dog-headed." The "cynocephali" provided an evocative image of the monstrousness and otherworld nature of people in distant places. This particular image ran, appropriately, along the margins of pages in the *Nuremberg Chronicle* (1493), a biblical narrative of world history. The "Cynocephalus" appeared in the Chronicle in Chapter 12 "Strange People." (Reproduced with permission from Morse Library, Beloit College, Wisconsin.)

people included the chest-headed men, the *Blemmyae,* who supposedly were far too common in the regions of Ethiopia, although they also emerged with regular frequency in travel accounts of Siberia. The one-eyed *Cyclopes,* the *Sciopods,* terrifying human-like creatures with only one leg, and the dog-headed *Cynocephali* (figure 1.2) all roamed the peripheries, driven to savage acts by their inhospitable environment.[18]

Renaissance cartographers enriched their texts by whole chapters from Pliny the Younger, who in the first century A.D. described in great detail the headless men and other nature-made creatures who occupied the distant places of earth. These "marvels and monstrous races" subsequently appeared with great regularity in colonial encounters with native peoples all over the world from the sixteenth century onward.[19] The ancient monsters and marvels fused with medieval folklore, aided by both print and travel to distant places. Non-European peoples, whatever their size, shape, or skin color, became quite interchangeable:

wild, non-Christian, and equally monstrous at the edges of the world, in Africa, South America, or Siberia.

The Siberian native peoples, however, carried the additional burden, reinforced through travelers' accounts, of inhabiting a particularly bleak and harsh environment, where only bare crude existence and mere survival were possible. While lush, abundant jungles kept the peoples of Africa or South America in a state of primitive indolence, the barren and desolate landscape had a similar effect on the natives of Siberia. From this European perspective, the temperate and moderate became the ideal of both climate and human nature, driving civilization.[20]

"PROMISCUOUS INQUIRIES, CHIEFLY ABOUT COLD"

Why would anyone voluntarily, without being forced by an evil government, move to Siberia, in prehistory or at any point in history?[21]

In the sixteenth and seventeenth centuries, Russia hovered on the margins of European awareness as a potential major empire, with only a few maps to give some visual guidance to its riches. However, the country loomed large in the imagination and curiosity of the emerging scientific community of England, France, and Germany in the early seventeenth century. The strangeness of the place was too hard to resist. The vast landscape to the east appeared a source of information on natural phenomena that were rare or impossible to obtain in Western Europe. The potential wonders of the East proved both an exploratory and an explanatory device. They enabled the search for knowledge and simultaneously explained why the distant places were so dramatically different.

For subjects related to the extremes of nature—of particularly great fascination and import in the formation of field sciences—the northern and eastern parts of Russia offered fertile ground. The emerging experimental philosophers of the mid-seventeenth century, fascinated by the mechanics of nature, saw the vast empire as a perfect setting for observations related to cold climate and its effect on various parts of the body.[22] Because unusual natural phenomena not encountered or found in many other places were in abundant supply, Russia held out the prospect of the wondrous and monstrous, observable yet safely distant. These phenomena indulged both the rational conception of scientific curiosity and the fascination of travelers for the strange, exotic, and supernatural. Siberia in particular was a place of natural wonder and horror, with plants and animals not seen anywhere else, such as the mythic "vegetable lamb of Tartary," a supposed plant-vegetable hybrid.

The increasing fascination with distant geographies as places that had to be visited and witnessed firsthand (or at least secondhand) combined with the interest in the mysterious interior of the body. Early scientists set about exploring the effect of cold on dead bodies and experimenting with injections of various substances into animal veins to observe the action of freezing cold on circulation. As Robert Boyle wrote in his introduction to *An Experimental History of Cold* (1665):

> It now concerns the inquiring World to take notice, that this subject, as it hath hitherto bin almost totally neglected, so it is now, by this Excellent Author, in such a manner handled, and improved by near *Two hundred* choice *Experiments* and *Observations*, that certainly the *Curious* and *Intelligent* Reader will in the perusal thereof find cause to admire both the Fertility of a Subject, seemingly barren, and the Author's Abilities of improving the same to so high a degree.[23]

His work was published in the very first volume of the *Philosophical Transactions of the Royal Society*. The Royal Society, founded in 1660, took explaining the purpose of natural philosophy to be one of its primary goals. Its members advocated experiments as a way to know nature and understanding the mechanical processes as a proof of the wisdom of God and the beauty of Nature. One of the central tasks of this new society was to establish the truth of scientific matters through experiments rather than through citation of authority. At the time, it was the only official scientific society in Europe but held the ambitious goal of creating an Empire of Learning, which would consist of a global network of scientists and correspondents, relying on the language of science as their lingua franca. Thus, travel to and communication with distant places were central and essential to collecting materials and facts.

Numerous gentlemen scientists, physicians, merchants, nobles, and members of embassies in distant places took up fieldwork with passion and zeal. The *Philosophical Transactions* published in every volume specific "inquiries" for travelers in remote parts of the world, questions deemed essential for the expansion of knowledge and "natural history." The questions emphasized nature when the travel was to the North, and a mixture of nature and curiosity about the inhabitants when the travel was to southern regions such as India or Brazil. The questions conveyed attitudes that reflected imaginative curiosity, assumptions about European superiority, and a desire for knowledge rather than simple affirmation. The distant places east of Moscow were viewed as not only culturally foreign and exotically different, but also full of fascinating phenomena that were either not common or never found in Europe. However, the northern and eastern parts of the Russian empire were seldom sought-after travel destinations for reasons other than curiosity. The one aspect that led to this reluctance—extreme cold—was also a problem of growing significance for scientists during the early seventeenth century, as Europe itself was experiencing the unusually cold periods later called the Little Ice Age.[24]

Thus, Robert Boyle, conducting experiments in physics and chemistry in the 1660s, asked travelers, "How in extreme Cold Countries the Bodies of Dead Men and other Animals may be preserved very many years entire and unputrefied? And yet, how such Bodies, when unfrozen, will appear quite vitiated by the excessive Cold?"[25] Boyle never visited Russia in person; instead, he relied extensively on the reports of various travelers for descriptions of the excruciating conditions that cold could induce.[26] One of his main correspondents, acknowledged by name and status as a source of much information, was Dr. Samuel Collins, a personal physician to czar Alexei I. Collins not only obligingly observed the cold and its effects on the body, but also helped Boyle with the "analysis" of the threatening environment of the frigid North. As one of the early foreigners who visited Russia not simply for adventure but with a more specific purpose of expanding knowledge, while working at the czar's court Collins contributed extensively to Boyle's *Experimental History of Cold* by providing answers to specific experimental questions, retelling anecdotes "unheard of anywhere else," and offering his own general observations as a scientist.

Collins lived in Russia for nine years and considered himself an expert, writing a treatise entitled *The Present State of Russia* upon his return to England. Published posthumously in 1671, the work began with the following introduction:

> Having had therefore fair opportunities, and good intelligence, I am the more willing to give you an account of this Empire. Indeed, hitherto no man of parts or abilities has been suffered to travel the Country. For the people are very jealous, and suspect those who ask them any questions concerning their Policy, or Religion, they being wholly devoted to their own Ignorance, and Education, (which is altogether illiterate, and rude, both in Civil and Ecclesiastical Affairs) look upon Learning as a Monster, and fear it no less than a Ship of Wildfire.[27]

Collins's text is a valuable commentary on Russia of the time. Yet read in the context of similar travel documents of the sixteenth and seventeenth centuries, it also reveals a particular emphasis on recording the scientific and the strange. Although the text proclaims its main focus as being "to survey the religion and manners of the inhabitants," seemingly extraneous details abound in its pages.[28] The work presents the inhabitants of Russia as a completely indistinguishable group, yet as completely distinct from other Europeans: "The Russians are a People who differ from all other Nations of the world, in most of their Actions."[29] The insistence on the uniqueness of the subjects under discussion was a common narrative trope of early anthropology.[30] Collins's vivid descriptions render Russia an appropriately exotic land. An abundance of jewels, cloths of amazing color and length not seen commonly in Europe, and rich furs all stand juxtaposed with the lack of manners—that is, English manners. This made the Russian wealth ultimately appear vulgar and lacking culture, rather than a sign of prosperity and high status:

> Since his Majesty has been in Poland and seen the manner of the Princes houses there, and ghess'd at the mode of their Kings, his thoughts are advanced, and he begins to model his Court and Edifices more stately, to furnish his Rooms with Tapestry, and contrive houses of pleasure abroad. As for his Treasure of Jewels, I think no Prince doth exceed him, yet he hath many foul Stones, but the Russians affecting greatness in Jewels, will upon that score dispense with small faults. The fashion of the Emperours clothes is like that of his Nobility, but only richer. That of the Empress is the like, only the tire of her head is higher, and her smock sleeves longer, about ten or twelve yards length, and her upper most Gown has wide sleeves like our Batchelors of Arts, which all her women of honour wear also.[31]

Collins's description of Moscow was one of continuous comparison and contrast with the English. The resulting impression was of an enormous distance separating England from the edge of Europe, where Russia was teetering. When Siberia came into view, the distance from Western Europe was beyond comprehension; it depicted as vast, barren, and cold—the end of the world:

> Siberia is a vast unknown Province, reaching to the Walls of Cataya. I have spoken with one that was there, who traded with the Chircasses, and amongst also who said he saw a Sea beyond Siberia wherein were Ships and Men in strange habits, like the Chircasses by their description, rich in cloth of Gold and Jewels, no Beards but on their upper lip. . . . 'Tis so excessive cold here, that water thrown up into the Air will descend congeal'd into Ice. The most Northern parts affort no Bread, but Fish in abundance, which they eat dryed instead of bread, and yet they live to a great age. They feed their Cows with Fish during the frost, which makes the milk taste fishy. The River Ob is a vast River, whose end is as yet unknown.[32]

The immense size and the unknown—and unknowable—nature of the land east of Moscow in the second half of the seventeenth century reflects continuing myth more than realistic observation. It was a myth that Collins and many writers from later periods helped perpetuate, successfully enough that elements survived well into the twentieth century. Beyond the question of whether such details were empirically true, their continuing popularity among even those who devoted themselves to scientific pursuits suggests both the force and inertia of imagination.

Collins himself recounted numerous stories of travelers meeting natives while crossing this vast land, commenting on their customs, appearance, and repeatedly upon the inhospitable environment. Soldiers, war captives, and merchants traversed Russia by the time of his writing, at the end of the seventeenth century.[33] Sailors made attempts to circumvent the land in valiant efforts to navigate the Northeast Passage.[34] Although not many soldiers or travelers wrote lengthy treatises on their experiences in the East, letters and briefs on the geography of the vast and cold expanse behind the Ural Mountains circulated through Western Europe.

The German writer Hans von Grimmelshausen in 1669 wrote one of the best-known picaresque travel novels of the period *Simplicius Simplicissimus*. Composed in the aftermath of the Thirty Years' War, it described the main hero's experience as a war captive in Russia, including a threat to be deported to Siberia:

> I made the acquaintance of the Germans that dwell in Moscow, some as traders, some as mechanics, and to them lamented my plight and how I had been deceived by guile; who gave me comfort and direction how I, with a fair opportunity, might return to Germany. But so soon as they got wind of it that the Czar had determined to keep me in the land and would force me to it, they all became dumb towards me, yea, avoided my company, an 'twas hard for me even to find a shelter for my head. . . . At that time there went out a decree that both among natives and foreigners no idlers should be allowed (and that with heavy penalties) as those that took the bread out of the mouth of the workers, and all strangers that would not work must quit the country in a month and the town in four-and-twenty hours. With that some fifty of us joined together with intent to make our way, with God's help, through Podolia to Germany; yet were we not two hours gone from the town when we were caught up by certain Russian troopers, on the pretence that his Majesty was greatly displeased that we had impudently dared to band together in such great numbers, and to traverse his land at pleasure without passports, saying further that his Maj-

esty would not be going beyond his rights in sending us all to Siberia for our insolent conduct.[35]

As this account makes clear, in addition to exceptional figures like Dr. Collins, a number of foreigners lived in Muscovy during the seventeenth century on a permanent or long-term basis, working in various positions. Furthermore, it is also apparent that by this time Siberia was part of the discourse of punishment, a place to settle the unwanted elements of society, be they war captives, undocumented foreigners, or landless peasants. Clearly a place with a name, a purpose, and a reputation, Siberia was part of the spatial imagination of the empire and its neighbors. Thus, the "vast unknown province" to the east was a state of mind of Western Europe rather than a geographically or historically accurate statement.

In the Middle Ages, Russia may have indeed been an isolated end of Europe with local wars around its edges, but Peter the Great was not the first ruler to change the outlook and relations with the rest of the world. Rather, the Russia that he adjusted and translated into a modern European image was a transforming and expanding empire long before Western Europeans came to realize the potential significance of the vast space to the east. From the mid-sixteenth century on, beginning with Ivan the Terrible (1533–87), Russia conquered and gradually acquired the lands of Siberia.[36] Through this acquisition, Russia connected Europe and Asia, becoming an Asian as well as a European power, its influence reaching all the way to the Pacific Ocean. Yet foreigners—and Western Europeans in particular—continued to perpetuate the myth of the land far away, still claiming one hundred years later that Siberia was a "vast unknown province."

THE STRANGE, THE ABERRANT, AND THE WONDERFUL

I had even eaten of the sweet and wonderous mutton of the Borametz plant in Tartary and, although I'd never seen it in my life, I could discuss its charming taste with my host in a way that made his mouth water. I said that its meat was like crayfish, and it had the color of a ruby or a red peach—and it had a smell, which could be compared to both a melon and an orange. . . .

But being hard at work and busied at night in a powder-mill outside the fortifications, I was in thievish wise captured and carried off by a horde of Tartars, which took me with others so far into their country that I not only could see the herb Borametz or sheep-plant growing but did even eat thereof: which is a most strange vegetable; for it is like a sheep to look upon, its wool can be spun and woven like natural sheep's wool, and its flesh is so like to mutton that even the wolves do love to eat thereof.[37]

Our fictional German travel guide, Simplicissimus, offered tales of foreign encounters and happenings in Moscow, threats of Siberian exile, and eyewitness accounts of the strange and bizarre in the distant lands of Siberia. The sheep-plant was but one such wonder that many had heard about, and a few, like our hero, even swore they had tasted. Aside from the incredible and oft-mentioned cold of the barren landscape, travelers to Siberia and the eastern parts of Russia continued to emphasize monstrous and wondrous life-forms. Although they expected and commented on the discomforts they experienced, they devoted far more ink to the aspects of the natural world that defied reason, the phenomena found on the margins that reminded them of the wonders of nature and God. Why might they have done so? What led to this persistent, fervent belief in the wondrous and monstrous at the eastern edges of Europe?

Wonder, as Caroline Bynum reminds us, is a way of knowing, of looking at the natural world; in the medieval period, wonder intertwined striking beauty, intricate artisanship, and horror.[38] Wonder focused on the aberrant, the exceptional, that which did not fit the rules and laws of nature, thereby simultaneously testing those rules and reinforcing the normal and the regular. It also engaged the senses, relying on the visual and imaginary, asking for suspension of belief in the rational. Renaissance courts, cabinets of curiosities, and eventually museums provided a stage for natural wonders, and they came to play a central role in the formation of Western science. The increase in travel to distant lands that was associated with the age of Columbus added a geographic dimension to the fascination with the aberrant and the unusual. The influx of marvels of the East into Western Europe found fertile ground for discussion of the normal, the less so, and their hierarchical relationships.[39]

Magnus's maps with sea monsters, mentioned earlier, carried on a classical tradition of representing distant places, which received renewed attention in the Renaissance. However, these sea monsters transformed into the natural objects of a far richer variety observed and described by travelers and sought after by natural philosophers of the seventeenth century. As Lorraine Daston has pointed out, unlike the supernatural, which was related to the works of God, the preternatural (beyond nature) served to elucidate that which was a part of nature.[40] These phenomena lay beyond the quotidian yet were still ruled by *some* rules of nature.[41]

Natural marvels were of particular interest to a form of science that sought to account for even the most marginal, corralling the curious and exotic sheep into the same scientific pen with their more common cousins. In the difficult balancing act of coherence of the *Wunderkamer*, the curiosity of sixteenth- and seventeenth-century scientists was combined with the collecting impulse of the wealthy. These cabinets of curiosities have been well described by historians of science.[42] Both these collections and the form of curiosity that led to their study constituted an essential part of the emergence of modern Western science. Their disappearance, as Daston notes, was not a "natural death."[43] Rather, later sciences cannibalized their preternatural philosophy, replacing wonder with diligence, and curiosity with utility.

Let us return then to our topic, the shamans of the East. In pursuit of such wonders or monsters, we need to extend our gaze to see what is behind the geographic mirror of strange objects from the East. When such marvels ceased to be marvelous, what happened to the place where they came from? Siberia did not simply transform overnight into a place of natural phenomena that are measurable and easily explained, an ordinary place similar to any other bucolic rural locale in Europe. Rather, Siberia continued to defy common sense, and it remained a geographical landmark for the marvels of nature. The story of Siberian native ritual practitioners connects the inhospitable, cold, barren landscape and strange plants of the Medieval and Renaissance periods with the later colonial fascination with the native peoples of the region, particularly with their rituals and the shamans who performed them. The larger geography of fascination may have changed over time, but it remained the overarching narrative associated with Siberia.

Take the Scythian lamb, for example. It was one of the wonders that came from the land east of Russia, attracting all the attention that a plant that grows animals on its stalks deserves:

> In the land of Tartary toward high Inde and Bacharye in the country of the Grand Can there groweth a manner of plant that is strange and wonderful indeed. This, which they call Barometz, meaning the lamb, grows from the earth in the likeness of a real lamb having head, eyes, feet and is attached at the navel to a root or stem. Its covering is an exceedingly soft wool. In height it is half a cubit and according to those who tell of this wondrous thing its taste is agreeable and its blood is sweet. It lives as long as there is

herbage within reach of the stem to which it is tethered and from which it derives its life.[44]

The story itself fit perfectly well within the medieval bestiary, and the narrative also ascribed particular attributes to the geographic and natural context surrounding this plant/animal hybrid. As with the sea monsters, the vegetable lamb claimed many faithful witnesses, who swore they had seen it growing like a flower in Tartary (the long-lasting name for Siberia and many parts of the land east and south of Moscow). But it increasingly demanded not simply observation but also explanation, which texts sought to discover in its surrounding conditions. A seventeenth-century French rendition of this wonder phenomenon, found in Claude Duret's *Histoire admirable des plantes et herbes esmerueillables et miraculeuses en nature* (1605), held that the air in this land was so dense and heavy that animal and plant had joined their efforts to survive in the inhospitable environment by becoming one strange creature. By the close of the eighteenth century in England, however, it was understood that only in Arctic cold air could such a fantastic creature emerge.

Indeed, Charles Darwin's own grandfather Erasmus memorialized this perspective in his poem Botanical Garden (1791).[45] Almost two hundred years after Duret, this poem was the rendition of a botanist who did not believe in marvels and wonders but instead focused on sexualizing the plant world, promoting science as a pleasurable, even slightly scintillating pastime so as to attract women to botany:

> Even round the pole the flames of Love aspire,
> And icy bosoms feel the secret fire!
> Cradled in snow and fanned by arctic air
> Shines, gentle Barometz! thy golden hair;
> Rooted in earth each cloven hoof descends,
> And round and round her flexile neck she bends;
> Crops the grey coral moss, and hoary thyme,
> Or laps with rosy tongue the melting rime;
> Eyes with mute tenderness her distant dam,
> Or seems to bleat, a Vegetable Lamb.[46]

For all that Samuel Taylor Coleridge admitted in 1796 that Darwin's poetry "nauseates him," the poem was highly popular and circulated widely.[47] Darwin's exaggerated verse, aimed primarily at translating and popularizing Linnaeus's classificatory system, mocked beliefs in mythical creatures while simultaneously evoking an exotic place from which such myths circulated, a place so distant that poetry and science merged into common inspiration. This land "cradled in snow and fanned by arctic air" was still capable of passion, a place entirely unlike English botanical gardens yet governed by similar emotion.

By the late eighteenth century, preternatural philosophy had lost its allure in scientific circles; the exceptional and marvelous gave way to the rule abiding and tested. Natural philosophy turned instead to developing categories to group phenomena and specimens by common features. In the years after Darwin's poem, few scientists cared any longer for the vegetable lamb of the East, even if it continued to exist in popular lore.[48] Yet such travel narratives from distant lands as well as the scientific reports regarding observations and experiments conducted there shaped these geographical locations in the imaginary landscape of early science.[49] These narratives of Siberia contributed to a spatial and cognitive perception of that place that far outlasted the vegetable lamb.

Visualizing, and consequently imagining as known, a distant place through travel and scientific descriptions is one of the tangible effects of science, particularly colonial science. This effect creates the place and imprints it with markers that are far more permanent than changes in history or scientific discoveries. Siberia was never quite the extreme opposite of Europe—the position of eastern Other was usually reserved for China or India—but it was never conceived of as belonging to Europe either. The "vast unknown province," in Dr. Collins's words, remained the vegetable lamb of geographic representations, a hybrid that did not belong to one defined category. Even after science had dismissed the lamb, the North, which once had sheltered it remained marked by those earlier accounts and the travelers' detailed impressions.

Centuries of images of a land of white death, extreme cold, and strange plants and animals all contributed to the representation of Siberia as the ideal place for banishment. It was a place between heaven and hell, and thus was a suitable purgatory for Russia's undesirables. Even after the sea monsters of the old maps and the vegetable lambs of the travelers' accounts had ceased to be geographic realities, Siberia remained a land apart, extending deep into the imagination. It would be rediscovered many times over, yet stubbornly remain a terra incognita, full of expectations, fears, and wonders. The shamans who once inhabited it would likewise play an enduring role. Unlike the vegetable lamb, they would persist as a scientific reality through ethnographic observation; then, after they had been described, they would leave Siberia, floating free through the world. As they traveled, they moved away from the maps of modern geography and onto the conceptual ones, to the extent that their specific origin could be forgotten. It is my goal in this book to bring the roots, strings, and loose tangents of the encounters and narratives about Siberia and its shamans together. I will not try to capture their essence or find the original shamans, for they are as elusive as the vegetable lamb, and equally no less real.

CHAPTER 2

Strange Landscapes, Familiar Magic

In my opinion, the most ordinary things, the most common
and familiar, if we could see them in their true light, would
turn out to be the grandest miracles of nature and the most
marvelous examples, especially as regards the subject of the
action of men.

—Michel de Montaigne (1580)[1]

By the eighteenth century, scholars and travelers throughout Europe
were familiar with Siberian shamans. Even if their understanding had no
depth, the term had resonance or at least sounded familiar.[2] Yet the stories about the shamans from earlier times did not emphasize a discovery
of new, unheard of sorcerers with unprecedented skills. To the contrary,
their existence did not seem to come as a surprise—they were almost
expected. How are we to understand this lack of surprise, the curious
anticipation of the existence of practitioners of mystical arts somewhere
else in the world, especially in a place that was described as uncharted,
untraveled, and stubbornly unknown? We might start by mapping the
landscape of magic through several preceding centuries. By tracing the
deeper genealogy of interest in magic and wonders of nature, it becomes
clear that Siberian shamans fit without difficulty into European perceptions at the time about the boundaries between human and divine, and
natural powers and forces. Puzzling as shamans might have seemed in
certain particulars of their skills, they still inhabited the edges of existing
imaginaries.[3]

Tales of shamans, told in remarkable detail in Western Europe during
the eighteenth[4] and nineteenth centuries, were a part of a historically
longer narrative about other practices, other worlds, and supernatural

powers. The cabinet of curiosities, a precursor of ethnological collections, was one such place where debates about the possibilities of the imaginary kind occurred, and connections between the fantastic and the natural were drawn. In Europe from the sixteenth century on, physical encounters between different peoples, religions, customs, and exotic objects intermingled easily with the fables about them, creating a setting for scholarly debates about mysticism, alchemy, and magic.

To illustrate my point, let us examine the legend of the Golem of Prague, a creature made by man to serve his needs and carry out tasks.[5] Allegedly a sixteenth-century tale of the consequences of abuse of supernatural powers, the story gives a frame for the space of inquiry that shamans filled. I suggest that the popular nineteenth-century version of the legend serves as a bridge between the world of alchemy of earlier periods and the concern with scientific rules, laboratories, and scientists that emerged later. The Siberian "sorcerers" remain interesting in their particulars, but before we explore claims about their differences, we should first recognize their similarities from the evolving European perspective. After all, many a golem creator, mystic, or practitioner of necromancy foreshadowed them.

It was a double move between difference and similarity that allowed the later portrayals to present shamans as ancestral: simultaneously related yet remote. Thus, in this chapter I focus on how and why these Eastern practitioners appeared relatively familiar rather than radically foreign to many students of Europe's own magic. The golem and the shaman were both figures that took up crucial space in the imaginary, both traditional and cultural, and they were also malleable enough to change shape over the centuries of tales.

THE MANY SPLENDORS OF THE WORLD

Early accounts of the strange and wondrous phenomena in far-away places invariably took the form of unique experiences presented in a first-person narrative. Yet these stories spoke a familiar language, which resonated with the interests of the natural philosophers of their time: the alchemists, the followers and practitioners of the occult, and the investigators of the rules underlying the world of nature.[6] Humanistic studies, early medicine, and natural history were all intertwined in an effort to understand the underlying rules governing nature and the universe, rules believed to have been laid down by God. It is in these interstices between nature, the divine, the human, and the otherworldly that we can situate the genealogy of responses to Siberian shamans.

By the mid-eighteenth century, stories of wild magicians living in the eastern parts of Russia were circulating throughout Western Europe. Heard, and on occasion also read, these implausible, fantastic tales described distant strangers who were possibly not quite human.[7] Yet they also resembled something familiar, resonating with undercurrents recognizable in many regions of Europe. At that time, the alleged spiritual powers of shamans, which are now seemingly beyond comprehension, echoed in an imagination for which a language had already existed since at least the medieval period. Supernatural forces were said to have acted on specific people or on whole villages for centuries. They manifested themselves not only as strange ailments, but also as artistic talents, medical skills, or visions of events past or future. Such powers were not always threatening; at times, they were admirable, instrumental, and possibly very useful. The invisible forces and beings that affected individual and collective lives have had a range of names. Thus, magic, spirits, witchcraft, sorcery, and the occult have all had a long tradition in Europe, and they are useful guides in understanding the reception of Siberian shamans once they had entered from the far side of the stage.[8]

However, to claim an uninterrupted continuity in thinking about magic from the Middle Ages to the nineteenth century debates on shamans would risk overlooking historical variations. The stories of shamanic experiences in distant places are more like threads of different color in a weave of histories about magic, healing, and studies of nature. Therefore, I frame the reception of shamanic encounters more as a loom, a frame of sorts that shaped these tales about distant others. Earlier stories of magic and supernatural powers provided a pattern within European imagination through which to incorporate the shamans when their time came.

THE COMFORTING FAMILIARITY OF THE STRANGE AND WONDROUS

European exploration in the late fifteenth century not only brought unimaginable riches but also pointed at new horizons. The travelers recounted stories about the wealth of other peoples and about animals, plants, and treasures of nature.[9] These discoveries created a simultaneous dilemma of comparison and curiosity. The curiosity focused on that which was new, unheard of, or supposedly unimaginable. Yet how did any of these wonders, strange and foreign, compare to the many mysteries at home? The discoveries resonated deeply with phenomena that had already been circulating for several centuries through Europe, long before men gave in to their yearning for the distant, in the form of a passion for travel and exploration as a full-time profession. Powerful magic and invisible forces, natural or spiritual, became popular topics of discussion among learned men. The discussions traveled widely across religious circles, among painters and their apprentices, and amid members of the court who pursued the education due their social position.[10]

To appreciate the impact of the new knowledge brought back to Western Europe by travelers, missionaries, and explorers from overseas voyages after 1500, we may wish to rethink the idea of Europe as a monolithic collection of Christian lands.[11] Catholics and Protestants fought tenaciously and brutally for the souls of peasants and nobles as well as for the territories of their sovereigns, each often accusing the other of heresy. But religion was not the only force that stirred the popular and historical currents. The makeup of Europe, even in this early historic period, was far more complicated.[12] Royal courts and cities in particular were places of great diversity in learning and religious practices. Abundance of contact between the cultures of the continent as well as between Europe and the wide Mediterranean world led to an exchange of stories, foods, material goods, and ideas. In this context, interest in natural philosophy and the practical aspects of natural magic resonated with the tales of distant lands, which found receptive audiences.[13]

Our recent history tends to focus on ethnicity and race as the defining characteristics of group identity, and we assume that nation states reflect natural affinities. From this general view, Europe appears a racially homogenous space, fragmented by ethnic conflicts along linguistic and cultural lines. Individual ethnic groups, who are portrayed as facing conflicts with other equally homogenous groups, are ultimately viewed as lacking true racial or religious diversity.[14] Yet as historians repeatedly point out, Europe has long had porous, contested boundaries, and the modern nation state only emerged in the nineteenth century.[15] Immigrants, travelers, and pilgrims moved from place to place, residents of nowhere and everywhere. Political and cultural identities were dynamic, defined as much by opposition to other places and peoples and religious affiliations as any certain sense of stable presence. As Slack and Innes stress, "There exists no one 'Europe,' whose history can be written in a linear fashion."[16] Nation states ultimately had to be built out of heterogeneous and resistant materials, conscious of their dissimilarities, and pulled in multiple directions. The southern parts of the continent in particular were exposed to influences from the Near East and North Africa as well as such distant places as China and India. The Mediterranean Sea washed diversity into a pattern, even if with shifting and waning shores.

The Ottoman Empire played a significant role in the cultural, religious, and political history of the world, and it had a major influence on learning in early modern Europe.[17] Looking at Europe from the East, it appears a strange, barbaric northern region adjacent to the much larger Muslim world. Aside from a loose religious mapping, Europe had no particularly defined sense of geographic space as a cultural entity until at least the end of the seventeenth century.[18] More accurately, Europe should be viewed as a historically changing concept: a construct.[19] As numerous historians have pointed out, the details of world regions and their peripheries belie many of our current assumptions.

Thus, when the pilgrims and crusaders of the Middle Ages brought home collectible wonders and marvelous possessions, these were incorporated and accommodated into the expectations of the time. These novelties may not have been common or pedestrian to the Europeans, but they did exist within their realm of what was imaginable. The strange had a place in their world, for common people and scholars alike. The wondrous and the strange spread widely through folkloric traditions, and even if some doctrines condemned curiosity as a sin, it found channels that allowed it to thrive just as fervently in learned circles. Alchemy and interests in the occult and practical magic intertwined quite easily with the new descriptions of natural and strange wonders in distant places.

INTIMATE STRANGERS

Until the late fifteenth century, a significant number of Arabs, Jews, and Christians lived in close proximity and interacted daily on the Iberian Peninsula, in what we would now call Spain.[20] Each of these religious and ethnic groups regularly felt at risk, both spiritually and physically, from the others. Their interactions were marked by intense violence as well as ongoing coexistence and intimate knowledge and awareness of the presence of the others.[21] Arabs and Jews were as much, if not more, a part of the circulation of knowledge in European royal courts as Christians. They had a major influence on debates about medicine, knowledge, science, and magic. Many scholars of the time considered magic a potential part of the arts in terms similar to grammar. Grammar, a serious subject of study, was viewed as essential in comprehending knowledge. By undergirding language and thereby all knowledge, it gave structure to thought and served the practical purpose of conveying thought. For early science, magic held out a similar prospect of providing an explanatory structure, a technical guide of how invisible forces worked. It had a useful purpose in applying knowledge acquired through the practice of specific skills.

The inclusion of magic in the arts reflected the influence of Arabic philosophy and learning, which was firmly established in Mediterranean scholarly circles by the middle of the twelfth century.[22] Pietro Alfonsi, a twelfth-century Jewish astronomer, physician, and theologian from Andalusia, who had converted to Christianity and received Arabic education attested to this:

> One of his pupils spoke to a teacher and said to him, "I would like for you to enumerate the seven arts, seven principles and seven gentlemanly pursuits in order." The teacher answered, "I will enumerate them for you. These are the arts: dialectics, arithmetic, geometry, physics, music, and astronomy. Concerning the seventh, many diverse opinions exist. The philosophers who do not believe in prognostication say that necromancy is the seventh; others among them, namely those who believe in prognostication and in philosophy, think that it should be a science which encompasses all natural matters and mundane elements. Those who do not devote themselves to philosophy say that it is grammar. These are the gentlemanly pursuits: riding, swimming, archery, boxing, fowling, chess, and poetry. The principles are the avoidance of gluttony, drunkenness, lust, violence, lying, avariciousness, and evil conversation."[23]

It is clear from this passage that while "evil conversation" was to be avoided, the roles of necromancy, prognostication, and grammar were open to discussion. While their relative status might be a subject of argument, their moral and religious standing did not preclude them from recognition. Both the temptation and the religious threat of magic lay precisely in its potential power. Necromancy, a divination practice akin to magic that involved invoking the dead, was rooted in the belief in the survival of the soul in the afterlife. Its inclusion or exclusion among the arts was based on the relative value given to the practice of predicting the future—or prognostication—as well as the study of language.

We now usually think about magic and witchcraft as synonymous, especially in the context of medieval Europe. However, it is important to recognize that magic was a plural form, and that its practitioners in different periods recognized many shifting varieties. It became associated with witches and evil deeds later on, but at one time magic played a vital role in European intellectual, scientific, and cultural life.[24] In the ancient Mediterranean world, magical practices were deemed morally neutral and could be used by an individual for beneficial or harmful purposes.[25] It was Christianity that developed an antagonistic relationship with magic, associating it with demons and relegating it to the domain of Satan. That however did not mean that with the rise of Christianity all magic simply transformed into acts of the devil. Rather, as Peter Brown notes, "the human agent is pushed into a corner by the demonhost."[26] Satan was the archenemy, and all energy in combating evil magic focused on defeating this particular evildoer. Ordinary human magic practitioners were insignificant in comparison, deserving scarce attention. Consequently, the rise in scholarly magic among the educated classes of Western Europe grew quite widespread during the Renaissance. Alchemy, astronomy, natural history, necromancy, and spiritual and demonic magic, rooted in Arab, Greek, and Jewish texts, enjoyed substantial interest among scholars and members of the royal courts of Europe.[27]

Amid such an elite, higher, educated class, an interest in magic and mystical forces not only continued but thrived, and this was the milieu in which stories about shamans would later take hold. The practice of courtly and scholarly magic differed quite significantly from the charms, spells, potions, and rituals that came to be associated with devilish rituals and witchcraft, even though the latter were practiced by large segments of the population, including many clerics. The scholarly pursuit of learned magic, where knowledge of Arabic, Hebrew, and Latin was essential, was an elite endeavor that involved complex practices and took years to learn and understand. When stories of shamans and their marvelous and strange deeds arrived in the West via educated travelers, the "foreign correspondents" of their time, the scientists and physicians, intrigued, popularized them. These tales resonated more with the existing traditions of scholarly practices and knowledge than they did with the local folklore, with its fear of witchcraft. Thus, shamans easily became seen as the scholars, wise men, and priests of the East. Although strange and foreign, shamans were already quite familiar and recognizable as a type to some, who regarded them as a piece of the puzzle, the shape of which to be explored and defined but with a perceived image that was familiar, expected, and ultimately unsurprising. For many, magic was an article of faith.

MULTICULTURAL ENCOUNTERS

Several historic events in 1492 had far reaching consequences for the multicultural environment of the later centuries. The most widely discussed affair was the overseas travel of Christopher Columbus on behalf of the Spanish kingdom. The subsequent discovery of the New World was well known among European merchants, migrants, explorers, and vast local audiences. The opening of new horizons was reflected in, but also driven by, the great interest in the exotic objects, animals, plants, and riches that accumulated in collections in many royal courts. Yet, as Flores points out, similarly great interest in exotic, strange, and "beyond imaginable" phenomena thrived in other parts of the globe outside Europe.[28] The meeting of the different, new worlds was not merely a creation of the Other for Europe, but also a recognition of connections between regions, continents, and peoples.[29] Therefore, we may view some of the encounters and tales about the distant worlds as cross-currents rather than a unidirectional flow. This notion of a back-and-forth of ideas is a productive angle if we wish to understand the European reaction to narratives about peoples with strange customs, which regularly featured descriptions of people who blurred the boundary between the human and animal worlds, just like shamans. As such tales circulated and recirculated, the characters within them became familiarly foreign, exotic acquaintances, whose presence attested to the distance traveled.

Other historically significant events of 1492 had similarly far-reaching consequences, particularly for scholarly and intellectual life. The Moors, Arabs from North Africa who settled in Iberia in the eighth century, were defeated in Spain in the summer of 1492. Together with the Jewish communities that had lived there for centuries, they were ordered to leave and were expelled from the entire peninsula. Many of the Muslims and Jews who remained in Spain converted to Christianity while continuing practice of their religion in private.[30] However, the great majority were banished, and they dispersed throughout the European continent, ending quite far in western but also central and eastern Europe. The educated elite of Europe had been familiar with Arabic and Jewish texts for some time, but after the fifteenth century, their scholars' reading materials were not only available but also their communities became a physical presence in great numbers throughout the continent. The rise in interest in mysticism and the occult in particular was to a significant degree influenced by this new personal level of multicultural exchange throughout the continent, a result of the presence of Jewish scholars, translations of Arabic texts, and the inclusion of Arabic traditions. In these philosophies, the occult, hidden powers, and mystical practices were deemed as operating within the natural rather than a supernatural order. Educated writers of the period cited such phenomena as works of natural magic, in effect reclaiming a classical sense of the term "magic."

"Magic" and "religion" were both common terms in medieval discourse, and not always viewed as opposites or even as essentially distinct categories.[31] The relationships, rather than contrasts, between spirits, nature, and life permeated scholarly discussions and allowed for an unprecedented degree of curiosity about distant places and remote experiences. The strange and wondrous appealed to the aesthetic sensibilities and nourished the scholarly imagination. As the historian Peter Harrison has argued, the term "religion" as we know it today is a nineteenth century invention, parallel to the emergence of science.[32] Following the lead of several historians of science, we might reasonably fold magic, science, and religion all back into a package that fits the "job description" of a shaman.[33] This is not to say that the historical figures we describe with that term undertook all the tasks of a modern professional in any given domain, from performer, to chemist, to priest. Rather, what we need to grasp is that contemporary distinctions between such categories were not obvious to our ancestors, on either side of encounters.

CABINETS OF CURIOUS OBJECTS

A number of European royal courts during the sixteenth and seventeenth centuries encouraged humanistic and philosophical research into the mysteries of the universe, natural wonders, and practical arts. However, it was the court of the Hapsburg emperor Rudolf II where such studies attracted particular attention. From the earliest period of colonial travel, the Hapsburgs were well known among all the courts of Europe as fervent collectors of objects and artifacts of extraordinary nature. A famous member of the family, Margaret of Austria (1480–1530) was one of the first beneficiaries of contact with the New World, accumulating in her palace a large collection of curious and rare ethnographic objects and specimens from the overseas explorations.[34] Hers was one of the earliest efforts to gather and display natural and cultural wonders together in one space, foreshadowing the widespread use of cabinets of curiosities in noble households. Furthermore, she combined and juxtaposed New World objects with Old World antiquities, a practice that attracted attention from courts throughout the continent. This eclectic collection signaled the appropriation of novelties as private possessions of a wealthy patron, but also highlighted connections between the mysteries and histories of the Old and New Worlds.

The driving impulse behind the collection and display of the objects in Margaret's royal house was an imperial gesture of claiming the newly discovered world as a subject. However, aside from a quest for status, newly emerging philosophical currents underpinned the custom. The recently discovered New World was not the only one that was peculiar and full of wonders, for the Old World collections also featured the curious and unique, such as fossils, deformed body parts, pictures of unicorns and supposed real unicorn horns, and gems and prehistoric stone tools. These objects were not collected for their practical value or any utilitarian purpose, nor were they mere playthings, pleasing the aesthetic sensibilities. Their value resided in their uniqueness, in the connection of art and nature in the pre-Enlightenment understanding of the world. Exotic, otherworldly phenomena and experiences were joined in one display. Paintings by well-known masters placed next to measuring instruments and fossil fish were a narrative about the workings of the world. The instrumental value of such collections was their insight into the mysteries of nature and art, and the possibility of affecting both by placing them together.

Margaret's display assembled a carefully chosen assortment of odd objects: "twelve pieces of exotic fabric, which were used for practical purposes such as curtains or bed hangings; twelve pieces of clothing for both men and women sewn with gold, fur, and feathers; twelve shields, decorated with items such as turquoise, plumes, gold, and gems; more leg guards also decorated with precious materials, feathers, and bells; seven ceremonial "helmets" (headdresses) elaborately decorated, as well as six arrows, four feather fans, three bracelets."[35] Locating the objects in the library, a place for perusing maps, letters, and printed materials about the travels, turned them into a recognized source of information. Such collections were not for mere viewing, pleasure or entertainment of anyone who walked into the residence; rather, they were a part of a discourse, an educated discussion on nature and the world in general. Knowledge, as much of it as possible, in strange combinations and associations, was on display for the purpose of visual and intellectual consumption: part performance, part self-fashioning, part conversation.

The spectacle served the purpose of distinction and indicated a proprietary sense toward other worlds. But it was also an invitation to philosophical, social, and diplomatic interactions. The objects were not an end point but the beginning of a dialogue, a conversation about a wider range of topics. Alongside the strange objects brought from distant places was a simultaneous explosion of interest in local discoveries of bizarre, natural, and unnatural objects, transmutations, fossils, and "artificialia"—objects made by human hand and considered equally fascinating. The culture of curiosity that materialized through such collections of wonders was not merely about material possessions to be had; it represented also a conception of the natural and the supernatural as part of the same macrocosm, which could be experienced through the senses or empirically observed. As Caroline Bynum has pointed out, the sense of wonder was at once an expression of curiosity about the world and a recognition of the unknown aspects that came into view: "To medieval thinkers, human beings cannot wonder at what is not there; but neither can we wonder at that which we fully understand."[36] Wonders were objects and phenomena to be collected, displayed, and discussed. Because they were not fully understood, these objects retained a core of mystery and magic.

The complex relationship among images, spirituality, and materiality in the investigation of nature was fully captured in the *Kunstkammer*—a separate room set aside as a space for wonder, the "cabinet of curiosities" that became all the rage in the sixteenth century.[37] A statement of worldview in which humans, animals, plants, and monsters all fit together, the Kunstkammer pointed at a search for truth and reality where magic and the supernatural intertwined as part of the same formula. Once the objects were moved out of the library, seen as sterile and not allowing a sensory experience, into a separate, specially designed space, they were recognized as a different source of information than a text. Their physical materiality and dimensions took precedence over the written word. Calling on other senses than reading, a display of objects in a Kunstkamera reoriented the debates about wonder and magic. The spatial display of art and nature together encouraged engagement between them and simultaneously created a laboratory and a theater. It was the performative aspect of both art and natural phenomena that resulted in wonder and magic. Thus, when shamanic performances as described by travelers arrived in Europe, they resonated deeply with the sort of engagements witnessed in the cabinets of curiosities as well as in scientific theaters and laboratories.

FIGURE 2.1. Mercurius as a Three-Headed Python. A 1760 reproduction of a fifteenth-century image from a manuscript by well-known alchemist Johan Isaac Hollandus. A symbolic representation of an alchemical process, a human-animal hybrid, the image illustrates early fascination with magic and the possibility of transformations between substances, beings, humans, and animals. Mellon MS. 110. (Reproduced with permission from the General Collection, Beinecke Rare Book and Manuscript Library, Yale University.)

For our story, an additional fact bears significance: these same cabinets of curiosity, with their mélange of magic and wonder, nature and culture, were precursors to ethnographic and archaeological museums, and thus to the broader history of anthropology as a field. Both the Ashmolean and the Pitt Rivers Museum at Oxford are descendants of such cabinets, which included the first stuffed, complete Dodo bird as well as Chief Powhatan's mantle and the cloak of Pocahontas's father all collected and displayed under one roof.[38] At the other edge of Europe, Peter the Great likewise accumulated ethnographic objects from every place he ever visited, heard about, or found curious. Objects from Siberia featured in many of his rooms in Saint Petersburg. True to his name and reputation, when the emperor revealed his collection in 1725, it was the largest building ever conceived for such a project. Later named the Peter the Great Museum of Anthropology and Ethnography, it remains to this day the largest museum of ethnography in Russia, and its collection of shamans' tools are still all in the same place.[39]

RUDOLF II AND THE POWER OF MAGIC

I now return to the Holy Roman Emperor, Rudolf II, of the Hapsburg dynasty for several reasons. Rudolf not only perfected the art of the Kunstkammer, but also enfolded it into a scholarly pursuit of all things magical, supernatural, and natural. His reign truly embodied to an extreme degree the vibrant, multicultural milieu of sixteenth-century Europe.[40] The emperor's court attracted an assortment of scholars of the day and encouraged a fascination with alchemy, creation of artificial life, and crossing boundaries between religious rules and mysteries of nature. Most nobles and royals of the period accumulated vast collections in their palaces, but Rudolf's Kunstkammer at the Prague castle was renowned as the most extravagant in all of Europe. Unicorn horns, fossil fish and plants, magic stones, ivories, and scientific instruments were piled up alongside thousands of paintings by renowned artists in rooms designated for such a purpose. The collections were a reflection of and a medium for discussions. Speaking to the mysteries of life and nature, to magic that could transform substances, and to treatises on the deepest natural philosophy, these objects were a vital part of not just the royal court but also the scholarly circles of Prague.

The familiar story of the golem, set during the time of Rudolph, offers a window into the world of courtly research into magical powers. At the same time, the nineteenth-century rendition of the tale illustrates the shift from including discussions of magic within the study of forces of nature to presenting it as a feature of folktales.[41]

> During the reign of Rudolph II there lived among the Jews of Prague a man named Bezalel Löw, who, because of his tall stature and great learning, was called "der hohe" [the Great] Rabbi Löw. This rabbi was well versed in all of the arts and sciences, especially in the Kabbalah. By means of this art he could bring to life figures formed out of clay or carved from wood who like real men, would perform whatever task was asked of them. Such homemade servants are very valuable: they do not eat; they do not drink; and they do not require any wages. They work untiringly; one can scold them, and they do not answer back.
>
> Rabbi Löw had fashioned for himself one such servant out of clay, placed in his mouth the Name (a magic formula), and thereby brought him to life. This artificial servant performed all of the menial tasks in the house throughout the week: chopping wood, carrying water, etc. On the Sabbath, however, he was required to rest; therefore, before the day of rest had begun, his master removed from his mouth the Name and made him dead. Once, however, the rabbi forgot to do this, and calamity ensued. The magical servant became enraged, tore down houses, threw rocks all around, pulled up trees, and carried on horribly in the streets. People hurried to the rabbi to tell him of the situation. But the difficulty was great; the Sabbath was already at hand, and all labor, whether to create or to destroy, was strictly forbidden. How, then, to undo the magic? The rabbi's dilemma with his Golem was like that of the sorcerer's apprentice and his broom in Goethe's poems. Fortunately, the Sabbath had not yet been consecrated in the Altneu synagogue, and since this is the oldest and most honorable synagogue in Prague, everything is set according to it. There was still time to remove the Name from the crazy youth. The master hurried, tore the magic formula from the mouth of the Golem, and the lump of clay dropped down and fell in a heap. Alarmed by this event, the rabbi did not wish to make such a dangerous servant again. Even today pieces of the Golem are to be seen in the attic of the Altneu synagogue.[42]

The legend of the golem captures the dilemma of mystical powers and scientific rules that scholars in the nineteenth century grappled with. Siberian shamans represented a solution to this problem, as practitioners of magic who could be cast as scientists and priests in one. In a historical study on the roots of the legend, Kieval shows that associating the golem legend with Rabbi Löw, the so-called Maharal of Prague, is likely a case of an invented tradition, the result of a later intersection of Jewish, German, and Czech political and cultural interests.[43] Yet even if we are dealing with an invented tradition—or even possibly because it was fresh and new in the nineteenth century—this tale has resonated broadly across literature and the arts.

I evoke the tale first and foremost to emphasize the important place of magic in central Europe of the sixteenth century. Natural philosophy, the investigation of the natural world as laid out by God, aimed to understand what the purpose of any given thing was. However, as Adrian Johns points out, natural philosophy remained a controversial practice, not least because it artfully appropriated non-Christian sources.[44] The influence of ancient, Arabic, and Jewish sources was transparently obvious to all learned scholars of the times. In Frances Yates's words, "Prague became a Mecca for those interested in esoteric and scientific studies from all over Europe. Hither came John Dee and Edward Kelly, Giordano Bruno and Johannes Kepler."[45] Alchemy, astrology, and astronomy, the occult and studies of the Kabbalah, all were encouraged and supported, giving magic a respected status and a home in the numerous institutions created by the emperor. Those interested in secret knowledge were deeply involved in the scholarly research of the period, investigating and establishing links between studies of nature and practices of magic.

The scientists of Rudolfine Prague were deeply invested in observations of nature, creating bestiaries and herbaria based on extensive fieldwork. Illustrations of nature, plants, animals, and minerals point at the seamless domain that included art alongside natural history. Herbal remedies appear in detail, and gardens not only sought to reproduce the possible designs of the Garden of Eden but also to replicate and analyze local environments and to understand "regional ecosystems." Peter Dear draws attention to this ambiguity in natural philosophy of the early modern period by pointing out that the field contained both contemplative and practical knowledge.[46]

Philosophical inquiries and practical magic of the seventeenth century laid out a space that was open to the reception of investigations of these same questions in other, quite distant contexts. To the extent that shamans were described by travelers as conjurers and magicians who simultaneously possessed knowledge obscured to others and acted on it in practical matters such as curing diseases or making remedies, they fit easily into Rudolf's conceptual cabinet.

In relation to the legend of golem, I want to emphasize continuities amid the European fascination with magic and mysticism on the one hand, while on the other, stressing the conceptual breaks with categories of the present day. The Golem of Prague can serve as a useful metaphorical guide to art, learning, religion, or practical magic. At the same time, the golem's uncertain origins—myth or reality, invented tradition or cultural history of a concept—reminds us of the multiple prehistories of an idea. When stories of Siberian shamans were incorporated into eighteenth-century discussions of the boundaries between creativity, nature, and human society, it was not a moment of a sudden discovery, or a break from previous times. To the contrary, these relationships had been of great fascination for centuries and had long resonated with scholarly interests. Recognizing this parallel historical process should help us understand the route by which shamans, religious leaders, scholars, and artists came to be accepted as all belonging to the same category, even while living in different contexts and in different lands.

The place of magic and the occult in the early modern period has become a topic of debate among historians and historians of science in an effort to define a break or a boundary between magic and science.[47] It also has opened the space to question the actual place and time of one of the major markers of European history: the Scientific Revolution.[48] My main interest in addressing magic and magical practices at such length is to outline the persistence of fascination with mysticism and its continuing practice, so as to explain the reception of the idea that magic existed in distant, foreign places. As Leigh Eric Schmidt astutely observed, "despite varied pressures of reform in the early modern world, magical practices proved highly resilient, particularly in their old dance with natural philosophy. The Enlightenment did not so much assault magic as absorb and secularize it."[49] Early modern European thought about nature, magic, the senses, experience, and human–animal relationships is misrepresented when recast in the modern language of religion, science, and magic. In keeping with recent scholarship on magic, alchemy, talking animals, and fairies that live in natural places, before deploying categories like "magic" in prehistory, we ought first to confront its historical understanding in Europe as well as in distant places. Meeting Siberian shamans is then not surprising per se. It is their persistence and durability that requires explanation.

CHAPTER 3

People in a Land before Time

The province of Siberia borders upon Permia and Viatka; but
I have been unable to learn whether it contains any cities or
fortresses.

—Sigmund von Herberstein (1530)[1]

Narratives of Russian expansion in the East are haunted by a persistent,
willful ignorance, what the historian Robert Proctor called "agnotology," a culturally and historically induced willingness not to know, a
stubborn desire not to find out.[2] Yet as Nancy Tuana and Shannon Sullivan point out, "we cannot fully understand the complex practices of
knowledge production and the variety of features that account for why
something is known, without also understanding the practices that account for not knowing."[3] A striking theme, repeated from the earliest
times of exploration in Siberia, was to emphasize the unknown or imperfectly known character of anything to the east of Moscow or Saint
Petersburg.[4] A 1572 Russian manuscript with one of the earliest descriptions of Siberia introduces the land with a chapter entitled "About the
Unknown People in the East and Their Various Languages," setting a
tone that was to last for centuries.[5] From the sixteenth century on, travelers, explorers, and geographers described in detail the rivers, animals,
forests, and people, who were geographically ambiguously called the
inhabitants of Tartary: their strange customs, and bizarre, disgusting,
generous or kind behavior.

Reports were filed, letters delivered, dairies published and read, maps
circulated, yet the accounts of Siberia continued to describe the land as
isolated, impenetrable, and unknowable. Writers and travelers, Russian
and foreign, began their narratives with an adamant proclamation—so
unknown is this land, that I will tell of glimpses that only a few have

caught: "Indeed, hitherto no man of parts or abilities has been suffered to travel the Country," claimed Samuel Collins in 1671.[6] Later in the same text he noted, "Siberia is a vast unknown Province, reaching to the Walls of Cataya. I have spoken with one that was there, who traded with the Chircasses, and amongst also who said he saw a Sea beyond Syberia wherein were Ships and Men in strange habits."[7] Almost a hundred years and many travelers later, John Bell testified in 1763:

> This vast extent of eastern continent is bounded by Russia to the west, by Great Tartary to the south; on the east and north by the respective oceans; its circumference is not easy to ascertain. Foreigners commonly are terrified at the very name of Siberia, or Sibir as it is sometimes called; but from what I have said concerning it, I presume it will be granted, that it is by no means so bad as is generally imagined.[8]

George Kennan's introduction to his 1876 essay, in which he described an arduous dogsled journey through northeastern Siberia and Kamchatka, is then to be expected as confirming the unknown:

> Few parts of the globe, and few races of men at the present day, are less known to science, to literature, and to the civilized public generally than the vast plains of Northeastern Siberia, and the wild tribes of natives who wander with their herds of reindeer from the Okhotsk sea to the low wind-swept shores of the Arctic ocean.[9]

The question that comes to mind then is this: if there were travel accounts of the land, why the insistence on the obscure and frightful nature of this remote and frozen tundra? Why did the writers provide such rich detail yet simultaneously insist that readers see nothing but a desolate, unfamiliar landscape? Was it to conceal, reveal, or engage the imaginary through tantalizing detail about what may lie at a distance?

This chapter charts the multiple motives—and the consequences—of the early accounts of Siberia that established it as an unknown space in the East. For all that the intentions of mapping and describing the region may have changed over time, the theme of the unfamiliar proved remarkably durable. My main interest here is to trace the emergence of Siberia's diverse native peoples from this fog of the unknown. The guides that brought them forward to Western attention were both foreign travelers exploring routes to China and Russian settlers moving east in a quest for riches.

The foreign accounts explored Tartary but continuously reminded the reader that this was a part of Muscovy, a foreign land in its own right. This compare and contrast frame resulted in travelogues that passed judgment on the Russians and on Muscovy even while describing the newly encountered native "hordes." In contrast, when the Russian government handed out the land, it claimed that "nobody" occupied the vast stretches in the east. When fur and taxes were collected, however, obstinate natives were everywhere—reluctant, resisting, and in need of coercion. Siberia was simultaneously the land of plenty, valued by the czar, and a barren reminder of the closeness of Russia to Asia. The end result is a case study of settler colonialism that was quite different from those of other empires. The anxiety about Russia's place in Europe, on the part of Muscovy itself and by western European rulers, shaped the treatment and representation of the landscape and the native peoples of the region as much, if not more, as any colonial aspirations or desires for the wealth Siberia possessed.

THE BEGINNINGS OF EMPTINESS, FILLED BY PEOPLE

European knowledge of Russia based on a first-person eyewitness account, an actual visit of the place in a traditional ethnographic sense, began with the sixteenth century writing of Sigismund von Herberstein.[10] An imperial army officer and a university-educated ambassador of the Hapsburg Empire, Herberstein visited Russia several times between 1516–18 and 1526, residing in Moscow for an extended period.[11] Herberstein's best-known treaty *Notes on Muscovy: Rerum Moscoviticarum Commentarii* (published in Latin 1549, in Italian in 1550, in German in 1557, and in English in 1577, with multiple editions in Latin and German in between) was based on his own observations, extensive readings, and a corroboration of other accounts.[12] His account of life in Muscovy is arguably the first true ethnographic description, repeated with great relish by many subsequent travelers, armchair or otherwise. The Hapsburg ambassador was not a passive observer; he certainly did not copy previous reports, and he actually frequently challenged them.[13] Yet his focus ultimately rested on the politics, religion, and trade of the capital city, Moscow, as he had arrived to negotiate a peace treaty, not to observe the customs of the natives, Russian or otherwise.

Herberstein's *Notes* (1551) was the most popular description of Russia in his day and remained so for centuries afterward. It was very quickly translated into many languages and was used by traders and rulers alike who were interested in conducting business with Russia. Yet the work had little to say about the vast land to the east. Although Herberstein traveled widely around the capitol and the adjacent provinces,

Siberia was weeks, even months away, and a space beyond imagination. Nevertheless, amid his astute assessments of the Russian ruling dynasty, history, trade rules, and social customs, Herberstein could not resist recounting the tales that he had heard. One such story featured a Siberian people from the region of the river Ob who died in the fall, exactly on the Orthodox holiday of St. George, only to come back to life in the spring: "It is said that a certain incredible occurrence, and very like a fable, happens every year to the people of Lucomorye, namely that they die on the 27th of November, which among the Russians is dedicated to St. George, and come to life again like the frogs in the following spring, generally on the 24th of April."[14]

Centuries later Russian folklorists explained this tale as a variation on a common folktale about seasonal changes.[15] Eighteenth-century German geographers, on the other hand, suggested that underground winter lodges could have accounted for this people's disappearance in the autumn and reappearance in the spring.[16] The story captured sufficient imagination that it was repeated regularly; as the event was increasingly witnessed by many, who attested to it, it became factual. While both interpretations of the fable are plausible, it is quite a bit harder to trace some of the other commonly circulated tales that Herberstein included in his accounts of Siberia, such as those of people with mouths on their chests.[17] With remarkably specific geographic locations, including rivers, their tributaries, and estimated months of his journey, Herberstein described people who resembled animals, just as hairy, others with heads like dogs, and yet another group with no heads at all.

> Moreover, from the sources of the same river, rises another river Cassima, which after passing through the district of Lucomorya, flows into the great river Tachnin; beyond which are said to dwell men of prodigious stature, some of whom are covered all over with hair, like wild beasts, while others have heads like dogs, and others have no necks, their breasts occupying the place of a head, while they have long hands, but no feet.[18]

Herberstein credited all descriptions to a "Russian traveler," and as he was moderately skeptical, he included the place names and urged others to visit Siberia and verify the accounts.[19] Marvels and monsters aside, if we read the text as a map of the empire, it is clear that in the sixteenth century Russia was really known only up to the Ural Mountains. The river Ob, in present-day western Siberia, was estimated to have taken weeks of journeying from Moscow. The bounds of the empire, described

FIGURE 3.1. Sigmund von Herberstein's map, 1549. A map of Muscovy based on an actual eyewitness account of Sigmund von Herberstein of the region surrounding Moscow. The limits of geographic knowledge are obvious with Moscow at the center of the map and only a limited region to the east recorded with any precision. At the same time, "Slata Baba" (Golden Maiden), the mythical carved idol of the native people living to the east of River Ob, is placed in the upper-right-hand corner as a geographic marker. The "Iuhra" native people later claimed as Yugra (or Khanty and Mantsi) are labeled in the very upper-right-hand corner east from the River Ob. The Bohdan & Neonila Krawciw Ucrainica Antique Map Collection. Uk-231. Record no. G7010.1549 H4. (Reproduced with permission from the Harvard Map Library, Harvard University.)

as vast stretches of frozen wasteland, expanded farther to the East and North. It was a place where one could only with the greatest difficulty distinguish between the Siberian native peoples, monsters and animals.

PICTURES FROM AN EXHIBITION

So what do we know about the people who lived in the space that the ancient Greeks—and almost everyone following their tradition during and after the Renaissance—deemed inhospitable, brutal, and full of monsters? Whence came this knowledge from reliable, eyewitness accounts? Who provided the other stories, the ones that were not fables of the Orient or folktales of unimaginable monsters?

Unlike in medieval Western Europe, mapping and knowing their territory was not an immediate or urgent concern for Russian rulers. A centrally organized state that needed the support of illustrated documents such as maps only came into existence in Russia later, and it would proceed at a much slower pace than in Western Europe or China.[20] However, this cartographic blind spot should not be interpreted as a lack of awareness of the physical surroundings or as a lack of a need of travel routes. Rather, this was the result of the different attitude of the rulers, the educated few, and the nobility toward their land, the subjects who occupied it, and the possession and representation of that space in a printed form. Although maps became more common under Ivan the Terrible (1533–84), it would be almost two hundred years later under Peter the Great (1682–1725) that the territorial expansion of the previous centuries acquired a new meaning.[21] In fact, the area to the east was almost as unreal to the Russians in the sixteenth century as it was to the Greeks, and they both viewed it as "uninhabited." It was of little imperial interest until conflicts with other empires and a market for sable furs brought the land into sharp focus as real and desirable. Furthermore, Peter the Great, while traveling extensively through Western Europe, encountered different concepts of the relationship between the state and land, and the ruler and the land.[22] He came to realize that having possession of a vast territory was not sufficient in and of itself for a proper sense of a state. By the early eighteenth century, sovereign power increasingly involved detailed knowledge about even the most distant and remote places and peoples living in the realm.

Although maps were occasionally mentioned during the sixteenth century, it appears that cartography was an unusual activity. A few foreign illustrative maps of Russia appeared during this time in Western Europe, particularly in Holland and Germany. These maps heavily focused on illustrations of the western parts of the empire and Moscow, where the European embassies traveled. Polish and German cartographers produced the very early products, and they rendered the images of narratives conveyed to them by military personnel and travelers. Thus, when looking at the maps from the 1500s such as those by Maciej of Michów, the Canon of Krakow, or cartographers of the Hapsburg emperor Maximilian I, it becomes quite obvious that the familiarity of travelers was restricted at most to Moscow and its environs, or that they never visited Russia at all but had relied on travelers' reports.[23]

As Valerie Kivelson notes, sketch maps (chertezhi) were the most common form of relating space for the inhabitants of European Russia until the end of the seventeenth century. These served "the most mundane and utilitarian impulses: the need to record property rights and

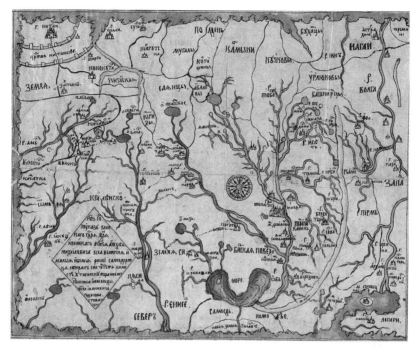

FIGURE 3.2. Godunov's map, 1666: the earliest *Russian* general map of Siberia, 1666 or 1667 "Godunov Map." Made under the administration of Petr Ivanovich Godunov, the governor general of Western Siberia. In the tradition of seventeenth-century mapmaking South is at the top and North (marked in the center at the bottom as "Cebep") is at the bottom. The Arctic Ocean runs along the bottom of the map. Samoyed people are marked on the map, just below the U-shaped body of water at the bottom of the page. China and the Great Wall are located in the very top-left corner. River networks and churches alongside them are the main navigational markers. Leo Bagrow Collection of Maps of Siberia (MS Russ 72). Houghton Library, Harvard University. (Reproduced with permission from Houghton Library, Harvard University.)

boundary lines for judicial and administrative purposes."[24] Mundane and utilitarian purposes notwithstanding, the maps also employed Orthodox iconography, expressing a particular religious view of the world, and every detail of a town or an estate was rendered through such a prism. These illustrations were a representation of property in a Russian Orthodox world; as such, they conveyed nature as a popular view of paradise, as it appeared in icons and images of religious texts rather than reflecting actual landscape. Hence, the focus remained on towns and the adjacent lands owned by people of the country, with little interest shown in the wilderness beyond the gates.[25]

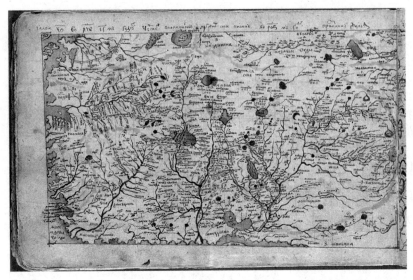

FIGURE 3.3. Remezov's map of Siberia, 1698. Semyon Remezov, a Tobolsk cartographer, made this map of Siberia on order from Moscow, specifically requesting that all Russian villages and native settlements paying tribute (iasak) to those villages be recorded. A much more detailed and larger map than the previous one (Figure 3.2), while still following the same cartographic conventions. The previously empty space was filled with names of peoples and settlements. The Baikal Sea is now the center of the map and Siberia, with China marked in red in the upper left corner behind the Great Wall. Remezov, Semyon Ulianovich, 1642–1720. Khorograficheskaya kniga [cartographical sketch-book of Siberia]. MS Russ 72 (6: seq. 202). Houghton Library, Harvard University. (Reproduced with permission from Houghton Library, Harvard University.)

Few maps of the seventeenth century furnished specific descriptive details of places farther east, even based on secondhand accounts. Rather, everything to the east past the mountains in the lands of Tartary was initially represented by rows of bushes and trees, with a scale that stressed the importance of the western portion of Russia. In the cartographers' renderings, a map of western Russia amounted to two-thirds of the space; the vast open space to the east took up one-third. Given that maps illustrate concepts, ideas, and current social conventions, the early maps clearly portrayed Siberia as being insignificant, inconsequential, and unknown.[26] Like *mappae mundi,* the popular European representations of the world by the late fifteenth century, Russian local maps did not depict the world as it was experienced but rather as it was imagined and desired. These maps were moral narratives conveying religious texts in a visual form. The harsh cold edges of Siberia appeared on the margin, beyond the events of Moscow or the world. The first, and for a while the only, comprehensive local map of Siberia appeared in the second half of the seventeenth century; the cartographer Semyon Remezov (1698) included a burst of detail as well as the names of ethnic groups such as the Land of the Ostiaks, the Voguls, the Land of the Yakut, the Land of the Tungus, the Gilyak empire (figure 3.3).[27]

TALL TALES AND DIPLOMATIC MISSIVES

Aside from maps, in the early period the descriptions of the native peoples who lived in the eastern regions of Eurasia came from two sources: foreign travelers and Russian collectors scouting the territory for furs. Foreign embassies had in their work assignment a requirement to submit regular descriptive travel reports, which now comprise the bulk of the literature on the Russian empire of the early modern period.[28] They were often the main source of knowledge for the Russian emperor himself. "Russia through the eyes of foreigners" is a subject heading that fills numerous shelves in all Russian libraries, suggesting a peculiar fascination with looking at themselves through the eyes of others.[29] This reversed mirror served as a source of knowledge, projection, rejection, and derision. Collected with great passion and continuously checked for "errors," these reports remain an anxious tradition with a long, familiar history even up to the early twenty-first century.[30]

Russia was a land of hazy details, some completely invented. Foreign travelers recounted their experiences of crossing Russia on the way to China or Persia, the destinations of choice for Europeans in the sixteenth and seventeenth centuries. They wrote about a Russian empire whose people, government, and landscape were all unfamiliar and provided novel experiences for anyone from Western Europe. However, as the historian Marshall Poe notes, it was very common in the sixteenth century to rely entirely on tales and secondhand accounts of the country.[31] Italian scholars of the sixteenth century, for example, wrote at length about Muscovy although many of these writers had never visited even the capitol; even so, they expressed strong feelings about the nature of Russians and Muscovy in general. It was the motivation for a tale, rather than its veracity as an eyewitness account, that gave it legitimacy and truth value, and travelers described the Russian empire from a Western perspective, which intermingled awe and disgust. But, like their Russian hosts, they saw Siberia as a very distant edge.

> What the distance between Tobolsk to the end of Siberia is, I cannot tell you with certainty; firstly I guess the distance is enormous: travelers from Tobolsk to Moscow who travel during winter return home in twelve weeks, that would be some three thousand Russian verst. Travelers going from Tobolsk to Dauria, to the most distant fort called Nerchinsk, usually do not return the same winter. (Anonymous traveller, 1680)[32]

Starting in the sixteenth century, Russian rulers sent out military and governmental envoys, emissaries, bureaucrats, and merchants to explore the empire and acquire new lands. They crossed the same space as travelers from Western Europe, but they viewed it with a different goal in mind, and thus saw through very different eyes. They focused on the riches of the land on the one hand, and the danger threatening their existence on a daily basis on the other. Imagined and real, these themes of wealth and fear permeated the writing of foreigners and Russians alike, yet they were expressed themselves quite differently. Russian interest in crossing the continent in the seventeenth century was purely and unabashedly economic.[33] The czar and his government directed the expansion from Moscow, interested in furs and minerals alone.

> The goods from Siberia flow to them through the Altai: sables, bobcats, foxes, beavers, otter, ermine, sacks of rabbit fur, leather in red, gold and silver; splendid cloth, ivory, large fish teeth, beautiful beads made in amber; Kalmycks also bring slaves, camels, all sort of horses and cattle; and for all those goods they can trade with the Chinese empire whatever they want, gold, all sorts of silver, precious stone, beads, tea and tobacco.[34]

The religious or ethnic affiliation of the different groups of people mattered little at the time (a group would be identified as "Mahometan" or "pagan") as long as they delivered the goods and did not threaten those who were moving them along. Nevertheless, official encounters with native peoples left behind a remarkable record of this early crossing of the continent, and it resonates with anxiety: the natives were ever restless. With every new settlement, new village, or new fort, the documents described conflicts with the locals, stealing by the tax collectors, desperate winter food shortages, and subsequent inevitable deaths. There was always the need to form alliances with a range characters, potential enemies and allies alike. Letters, reports, and orders traveled back and forth between Moscow and the frontier documenting the tensions with a remarkable frequency.

NONBELIEVERS BUT PAYING THEIR TAXES

Over the course of a mere seventy years at the end of the fifteenth century, the territory of Muscovy increased impressive six and a half times, attaining the size of almost 3 million square kilometers.[35] In terms of ethnic composition, however, the empire remained relatively homogeneous. This situation changed dramatically in the mid-sixteenth century when Ivan IV, the Terrible, conquered the khanates of Kazan and Astrakhan, followed by Siberia. Native peoples of tribes large and small fell under the control of the Muscovite state, even if, for the most part, they did not know it. Their fate for centuries thereafter would be tied to Russia. Neither subjects nor conquerors knew much about each other. Russians knew that native peoples populated the eastern regions, but what they looked like, what customs they had, and how they lived was an exercise in imagination that changed with some regularity while retaining the same uncivilized, primitive central features.

At first, the lands east of Kazan were simply described as uninhabited and empty. No one paid taxes, no one registered in the census, and no one worked the land. The only way a person could truly exist in sixteenth century Russia was by being a settled farmer—at least occasionally tilling the soil—and registering as a tribute-paying subject.[36] With such definition of the imperial subject, hundreds of thousands of nonagrarian native peoples were nonexistent and not recognized. Yet these nonexistent people retained a place in the Russian imagination, always lurking just around the bend as a threat. As they revealed themselves as a potential source of wealth in the form of silver and furs, the natives were referred to as *inovertsy*, "other-believers" or non-Christian heathens, who required more than merely settling down to become respectable people.[37] Nevertheless, in the early days of Russian expansion eastward, the Orthodox Church was not on the forefront of the colonial effort. The empire absorbed the natives as they provided access to furs, and it did not matter that they often swore allegiance to the czar according to their own religious traditions.[38]

Czar Ivan the Terrible first certified the official nonexistence of Siberian native peoples in 1558 in a land-granting document:

> I, the Tsar and Grand Prince Ivan Vasilevich of all Russia, have been asked to grant to Grigorii Anikevich Stroganov that for which he has petitioned, namely: the *uninhabited* lands, black forests, wild rivers and lakes and *uninhabited* islands and marshlands in our patrimony which extend for some 88 versts, along the right bank of the Kama from the mouth of the Lysvaia, and

along the left bank of the Kama opposite Pyznovskaia backwaters, and along both banks of the Kama to the Chusovaia River. These *uninhabited* lands extend for 146 versts. To the present time no one has worked this land nor established homestead here. To date no tax revenue has been received from this area into the Treasury I hold as Tsar and Grand Prince. At present the land has not been granted to anyone, nor has it been entered in the census books, nor in the books of purchase, nor in legal records. . . . This man from Perm, Kodaul, has told our Treasury officials that the region for which Grigorii petitions us has been *uninhabited* from time immemorial, that it has brought no revenues into our Treasury. . . . He may build a small town in the black forest, in a secure and well-protected location, and emplace cannon and defense guns in that town to protect the town against the Nogai people and other hordes. (April 4, 1558)[39]

Grigorii Anikevich Stroganov, a member of a Novgorod merchant family, was a useful ally to the czar. His family's commercial interests in the east coincided with imperial preoccupation in the south, in Crimea. Not having the forces to guard the eastern frontier, the czar made a calculated transaction and handed over the control of the eastern edge of the empire to a private merchant company, the Stroganovs. Having acquired the land "uninhabited from time immemorial" initially for twenty years, the Stroganovs settled in and immediately cast their gaze eastward for more. This was granted every twenty years or so, each time with a new petition stipulating new qualifications and obligations, all of which the Stroganovs easily ignored, being separated from the czar by months of travel. They hired a troop of Volga Cossacks, led at the time by one Ermak Timofeev, for protection. By the late 1570s, Ermak was not only protecting the Stroganovs' property, but also conducting his own raids further into Siberia with increased frequency.[40]

In 1558, only the Nogai people, a Muslim group with ties to the Mongolian khanate, were worth mentioning as a potential threat, but less than twenty years later, a document from 1574 was replete with the names of other native groups. The Stroganovs were voracious as well as entrepreneurial, and they demanded goods from an increasingly larger circle of peoples. The Ostiaks, the Voguls, the Iugras, and the Samoyeds all found themselves caught between the Russian czar and the Muslim rulers in the south who were vying for the same territory, each demanding taxes, *iasak* (a tribute in fur), and allegiance.[41] Official documents now referred to the various groups as "our," indicating a clear sense of ownership. The native peoples were no longer a part of an uninhabited landscape but imperial subjects, coerced into a relationship with the growing Russian empire:

In the past the Siberian sultan killed *our* [tax] paying Ostiaks, Chagir and his men, in these same areas where Iakov and Grigorii [Stroganov] are carrying their enterprises. The Siberian also took some of *our* paying subjects prisoner, and killed others. He will not allow *our* Ostiaks, Voguls and Iugras to pay [tax] into our Treasury. He is forcing the Iugras to go into boats to fight these Ostiaks and Voguls. Any Ostiak who will turn against the Siberian and pay [tax] to us are to be protected against the Siberian. . . . Iakov and Grigorii [Stroganov] are to offer protection in their forts to these [tax] paying Ostiaks, Voguls and Iugras and their wives and children, against the attacks by the Siberian. (May 30, 1574)[42]

The native peoples whom the Stroganovs encountered in their expansion eastward were recognized as a potential source of revenue, allies in the perpetual conflicts with their southern Muslim neighbors, and a labor force in hunting and mining. In a mere twenty years, the previously uninhabited space turned into a place teeming with people of distinct names, who were simultaneously potential enemies and tax-paying foot soldiers. The czar specifically instructed the Stroganovs on how to interact with an exhaustive range of travelers, emissaries, boyars, tax-exempt peasants, plaintiffs, defendants, willing-to-be-subdued natives and their wives and children, as well as runaways. Although previously the emperor had gladly certified the land uninhabited, he—and his officials—intervened in later periods on behalf of numerous individuals. At the same time, the distance between Moscow and the forts that the Stroganovs built further and further east allowed them to ignore most of the rules and act on their own impulses in response to the changing frontier situations. Although the czar gave strict orders to deal with the Siberian khan only after consulting with Moscow, and only on his order, in 1582 the Cossack Ermak Timofeev went on the attack, defeated the khan's army, and conquered the capitol Qashlik.[43]

This "conquest of Siberia," and Stroganovs' establishment of Tobolsk as the capital, has been commemorated in Russian history as the beginning of the eastern expansion across Siberia. Ermak came to be venerated in Russian history and literature despite (or because) of the gruesome mercenary activities during his time (figure 3.4). The nineteenth-century painter Ilya Repin etched the Cossack into the national imaginary through several larger-than-life paintings, which hang to this day in the Russian National Gallery. Ermak remains a permanent character in Russian books and in popular culture, a part of the heroic national struggles through history.

The victory was a defeat of the Muslim rulers in the south who had been eyeing the native land with an equal hunger for its wealth. Unlike

FIGURE 3.4. Ermak Timofeevich, Conqueror of Siberia, 1887: an illustration of a historical event—Ermak conquering Siberia—but the image is a "lubok" print. A humorous and satirical form popular from the seventeenth century on, similar to cartoon illustrations, lubki (pl.) illustrated historical events, familiar tales, and religious texts. Circulated as woodcuts and easily reproduced, the prints were used by various groups for political messages. Ermak's conquest of Siberia was a popular theme for nationalist paintings during the late nineteenth century, usually depicting a victorious mass slaughter of the indigenous populations. The lubok represents a marching army of soldiers without any natives present, suggesting a military advance rather than a victory in a battle. Russkii narodnyi lubok; albom. 1873–1888. Record no. 294950. Print Collection, Miriam and Ira D. Wallach Division of Art, The New York Public Library, New York. (Reproduced with permission of the New York Public Library.)

the Russian conquerors, however, Muslims had made numerous earlier concerted efforts to convert the indigenous groups. Their defeat thus meant the native faith practices had a much longer tradition, as the Russian Orthodox Church made only a feeble, and largely unsuccessful, attempt at conversion.

Those honorable men, Semen, Maksim and Nikita Stroganov, captured and subjugated all the Siberian land. They pacified Busurman natives such as the Siberian Tatars, the Ostiaks and the Voguls. And they accomplished this through trade and with the assistance of the brave and the valorous, good and noble warriors, Ermak Timofeev and his Volga atamans and Cossacks. These honorable men also succeeded in winning over the Busurman people who live near the Stroganovs' towns and ostrozheks along the Kama, Chusovaia, Usva, Sylva, Iaiva, Obva, Inva, Kosva and other rivers. They brought all of these Busurman people to swear an oath to serve the Sovereign Tsar and Grand Prince Ivan Vasilevich of Russia, to commit no treasonable acts, to obey the Sovereign in all ways, to keep his interest foremost, and to pay him iasak. (Stroganov Chronicle 1582)[44]

The subjugation of the different tribes and groups living in Siberia, and their gradual incorporation into the Russian empire, may have been triggered by Ermak's defeat of the Siberian khan.[45] The Cossacks pushed through the barriers to the East that the Mongolian and Tatar empires had held until then. They showed that it was possible to march farther east, despite the presence of powerful southern empires and savage "hordes."

What did this push eastward mean in human terms? Aside from the political sense of an expanding empire, what was the Russian experience of "contact"? In contrast to the earlier foreign descriptions, did the Russian officials distinguish between the diverse groups of people they encountered on their way to the Pacific?

First and foremost, the colonial administrators demanded tribute; *iasak,* formerly a Mongolian imperial custom, was heartily embraced by the Russian rulers and many native groups. They also demanded native labor. They interacted with members of native populations solely through conflict resolution or by addressing the complaints of various constituencies. Their bureaucratic decisions had the tacit approval of Moscow, and they were free to do as they pleased. Occasionally we get a glimpse of the contentious relationships in the colonial attempts to show authority, as shown in a letter from 1601:

We have received a petition from a newly baptized man, Stepan Purtiev, against a Berezovo Ostiak named Shatrov Luguev, in which it is stated that in 1595 three women slaves Purtiev had bought ran off to this Shatrov. One woman was a slave from Nerym, another was from Tymsk, and the third was from Voikarsk. They ran away because they had learned of Shatrov Luguev's treasonous attack on the town of Berezovo. After Shatrov Luguev's treason, Stepan went to Shatrov to reclaim his runaway women, but Shatrov would not return these women to him. He is keeping them by force. Stepan petitions us to order Shatrov be brought to justice. It is decreed that this be done, as the newly baptized Stepan Purtiev has petitioned us. . . . Done in Moscow April 28, 1601.[46]

The letter illustrates the general tenor of seventeenth-century correspondence between Moscow and the distant provinces: replete with accounts of violence. This letter features kidnappings of women and children from the indigenous groups, and the problem was grave enough that it required official attention.

The great majority of the colonizing forces were military men, traders, mercenaries, and peasants, men without families or wives. Even the few Russian women sentenced to exile in Siberia for murder outnumbered the men's female relatives, creating a gender dynamic rife with violence, disease, and unwanted children. Relationships with native women were common and just as fraught with all the power dynamic of colonial settings. By the end of the seventeenth century, the possession of captive women and children as well as the holding and selling of slaves had grown so common that the czar grew concerned enough about revenue to issue regulations protecting the extended families of tribute-paying natives. Daughters and wives of native leaders were kidnapped on a regular basis, requiring interventions by the local official, which solved the issue only temporarily. The czar periodically issued guidelines, seeking to enforce his authority, but captivity, hostage taking, and various forms of slavery remained common on the Russian frontier.[47]

The institution of slavery, however, was not the real point of contention in these official communications. Rather, concern centered on the property rights of Christians and tax-paying subjects. As Robin Blackburn has noted, "If slavery had largely disappeared from western and northern Europe, the same could not be said of Muscovy, where slaves comprised as much as one tenth of the population in the late Middle Ages and early modern period."[48] Michael Khodarkovsky claims that "after West Africa, Eastern Europe—Russia in particular—was the second largest supplier of slaves in the world."[49] Historians have noted that from the tenth century onward Russians regularly sold slaves to Viking and Italian traders. Beginning in the sixteenth century, Russian slave traders regularly engaged in hostage taking and captivity of natives during their expansion east.[50]

The moving eastern frontier produced a setting where rules and social mores were alternately modified, circumvented, or ignored, and only occasionally followed. The brutality vividly described in the nineteenth- and twentieth-century exile literature about Siberia has a long history, and the native peoples played a major role in it. Amid their geographically immense empire, Russians of this period rarely made distinctions between the various "small peoples."[51] Consequently, Russian colonization of Siberia and northeast Asia often appears as an un-impeded move across a sparse, inhospitable landscape. Yet the letters and official documents tell a more complicated story. Accounts of ongoing attacks by the natives, including sieges of towns and settlements by the Tungus, the Ostiaks, or the Kalmyks in different regions of the realm, make it clear that the "contact" between the various agents of the empire and the native peoples was generally a violent affair, infused with fear on all sides. After initial overtures with the new settlers, it appears that the native groups put up strong resistance to the encroachment. A warning from the early seventeenth century advised: "Be extremely cautious. Increase your guards and sentries. Keep surveillance over the mobility of the natives."[52]

The early letters and official documents provided little detail about the lives, similarities, or differences of the Russians and the newly encountered natives. The only distinction that really mattered was who paid taxes and who delivered tribute. Those who swore allegiance to the sovereign and regularly paid tribute were deemed as deserving protection from the colonial foot soldiers. Their particular customs, eating habits, or social arrangements did not attract any attention or scrutiny; the lens of economy was the only looking glass. The letters and missives tell us vastly more about the lives and behavior of the colonizers, the unruly subjects of the ruler who periodically needed to be reigned in:

> Did these servitors and other persons acquire native women and young girls and children through pawning or purchase, or by force? Did they sell them? . . . If your investigation reveals that certain servitors, traders or *promyshlenniks* [fur trappers] have taken women, girls and children, and that these women and girls have been taken from *iasak* people who have paid their iasak to the Great Sovereign, such persons are to be punished by being beaten mercilessly for their crime, and they are to be fined, and the money from the fines is to go to the Great Sovereign. The women and girls and children of the *iasak* people are to be returned to the native *iasak* people from where they were abducted. If any have been baptized into the Orthodox faith, such women and girls and children are to be taken from their abductors and sent to Iakutsk *ostrog* [fort]. . . . A list of these females is to be prepared and sent to Iakutsk over your signature, as well as a list of the [Russian] men from whom they were taken, and the marks of those persons to whom they are to be returned. All this is to be written down in detail. (August 13, 1676)[53]

The seventeenth century colonial expansion consisted of small parties of men who advanced into a new territory, set up camp, captured hostages, and demanded payments and labor for their release. Periodically the captives resisted and refused to provide any information about the local people, their rulers, or their alliances, and were unwilling to take the Russian soldiers to their settlements. Torture and death were common tools of persuasion. All this was driven by a desire for economic gain with little attention to the culture of the group at hand. "New rivers" led into "new lands," which contained "new foreigners" (*inozemtsy*), and new foreigners were only useful if they could provide profit for the czar. Profit was measured by the size of the tribute. However, tribute-paying natives remained "*inozemtsy*" and were largely allowed to keep their own names, gods, and "oaths" rather than being expected to adopt Russian ones.[54] Official documents and transactions described in great detail the gruesome punishments inflicted on the unwilling subjects, and there is minimal attention to the particulars of their lives, social customs, or religious practices. The colonial advance of seventeenth-century Russia was not a civilizing mission, and had no religious or ethnic motive. While the ruler wanted more subjects, the allegiance of these subjects was a part of a business transaction, not a matter of state or ethnic formation.

Yet by the middle of the seventeenth century a more varied image of the native peoples begins to emerge, as the colonial officers began to distinguish among the groups. Imperial bureaucrats established records of the composition of every settlement. Although the motive was still to track which groups paid tribute and which ones resisted, in addition to establishing head counts, through their record keeping the officials gradually recognized that they were negotiating with culturally different entities. The relentless violent skirmishes likewise contributed to the permanent paper record. Once Russian settlers established homesteads in the region rather than transit stations, officials filed regular reports, and among other details began to note the religious customs of these foreigners. Amid negotiations and assessments of who might be a fierce foe and who a temporary ally, the Russians' recognition of cultural differences slowly grew.

An acknowledgment of significant differences between the Russians and the natives appeared, for example, in instructions from 1650 on how to subjugate the land of the Daur.[55] While anticipating mass killings of villagers, the document also advised that the swearing of the oath be conducted "according to local religious practices." Subjugation, even without conversion, might prove preferable as far as taxes were concerned:

Some will be hanged, and others will be ruined. After they [the Russians] have totally destroyed them, they will take their wives and children into captivity. But if the non-*iasak* people bow down and are in every way obedient to the Sovereign, then in accordance with their religious practices, these people are to be brought to swear allegiance so that they will be personally under the Sovereign Tsar's mighty hand in eternal *iasak* servitude, for all time undeviatingly, and pay *iasak* for themselves and for their *ulus* [village] subjects without interruption.[56]

In this particular case, the instructions appear to have been executed quite conscientiously. According to records of the establishment of the first Russian settlement Albazino on the Amur River in 1651, the endeavor began with over six hundred Daur men killed, and two hundred forty-three women and one hundred eighteen children taken prisoner. Following this mass slaughter and capture, Russian officials conducted the swearing of allegiance to the czar in a Daur traditional form, "respecting their local customs."[57] This was not done out of any deference to local religious practices, which remained of minimal interest to the merchant enterprise; rather, the Russians considered an allegiance established in terms of local customs to be more sincere and therefore more durable.

Nonetheless, the peculiar details of the customs that were increasingly noted and described not only identified points of difference between the Russian frontiersmen and the newly conquered peoples but also between the native groups themselves. For example, "the Yakut cut a dog in half and the oath-taker walked between the two parts, supposedly inviting the same fate as the dog if breaking the allegiance, while the Ostiaks performed a similar ritual in front of a bear skin."[58]

By the end of the seventeenth century, customs and traditions were a common topic in letters and travelers' accounts of crossing Siberia. The growing curiosity about others was not simply reducible to a direct political desire by imperial officials to get to know the people with whom the emperor had dealings. Neither was it an effort to impose a unified system of official customs and rituals. As Yuri Slezkine pointed out, "there could be no New Muscovy after the fashion of New France or New England because old Muscovy had no clear borders (in time or space) and because the 'new lands' in the east were being incorporated without being fully appropriated (christened, Christianized, and conquered)."[59] Rather, the impulse emerged out of the development of new scientific traditions that focused on classification, categorization, and difference. Upon his return from Western Europe in 1697, Peter the

Great took it upon himself to westernize Russia in multiple ways: from ordering that all court officials and boyars cut their beards to moving the capitol to a newly built city closer to the northern coast. The czar also established a new venue for scientific research, the Imperial Academy of Sciences. Counting and describing the subjects of the empire became the task of a new branch of science as well as the work of the administrative officials.

RELIGION: PRACTICES AND IDENTITIES

The early accounts of the native peoples noted their lack of civilization and strange eating habits—ranging from incomprehensible to utterly disgusting—as well as their means of transportation, including traveling by reindeer, dogsled, or occasionally horses. Initially, the official documents were merely tribute reports. The only distinguishing feature of any native group was their tax status—"*iasak* paying" or "non-*iasak*" people. Yet eventually the native peoples' diversity in their appearance and habits turned up with increasing regularity in a range of other accounts, particularly the records of military captives and exiles. The travelers' descriptions of all Siberian groups commonly mentioned several supposed defining features of the people: polygamy, large herds of animals, odd appearance, and an intimate knowledge of the inhospitable environment.

Rivers as the only routes of transport appeared in every account. In 1658, a Polish artillery soldier named Adam Kamensky-Dluzik who was traveling with a group of prisoners sent to exile in Siberia recorded an encounter with the Tungus people at the near the Angara river: "They walked around naked and their faces were painted with various colors."[60] Eating habits, extensive body tattoos, and family relations loomed large in the account, but so too did the kind treatment that exiles received from the newly met people: "The Tungus were very generous to the prisoners, fed them and provided them with meat and furs for their journey. They were polygamous, some had as many as nine wives. Their reindeer herds were in the thousands or more."[61] From the perspective of the prisoners headed into exile, the natives lived in abundance, free to act as they wished, and move anywhere in this vast space.

In addition to their wealth, religious customs were another defining characteristic of the cultural groups, much in the same way that the Orthodox religion was seen as characterizing Russians to the outside world. Increased contact between Russians and Western European travelers and merchants had created a conscious sense of cultural difference through the prism of religion. As far as Western Europeans were concerned, Orthodox religious practices described the essence of being Russian. Their eating, clothing, and monthly calendar all expressed adherence to a distinctly different form of Christianity than that practiced in Western Europe. Similarly, when Russians turned their eyes to the East, they began to remark on the difference between themselves and the native peoples in Siberia in terms of religion, which fused into the description of the geographic place and the identity of the people therein.

Amid colonial expansion and the everyday realities of the colonial experience, when Russians began to record the Siberian religious diversity, it was as a distinctly gendered phenomenon. There had been few efforts to bring groups as a whole to Christianity, but native women were another matter. The main reason for this distinction was purely utilitarian: upon being Christianized, the women immediately became eligible for marriage with servicemen.[62] The custom of converting women grew more common over time, as more Russian men settled in the new territories. Although kidnapped women also could be traded for sable furs, settled Russian men aspired to marital bliss—or at least social recognition of their household and offspring.

However, the actual religious practices in these domestic settings did not always correspond with the official number of recorded Christian souls. As Sunderland noted when discussing a later nineteenth-century context, Russian men marrying native women most often resulted in the men "going native" and adopting the local customs and language.[63] When visitors in the late imperial period made their way to these northerly places, they reported finding Russian men who spoke Siberian languages better than their own, ate raw meat, practiced "shamanism," and looked so strikingly "alien" that they seemed virtually indistinguishable from the Iakuts, Ostiaks, Samoeds, and other "primitive" Siberians who lived around them.

By contrast, the Russians made little or no attempt to convert native men, who were generally described as belonging to the "shamanic religion." The result was the gender-skewed demography collected by imperial officials: the Christian men had all arrived as settlers, the Christian women were largely native converts, and precious few appeared to attend any church services. Instead, native groups held firmly to "shamanism," which also gained many Russian practitioners.[64]

CANNIBALS AND SHAMANS: ENTER STAGE EAST

In the context of defining, describing, and categorizing the different indigenous groups according to their religious customs, "a shaman" emerged. Sigmund Herberstein in the 1530s had provided many a lurid tale of customs and appearances, but religion had received short shrift; in two volumes, merely a brief passage appeared:

> Although of theyr own institution and custome receyved of theyr predicessours, they are Idolatours, honouryng that lyvyng thyng that they meete fyrst in the morning, for the God of that day, and divinyng thereby theyr good luck or evyll. They also erecte Images of stone upon mountayns, whiche they esteeme as Goddes, attributyng to them divine honour.[65]

Writers who plagiarized—or repeated—his accounts during the following decades did not seem to view native religion or practices worthy of much note, mentioning idol worshipping without much detail or attention. In Jan Huyghens van Linschoten's 1598 map of the northern coast (figure 3.5), a pictorial description of Willem Barentz's ill-fated search for the Northeast Passage, the carved idols of the Samoyed appear as an image, an essence of their identity. The carved idols reappeared in the work of early seventeenth-century cleric Samuel Purchas, who brought travel writing into popularity in London, in his description of the northern edges of Russia:

> The Hollanders in the year 1594, sent to discover a way to Cathay and China, by the Northeast, which by Master Borough, Peet and Iaeman Englishmen, had beene long before in vaine attempted. William Barentz was the chief pilot for this Discovery. This year they sailed through the Straits of Vaygats, and thought themselves not farre short of the river Ob. The next yeare they returned for the same discovery. They landed in the Samogithians or Samoyeds country, and named a place, because they there found images carved of wood, Idollneeke. They gave names to places long before discovered by the English, as if they had beene the first founders.[66]

The absence of proper Christian faith fascinated foreign travelers from the late sixteenth century as a marker of difference, and they ranked the Russians' Orthodox Christianity a great deal lower than the religious practices of Western Europe. As the German geographer Adam Olearius noted in his diary in 1636 regarding the Russian Orthodox sacred texts,

> They have made a certain Book, wherein they treat the Histories of the Gospel after a strange manner and adulterate them with so many fabulous, implausible and impertinent circumstances that it is not to be much admired

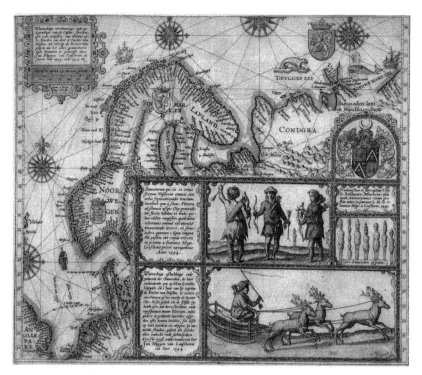

FIGURE 3.5. Jan Huyghens van Linschoten's map with Samoed figures, 1624. Jan Huyghens van Linschoten participated in two Dutch voyages (1594, 1596), led by Willem Barentz, in search of the Northeast Passage. This map was made on the first voyage when the ships had to land and the crew attempted an (unsuccessful) overland crossing. Samoied, the indigenous people of the coastal region, were illustrated for the first time, as were their carved idols (right side of the map). This early cartographic convention still included measurements, geographic information, and stories from encounters in a representation of the newly discovered region. Jan Huyghens van Linschoten. Map of Scandinavia and the White Sea area. Made after the first Barentsz voyage of 1594. Linschoten, Jan Huygen van. 1624. Voyasie, ofte Schip-vaert van Ian Huyghens van Linschoten: van by noorden om langes Noorwegen de Noordt-Caep, Laplandt, Vinlandt, Ruslandt, de Witte Zee, de Kusten van Kandenoes, Swetenoes, Pitzora, & c. door de strate ofte enghte van Nassouw tot voor by de Reviere Oby ... Anno 1594. ende 1595. T'Amsterdam: By I.E. Cloppenburg. Image in public domain. (Reproduced courtesy of the Tromso University Library, The Northern Lights Route Project.)

that vice and sin reign among them when they are furnished with examples thereof in their Book of Devotion.[67]

In view of the marked deviations of Russian Orthodox practice from European standards, the foreign travelers were not altogether surprised when they went farther east and encountered a total lack of belief in one God and no interest at all in Christianity—the idolaters in the colonies were only slightly stranger than the Russians. Reminiscent of the images of monsters in the early sixteenth century, the local native religion was painted with broad brushstrokes: the idolaters knew nothing of Christianity, practiced polygamy, worshipped trees, and did not fear sin or death. The Samoyed, a native people in the westernmost part of Siberia closest to Moscow, received the earliest and most attention. Every travel account that discussed the Samoyeds described them as cannibals, as *samo* in Russian means "self" and *yed* is "to eat." From the earliest times, this translation had been repeated, misspelled, and mangled, but was always "helpfully" explained because it fitted well with the "men with mouths on their chests" narratives.

In 1575, the French geographer Andre Thevet provided his own insight: "towards the 'Stone Range' mountains, as well as by the coast and on the adjacent islands, live all kinds of peoples, whom the Russians uniformly call Samoyed; which means people who eat each other (Samoged, qui signifie se mangeant soy mesme)."[68] Giles Fletcher, the English ambassador to Russia in 1588, captured the essence of such tales in his *History of Russia*:

> The Samoyt hath his name (as the Russe saith) of eating himself; as if in times past they lived as the Cannibals, eating one another. Which they make more probable, because at this time they eat all kind of raw flesh, whatever it bee, even the very carion that lieth in the ditch.[69]

As to their customs and religion as well as those of their other northern neighbors, Fletcher stated: "The whole nation is utterly unlearned having not so much as the use of any Alphabet, or letter among them. For practice of witchcraft and sorcery, they parallel nations in the world."[70] The significance of both statements resides in "as the Russian says." The linguistic attribution of the term "Samoyed" is a Russian word, not a native term. In these traveler commentaries on the complicated relationship between the indigenous populations and their Russian colonizers, the Russians served as the intermediaries and the interpreters.

Everyone agreed that idolatry and sorcery were the common characteristics of the native religion. After more excursions farther to the south and east of Moscow, and greater exposure to a diversity of native peoples, the term that would emerge by the middle of the seventeenth century in reference to indigenous worship was "shaitan." This Arabic loan word for *devil* had been taken from the Muslim populations.[71] An anonymous writer, likely from Germany, included it in his 1666 description of the Ostyak people, along with an unusual amount of information about their religious practices:

> These Ostaykas know nothing about God, neither about any of his commandments; they have no books, no writing, no alphabet; they bring offerings and pray to "shaitan" (Scheitan), which means the devil, for whom they build a sacrificial place in the woods under a tree. When the shaitan appears with a swishing noise and rustling, they fall to the ground or to their knees and beg not to loose any horses; they bring him offerings of ermine, foxes, weasels and anything that they have. They have a priest of sorts, called shaitanik (Scheitanik) who responds to the shaitan; that is a veritable sorcerer (koldun) or wizard of evil arts (Hechsen Meister oder Teufels Banner). These people live to the north of Tobolsk in huts, barely scraping by, subsisting on fish.[72]

Anonymous writers were the norm, frequently German, Swedish, or Danish captives; among them, by the second half of the seventeenth century, "shaman," "saaman," and "shaitan" were established as interchangeable terms, applied to all groups living past the Ural Mountains. Later ethnographers would suggest that the term "shaman" was specifically of "Tungus origin," but in mid-seventeenth century the Tungus were one of many assorted groups living in the vicinity of Ob and Angara rivers, not a distinct ethnic tribe.[73] These seventeenth-century travelers reported "shamans" everywhere, among every group they met, transcribing into German the terms of a people who lacked orthography:

> This northern region and its edges are settled by all kinds of nations, and each one speaks its own language: such as Voguls, Ostiaks, Zyrians, Bratsk, Daur, and others. They all are heathens. (They worship wooden idols, which were seen by the Dutch who tried to get to China via the Arctic Ocean, between Nova Zemla and those regions of Siberia.) These idols are nothing else but wooden carvings, standing by the side of the road; the top of the carving resembles some kind of head. . . . The Tatars called the priests of these nations "shaitan," they call them shamans; the majority of them are fortunetellers (that is servants of the devil). If any Russian turns to them to find out his fate, the shaman tells the inquirer to stab him in the side with a sword or a lance. The weapon stays in his body and in about an hour the shaman is twisted in pain and foams at the mouth. Finally he tells the inquirer to take the weapon out (nobody else can do this instead); yet no blood appears and the weapon is so hot as if taken out of a fire. Then the shaman tells the fortune. Needless to say, anyone who attended such event was not merry and ended his life under some unfortunate circumstances. (Anonymous 1680)[74]

Sieved through earlier encounters with Muslim Tartars and Russian Orthodox settlers, the emergence and stabilization of the image of shamans does not give much support to the claims of origin. We may recall this tangled colonial history when discussing where shamans came from or even what a shaman might be. Judging from the historical evidence, the word itself is a generic label of Slavic origin via German transcription with negative connotations. Our search for indigenous spirituality and practice should thus not be guided by such a colonial heritage.

CHAPTER 4

The Invention of Siberian Ethnology

The Countrey of Siberia is the Place whither the Czar
banishes capital Criminals and Offenders never to return.

—John Perry (1716)[1]

There is hardly a set of people that love moving about better
than the Siberians; they have a natural curiosity, that always
prompts them with a desire of making new discoveries,
Government has taken pains to encourage this inclination,
and to it Russia is indebted for the wide extent of territory
she possesses, from the river Irtisch to the Kourille islands:
most of these conquests have been made in winter.

—Catherine II (1772)[2]

At the beginning of the eighteenth century, Siberia appeared as a dismal
land of exile to John Perry, the Englishman working for Czar Peter the
Great. Only a few decades later, Peter's successor, the Empress Catherine, could see it as a region where happy, nomadic people colonized the
land for the benefit of their benevolent rulers. Needless to say, the difference in the opinion stemmed partly from the station of the two authors.
Perry, who spoke for the many foreigners living and working in Russia
in the early eighteenth century, was indebted to the czar and wished to
stay in his good graces. The Empress expressed the official view of the
government, and her intended audience was located abroad in Western
Europe. Nonetheless, the shift also reflects the newfound importance of
Siberia's people, who went from being the invisible residents of an "uninhabited" land, aside from moments when they posed an obstacle to

Russian settlements, to an object of curiosity and a topic of more careful study.

In this chapter, I offer an account of the degree to which descriptions of Siberian native peoples changed with their newfound scientific significance. Who came to be the most authoritative voice representing them? Which topics captivated the attention of early scientists and their readers? Why did even the empress herself feel compelled to comment on life at the far eastern edges of her empire? Catherine never visited any of the native hunters, yet she felt called upon to write about them, composing *The Antidote* in response to a critical French account of Siberia, and even penning a play called *The Shaman*. How did Siberia become a measure of *Russia's* civilization, when just a few decades earlier it had been a frozen land, unknown and unknowable? Walking back in time through the Siberian landscape, we can begin to see how the empire needed the science of its subjects, and how, in order to become truly European, the Russians needed the Siberian natives.

In tracing the descriptions of Siberia and its native peoples at this time, the most striking change is the emergence of systematic descriptions of other cultures and foreign peoples. As several writers have suggested, the roots of anthropology as a methodical study of cultures through personal observation extend deeper into the eighteenth century than is sometimes acknowledged.[3] Furthermore, they involve quite a different geography than that of Western Europe's empires. Vermeulen has tracked the origin of the term *Völkerkunde*—ethnology—and convincingly shows that its prototype *Völker-Beschreibung*—description of people— was a standard orientation by the middle of the eighteenth century for writings about Russia.[4] German scientists, sponsored by a newly minted Russian research academy, constructed Siberia through detailed descriptions of its people and their customs, beliefs, and history. In so doing, they helped provide a foundation for later developments, such as the British and French nineteenth-century ethnographies that expanded upon this existing German tradition. They also transformed the image of the oft-neglected region of Siberia, filling it with people and helping the shaman to venture out into the world.

THE LAST ENGLISH CAPTAIN

Rather than begin with a sober German scientist, I will start with a disgraced English sea captain: John Perry will be a good guide through the early period of Siberian ethnography. He was one of the last of the non-expert travel writers in the grand tradition of the seventeenth century, who depicted the whole vast empire as Russia, even while paying significant attention to places outside Moscow. Yet he was also one of the first of a new eighteenth-century breed of writers, who referred to the specific ethnic tribes of Siberia by name, visited and spoke to them in person, and reported on their thoughts, however mistranslated they may have been. As a transitional figure, he merits particular attention.

A former naval officer, Perry had been court-martialed for negligence in the sinking of a ship, so he needed employment somewhere other than his native England. He thus accepted an offer from Peter the Great in 1698 to build a canal between the Don and Volga rivers. Perry was hired for his engineering skills, not his ability to observe the world around him. Still, he wrote an account of his travel experiences in Russia, and published it upon his return to England under the title of *The State of Russia, Under the Present Czar* (1716). The work became tremendously popular throughout Europe. Read by the educated casual readers who developed a passion for distant shores, the text was also favored by natural historians and scientists intent on discovering the land for themselves and preparing for a research journey.

Perry's book bridged the century divide and marked a change in travel writing about Siberia. He provided a narrative rich in detail, and used the native people of the empire for contrast and comparison with Muscovites and people living in the western part of Russia. His was one of the last accounts to describe everything on the eastern side of Europe as "Russia," but he also paid close attention to the native people rather than solely extolling or condemning the Russian military and trade settlers, as had been the custom earlier. The everyday and the mundane became just as noteworthy as the sensational, a result of Perry offering far more information based on his own experiences than had writers of the previous centuries. After Perry, subsequent publications would examine increasingly smaller segments of the empire and describe them with a growing awareness of the difference between Russians and those who lived in the East.

Perry's writing also signaled another new trend: he showed far more sympathy for the inhabitants of the empire than any of the previous explorers. John Perry was an engineer, an educated man who traveled to the eastern parts of the Russian empire out of particular curiosity, not out of necessity to get somewhere else as had been the case with previous writers en route to China, India, or Japan. He wrote with a perceptive eye; he noted differences and observed local customs as well as village layouts and modes of transportation. However, like other foreign writers, his relationship with the native people was mediated by his views of the Russians. He observed his hosts with a heavy dose of suspicion, at times boarding on open abhorrence:

> Upon these considerations, it is no great wonder that the Russes are the most dull and heavy people to attain to any Art or Science of any Nation in the World, and upon every opportunity are the most apt to rebel, and to engage in any of the most barbarous cruelties, in hopes of being reliev'd from the slavery that is hereditary to them.[5]

His decade of service for the Czar had been fraught with conflicts over pay—or the lack thereof—a circumstance that inclined him to a more sympathetic attitude toward the non-Russians he met along the way.

By the eighteenth century, the topics of interest among travelers in remote parts of the world had narrowed down to a set of specific inquiries and key terms that could define societies in comparative terms: food and eating habits, relationships between men and women, and religion.[6] Perry paid due attention to all these, highlighting religion and local customs in his writing. He stressed the significance of these themes in explanatory subtitles, such as "Also an Account of those Tartars, and other People who border on the Eastern and extreme Northern Parts of the Czar's Dominion, their Religion, and Manner of Life With Many other Observations." The flow of these lengthy titles also signaled a shift from travel narrative to ethnographic observations. Although Perry still referred to the natives as "Tartars," the generic term for all inhabitants living to the east of Moscow, he included "other people" in his account. The geographic location remained vague and uncertain, defined as the territory that bordered the east and the north of the czar's empire. The "Samoiedes," one of the groups living close at the western edge of Siberia, were the only ones whose name was not interchangeably used with "Eastern Tartars."[7] A decade after Perry's publication, a number of ethnic groups in specific geographic locations would take center stage; in his text, they waited in the wings.

Judging from his writing, Perry was certain of the "English way of Christianity," and he used every opportunity to condemn papists and display an impressive dose of religious tolerance toward non-Christian faiths. On the other hand, his bias against the Russian version of Christianity was firmly rooted in his dislike of Russian cultural practices, including "the superstitious manner" in which attempts to convert the natives were carried out. Although he refrained from commenting extensively on the "heathen habits" of the natives, Perry's account is still notable for its incorporation of detailed personal narratives, a novel attempt to report the worldview of the Samoyed. Gone were the observations of earlier travelers filled with fascination and disgust; those depictions also had been based on personal encounters, but they involved no attempt to ask the people what their practices meant or why they were conducting themselves in a particular way. Perry's work was one of the earliest efforts to understand why the local people would not embrace Christianity or even show the slightest interest in it. As Perry noted about the Samoyed,

> They acknowledge Obedience to the Czar but refuse to embrace the Christian Faith, in the superstitious manner as the Russes represent it to them; and for the same Reason, as afterwards I shall have occasion to mention, the Christian Religion is refused even by many of those people who live immediately within the Districts of the Czar Government. I have discoursed with some of the said Samoiedes, who have told me, that they have no established form of religion, nor Order of Priesthood amongst them, but take their Rules of Life from such of their Elders who have lived justly, and acted righteously amongst them, and to whose judgment they also submit in case of any controversy between Man and Man, electing such Persons by common consent. They believe that there is a God that rules the Sun and the Stars, and that blesses them with health and length of days, according to the equity and justice of their behavior to each other.[8]

The approach taken in Perry's account suggests a nascent comparative study of religion, where the belief system of the local population was presented in a far more favorable light than the dominant religion of the surrounding empire, if not that of the author. The native belief constituted a rational system that resembled other traditions, intelligible to outsiders:

> Their Faith is something like the Mahometan; they explain their notions very rationally. . . . As to these Tartars, I must do them this Justice, that as often as I had the occasion to trust, or make use of them, both I and all my assistants have observed that we have found them sincere and honest in their lives, and ingenuous in their conversation, above what we have in the Russ Nation.[9]

Such statements established a precedent for other foreign writers and scientists throughout the eighteenth century. Russians and the subjugated populations of the empire appear as distinctly different, but within the same comparative frame.

The native peoples might still be viewed as ignorant and filthy—probably the most common adjective used by even their most ardent admirers (who were, we should recall, none too fond of bathing themselves)—but they were recognized as having their own system of logic, rationality, beliefs, and way of life. At times, a tone of distinct admiration even creeps into these accounts. Thus, less than a decade after John Perry's return to England, John Bell, another traveler to Siberia, noted in 1721: "Their language contains none of those horrid oaths common enough in tongues of more enlightened nations. They believe virtue leads to happiness, and vice to misery; for when desired to do what they think wrong, they reply, in a proverb, 'Though a knife be sharp, it cannot cut its own handle.'"[10]

EMPIRE, NATION, AND THE TOPOGRAPHY OF CIVILIZATION

Even as writers acknowledged the existence of diverse populations at the eastern stretches of the empire, Siberia continued to be represented as a place of tremendous contradictions. Labeled as empty but also filled with riches, it was a land available for exploitation but also inaccessible, difficult to settle yet replete with all manner of indigenous peoples. However, the most significant change compared with previous centuries was the sense of Siberia as a known entity. While it was still viewed as vast and a place of no return, the name no longer suggested an unfamiliar realm built solely out of wild imagination. Rather, it was an endless space crossed numerous times by travelers, missionaries, traders, and the military. During the eighteenth century Siberia became a destination. No longer a frozen, miserable passage to reach China or other distant, more alluring places in Asia, the land and people emerged as a growing focus for scientific research. Uncultivated nature did not immediately imply barren wastes and forests teaming with wild beasts; instead, systematic mapping and careful description of the flora and fauna, with each species listed item by item in scientific tables printed by the Imperial Academy, made Siberia real—tangible and imaginable in a whole different way. Constructed through careful accounting of the natural world, the columns of facts in treatises and dictionaries rendered Siberia into a real place and an object of continuing study.

As numerous historians of Russia have noted, the beginning of the eighteenth century represented a dividing line between "Old" and "New" Russia.[11] A new way of looking at Russia had particular implications for the vast eastern territories and the peoples living therein. The central concern for rulers of European kingdoms, empires, and principalities was the constitution of a "European empire." Russia of the eighteenth century was a perfect if exaggerated example of the difficulty of such a project in territorial, civilizational, religious, political, and most importantly human terms. Given its large geographic body, Russia wished to be regarded as an equal with the major players of Europe yet to retain a special status due to its scale.[12] These contradictory desires appear front and center in the writings of the day: insistence on the European nature of Russian culture, yet uncertainty whether those same features should also count as distinctly Russian, unique to their local place and space. This was a pressing issue from the perspective of Russian pride because a widely shared opinion throughout Western Europe was that Russia had arrived on the world stage about thousand years later than everyone else and thereby was a crass latecomer to civilization: "these last comers upon the old theater of the world, engaged my mind during the whole time of my stay among them."[13]

Was Russia sufficiently "civilized" to be considered European? Was Russia already European or merely hoping for a European future? Amid such questions, the territorial presence of native people proved crucial. Starting with Peter the Great, Russian rulers enthusiastically emulated Western European empire-building missions, comparing their own efforts in Asia to the overseas colonial expansion of Britain, France, and Spain. Anything in the steppes of Asia was so distant and remote, after all, to be a metaphorical ocean away. As Mikhail Lomonosov enthusiastically wrote in 1747, the river Lena was just like the Nile, and Asian territories just like Brazil or Mexico—colonial outposts reflecting the grandeur of the empire, rather than any geographic reality.[14] The East stood distant, wild, and available.

Yet it did not go unnoticed to Russians that their country itself was at times treated as an outpost of Asia, the only European empire to "colonize itself."[15] This marginal position encouraged ongoing angst over civilization, with the need to affirm that Russians had been "European" all along, while insisting on a distinct nature and national character—nation and empire, facing each other. Consequently, the outpouring of eighteenth-century ethnographic tales about Siberia served to narrate the European-ness of Russia by describing the "other" living next to them in Asia. In this sense, Russian emperors needed Siberia and its native peoples to confirm their own civilization and their belonging to the West.

Siberia embodied the geographic and the conceptual space where the nation and the empire were in direct contact. As a separate but connected colonial outpost, it served as a reminder, a threat, and a marker of Russian identity. The Ural Mountains—until then viewed as a rather modest mountain range—emerged at this moment as an increasingly significant physical boundary and gave shape to a new topography for the aspiring European empire. As Mark Bassin noted, Vasilii Tatishchev, an aristocrat, a historian, and most importantly a skillful diplomat in the service of Peter the Great, expressly recognized the connection between geography and history, and the importance of a defined geopolitical space.[16] Charged in 1720 by the emperor to create a map of Russia, Tatishchev identified the Ural Mountains as the natural boundary between the continents of Europe and Asia.[17] This proposition gained enthusiastic acceptance, having arrived at the right historical and political moment.

The division of the empire into Europe and Asia along the Urals provided a new geographic canvas upon which the West European imperial model could be painted. The Urals took the place of an ocean, a natural boundary that required time and effort to traverse. The relationship between the territories on either side of the mountains could now be characterized in properly European terms of continental and civilizational contrast, as if the empire existed in different parts of the globe. In this spirit, scholars began to emphasize the foreignness in all regards of the lands east of the Urals vis-à-vis European Russia, which included the physical geography, climate, and plants and animals as well as the inhabitants and their cultural development. The divide displayed the essential contrast in terms that corresponded to the respective métropole—colonial distinctions drawn by empires in the West.[18] Thanks to Siberia and the modest physical boundary of a mountain range, Russia could be European, a part of the "civilized" continent.

The emergence of the Ural boundary had an equally meaningful effect on the Asian part of the empire. In writing, legal documents, and travel narratives, Siberia began to emerge in much greater detail, yet increasingly became a part Asia, obviously distinct in all aspects worth discussing. The topography of a mountain range created a sense of civilizational divide above and beyond the cultural and religious differences. Furthermore, this geographical feature was also a marker of time and history. It separated the ancient—in words of many eighteenth-century travelers, the "Scythian"—from the merely old, divided the unchanging wilderness from the civilized, settled, and increasingly urban European Russia.[19] Siberia remained uncultivated, a place of hunting peoples who would not settle, who were impervious to civilization.

Such "ancient inhabitants" were so unlike the Russians of the European part of the empire that they required scientific studies and detailed descriptions. To become comprehensible subjects of the government, they had to be counted, described, and catalogued alongside the physical features of the landscape. Just as with the abundant and heretofore unknown plants, animals, and minerals, scientists began to classify the native people through their discernible features. The Tungus and the Samoyed, formerly hunters and fishermen, fur trappers and reluctant trading partners, were transformed into anthropological objects with peculiar customs, religious beliefs, and marriage customs.

Representations of nature in Siberia now included the indigenous peoples as a part of the wilderness. Yet unlike most European colonizing adventures in the New World, the Russians made no serious attempts to civilize these newly discovered subjects. The uncivilized natives were allowed to remain just like the spaces of nature, untamed and wild, untouched by culture. Siberia served as a counterpoint to metropolitan Russia, which by comparison appeared civilized, almost European. Early Siberian ethnography thus not only catalogued the different ethnic tribes and ancient peoples but also defined urban European Russians by contrast, transforming both groups in the process. By shifting the ethnographic focus to Siberia, Russia moved much closer to the European empires it wished to resemble. Now in possession of colonies, the Russian imperial court and ruling class could point to the natives who were less civilized and far more peculiar. Moscow lay securely west of this unstable East.

THE BEGINNING AND THE END

On March 14, 1692, the Dutch artist, traveler, and scientist Cornelius de Bruyn wrote in his diary,

> Muscovy is now grown to be very considerable in the world, and has for some time been so much the subject of discourse, and the Prince at present on the throne having made himself famous for his conduct, his victories and care he takes to cultivate the minds and manners of his subjects, by introducing into his dominions all that can contribute to their advantage, all Europe is attentive to what concerns this great empire, and inquisitive to know what passes therein.[20]

The enlightened prince in question was Peter the Great. The czar found a great reception in Holland and England during his "Grand Embassy" of 1697. While living "anonymously" in Amsterdam, he learned shipbuilding skills and drafting. He likewise came to appreciate the new fascination with natural history and geography. Amsterdam's mayor at the time, Nicolaas Witsen, a wealthy politician and one of the earliest collectors of ethnographic details, provided Peter the Great with a team of Siberian surveyors and natural scientists. Upon his return home, the czar implemented a host of social and political changes. In addition to moving the capital away from Moscow to a new location on an island in the northern marshes, he founded the first Academy of Sciences, which was devoted to research and collecting. This last institution was the most significant change in respect to the vast empire and the countless ethnic groups of Siberia. Peter's decision to reorient Russia, to open the empire to Europe, and to invite Dutch and German scientists to help with the modernizing process marked a new point not only in the history of Russia, but also in Russian colonial expansion into Asia.[21]

However, the relationships among seeing, knowing, describing, and appropriating colonized eastern territories would remain distinctly Russian, particularly when compared with European colonial ventures in other parts of the world. The Russians lacked any interest in civilizing or Christianizing the indigenous peoples. Still, Peter the Great aspired to acceptance in Western Europe, and his imperial imagination, influenced by German and Dutch scientific sensibilities, marked a new turn in Russia's territorial ambitions. The result was a sudden, systemic surge in the search for information about everything in the eastern and northern parts of the empire. Descriptions of plants, animals, rivers, mountains, and people as well as collected samples and drawings were deposited in the newly founded Imperial Academy of Sciences. The previous century and a half of plunder and fur trade had generated unprecedented wealth for the empire, which helped fund the new scientific ambitions.

Whereas documents from the previous centuries had been largely formulaic and uninterested in specific details, those from the eighteenth century marked a turning point in ethnographic accounts of Siberia. Travelers, war captives, merchants, geographers, and newly hired scientists all combed through the land for accounts of peoples with strange customs, remarkable body types, and fascinating, if revolting, eating habits. No longer were the native groups in the vast eastern empire a mere source of furs and minerals and a ready supply of slaves. Rather, they became subjects with knowledge in their own right, revealed through detailed descriptions of their lifestyle, customs, and collections of their material culture.

The emperor hired geographers and natural scientists and sent them to the East with a singular mission: document everything about these imperial subjects. Thus, the landmark publication from the Danish diplomat Evert Ysbrants Ides, "Three Years Land Travels of His Excellency E. Ysbrants Ides from Moscow to China," featured the following dedication:

> Most Illustrious and most Potent Czar and Monarch, Most Gracious Sovereign. 'Tis well known to all who are acquainted with the Descriptions of the World, that your Czarist Majesty governs with a Sovereign Imperial Sway a considerable and conspicuous part of Europe. And considering that the insufficiency of my head and my pen would not allow me to describe the whole State of Great, Little and White Russia, I have here attempted a short view of your Majesty's Kingdoms of Sibiria and Daour.[22]

Over the course of nearly three hundred pages, Ides's work provided an early detailed ethnography of the eastern parts of the empire. As it was subsequently translated into multiple languages, its success also indicated the growing interest throughout Europe in Russia, and even more in its eastern territories. The tome served as a guidebook for later travelers, as Herberstein's work had before, and it became as a scientific source document for early anthropologists.

Ides was a Danish diplomat, so his national origin and professional station gave him a significant amount of credibility. An educated man, he represented not only Nordic sensibilities but also the institutions that Peter the Great admired and wanted to emulate. Like Holland and England, Russia's Scandinavian neighbors Sweden and Denmark, although regularly at war, had a major influence on the czar's decision to establish educational, research, and military structures separate from the hierarchy and influence of the Orthodox church. Peter distrusted theological philosophy, and he had great interest in knowledge based on observation and experience, as diffused through scholarly debates.[23] Ides, who was crossing Russia on a mercantile mission to China, was just the man for Peter. A skilled, educated observer, he did not merely repeat the stories of other travelers but rather visited the places himself and provided eyewitness accounts. He maintained a firm belief in the superiority of European civilization, but Ides also was fascinated with barbaric behavior, and he recorded a wealth of curious customs in an unprecedented detail:

> For this country [Siberia] having never been travelled by Geographers, much less measured by Miles, I have only as carefully as I possibly could taken the

Altitudes with Mathematical instruments, and from thence marked the Places, leaving to my Successors in these attempts, the more thorough search and discovery of these untraveled Countries. I have indeed broke the ice for them, being the first German that ever went through this vast Country to, and returned from China. I must acknowledge that I am obliged for the first light of a good Sketch of a general Map of these Lands, to the highly Honourable and Worthy Nicholas Witsen, President Burger-master of the City of Amsterdam, whose Memory will be perpetually reverenced by all the Learned World; He having first discovered to the Europeans all Siberia.[24]

The emperor who had dispatched Ides across Siberia to China was a passionate collector of things strange and anomalous. Peter's vast *Kunstkamera,* a cabinet of curiosities in the most expansive sense, contained hundreds of human embryos in various stages of development; a skeleton of a giant; stuffed birds and animals, plants, and shells; and an impressive collection of books in many languages.[25] Although Ides wrote his travelogue for the emperor's collection, he recorded information of great interest to a much wider European audience. In fact, the focus and attention to detail were strikingly similar to accounts of distant encounters throughout the eighteenth century, providing an early example of ethnography in colonial settings. Clothing, food, appearance, customs, and marriage patterns were all central topics in this emerging genre of travel writing.

Ides devoted considerable detail to the Ostiaks, a western Siberian people who lived near the river Ob as "fish folk."[26] Not only did they subsist entirely on fish, but according to the Dane they also wore clothing and shoes made from fish skins. In one of the early explicit discussions of religion among the native peoples, Ides wrote that the Ostiaks were "heathens who have their own Gods made of wood and earth, in several human shapes. Some of the richest amongst them dress these Deities in silken cloaths. . . . They call their Gods Saitan, and might indeed very well say Satan."[27]

The suggestion that the words *shaman* or *Saitan* and Satan were actually synonyms was a common theme by this time, particularly in Dutch and German writings. After a visit to a "Tungus shaman," Ambassador Ides offered details of the encounter, a description that would end up being quoted for decades, even centuries, as an example of a veritable shamanic experience:

> Some miles upwards from hence live several Tunguzians, amongst which is also their famed Schaman or Diabolical Artist. The reports which passed concerning this cheat made me very desirous to see him. Wherefore in order to gratifie my curiosity I went to those parts, to visit him and his habitation.

I found him a tall old Man that had twelve Wives, and was not ashamed of the Art he pretended to: he shewed me his Conjuring Habit, and the other Tools which he used. First I saw his Coat, made of joined iron work, consisting of all manner of representations of Birds, Fishes, Ravens, Owls, besides several Beasts and Birds Claws, and Bills, Saws, Hammers, Knives, Sabirs, and the Images of several Beasts, so that all the parts of this Diabolical Robe being fixed together by joints, might at pleasure be taken to pieces. He had also iron stockings for his feet and legs, suitable to his robe, and two great bears claws over his hands. His head was likewise adorned, with such like images, and fixed to his forehead were two Iron Bucks Horns. When he designs to conjure he takes a Drum made after their fashion in his left hand, and a flat staff covered with the skins of mountain mice in his right hand; thus equipped he jumps cross legged, which motion shakes all these iron plates, and makes a great clangor, besides which, he at the same time beats his drum, and with eyes distorted upwards, a strong bearish voice makes a dismal noise.[28]

A lengthier discussion of the ritual itself followed this vivid description, conveying the respect the shaman enjoyed among his people and his wealth and skill. Ides inserted a note of skepticism throughout the pages, but the text exhibited considerable fascination with these practices, which were exotic yet of scientific interest to the natural philosophy of the day.

Bodies of Differences and Ethnographic Genders

A striking aspect of the early writing was the curiosity about the lives of Siberian women. A great deal of attention was paid to native women and their apparent distinction from women in European societies. Travelers remarked on the position of women in relation to men and the number of wives a man had, as well as the clothing women wore and the activities they engaged in. In the case of Siberia, a perceived lack of distinction between men and women among the groups in Siberia attracted particular interest. According to these accounts, men and women often engaged in the same activities and wore the same clothing, or they went without clothes all summer long and decorated their bodies with similar tattoos:

Both Men and Women go naked in the Summer, excepting only a Leather Girdle of three Hands breadth, that they deeply cut In the shape of Ribbands, which they wear about their wast, and covers their Priivities. . . . These People are great admirers of Beauty, according to their notion of it. To improve which, they adorn their Forehead, Cheeks and Chins in the following manner: They with a needle run Threads greased with black Greace

through the Skin, in representation of several Figures, and leave the said
Threads therein for several Days, after which they draw them out, and
leave their traces behind them, and very few of them are without this
Embellishment.[29]

In comparison with earlier texts, Ides' account stands out in terms of
his recognition that standards of beauty might be culturally defined.

The early eighteenth century was still a period enamored with the
different and monstrous in distant places, although all these phenomena were seen as a part of God's creation. A nascent desire to classify
and categorize began to appear among the traveling scholars, and although the exotic and strange remained the focus, details of daily life
started to take on a larger role. Travelers commonly noted the lack
of hygiene or expressed disgust with the natives' habit of eating food
"barely cooked." Ides foreshadowed the emerging new generation of
educated, scientifically minded natural philosophers who approached
the world as a curiosity while detailing the differences between its
parts in a more systematic fashion. The eighteenth-century ethnographies of Siberian native peoples were no longer mere collections of everything bizarre.

The wide-eyed travelers commented increasingly on customs, detailing the lives of men and women and their gender norms and differences.
In 1701, Louis Moréri, who had never been to Russia, wrote about the
Samoyed people for the *Great Historical Dictionary,* describing them as
a group living to the northeast of Muscovy by the Frozen Sea and noting that the women commonly engaged in what he perceived to be
men's activities: "Their women are very nimble, and take much pains to
teach their children to hunt. They are clothed like the men, save only
that they have no furs upon their shoulders. They go hunting with a
quiver full of arrows, and a bow in their hands."[30] Moréri's attention to
Samoyed women's hunting spoke to a common theme of "savage societies" that captivated the political philosophers of the eighteenth century,
who considered the native groups to be the starting point of natural history for all humanity.[31] The topic of natural sex difference, its emergence
in human history, and the social circumstances under which such distinctions might have appeared attracted particular attention among gentlemen scientists. Travelers also noted the gender divergence of the native men from what they considered a proper masculine norm; particularly
noteworthy were an absence of body hair, a lack of gender-specific clothing, and peculiar hair arrangements.

Divergent gender characteristics at times evoked more than simple scientific passion. For example, the Danish traveler Ides recounted a visit to a group of Tungus living near the Angara River. While there, he met a "local prince named Lilliulka," whose most distinguishing feature was his remarkably long black hair, arranged three times around the shoulders.[32] Enticed by the sight, the Danish scientist proceeded to intoxicate the prince with brandy "by which civility [I] obtained the favor of having his hair loosened" and found it to have been "all his natural hair only." Ides then used a scientific instrument to record the exact measure of "four Dutch ells."[33] He determined that the remarkable hair was not a wig, as any European accustomed to princes and courts might have suspected. Thus carefully recorded and never reflected upon, the incident marked the beginning of the physical scientific study of native bodies, not merely their customs, as a part of the natural history of Siberia. The strange and curious still attracted the attention of the traveling scientists, but the step to physically measure and verify suggested a new way of meeting the world. People, plants, and animals could be described, illustrated, measured, and collected. No longer was the world merely an assortment of wonders; it became a laboratory with instruments, scientific methods, and meticulous records with uncensored detail.

The activities of the traveling scientist took a gendered turn not detected earlier, and the passion for scientific discoveries at times resembled a sexual encounter. The description of "a prince" with very long hair, who had to be intoxicated so as to have his hair untied and touched, defined the native man not only as a colonial subject but also as a scientific specimen. Ides had dined with a "Siberian prince," but once his body came into focus, the description of the Tungus man became that of a woman who was seduced and whose hair was then measured with a scientific instrument. In the text—situated between a detailed discussion of fish species, their numbers and sizes, and followed by a description of river flows—the Danish scientist's description of the very long hair treats it as an unusual natural phenomenon. But the intimate context of an evening meal in a native tent followed by intoxication evokes less distance than such comparisons might suggest. As the historian Londa Schiebinger has noted, colonial science as a description and measure of a distant world was a highly gendered enterprise, which reflected upon the European gender norms and arrangements of the time.[34] The new worlds in the process of discovery, description, and measurement were treated as bodies to be intoxicated, subdued, and conquered.

Остякъ при рѣкѣ Объ.
Ein Ostiacke am Ob Fluß.
Ostiak a la rivière d'Ob.

FIGURE 4.1. "Ostyak man," from Johann Gottlieb Georgi, 1799. Georgi's richly illustrated text offered detailed information about numerous indigenous groups in Siberia. His illustrations reinforced the impression that men and women in Siberia were interchangeable. The Ostiak man—"man of the East"—mirrored the illustration of the Otsiak woman, with hands turned upward in a dance-like figure, bonnet, and a woman's fur coat reinforcing the notion of man devoid of masculinity. Georgi, Johann Gottlieb. 1799. Finskie narody: Ostiak pri reke Ob'. Image no. 1241932. Slavic and Baltic Division, The New York Public Library, Astor, Lenox and Tilden Foundations. (Reproduced with permission of the New York Public Library.)

Given the striking similarities they saw between men and women—their identical hairstyles, lack of body hair, and indistinguishable body decorations and clothing—early travelers searched for signs of sex and gender as markers of civilized behavior: the Tungus or Chukchi men may have been hard to tell from their women, but surely they were still masters of their families. As if to confirm this order of things, the early ethnographers recorded the marriage patterns and relations between the sexes in every village and settlement. Although regularly condemned in Christian societies, polygamy was a topic of great fascination to all European travelers, and it was regularly commented on. The higher the status a man had in the native society, the more wives he was claimed to have, in the case of the Tungus shaman even reaching twelve, a number oft repeated for any man perceived as being of high standing. Sexual mores, appetites, and their regulation, and gender codes and markers in newly encountered colonial settings provided a mirror for European sexual arrangements and the standards of proper masculinity and femininity. The lives of Siberian natives hinted at a possible ancestral past and what had gone before: nudity, polygamy, and uncontrolled consumption.

Beyond providing a map of the Russian empire, travel writing from this period also contributed to the debate about European ancient history. The early accounts, eighteenth-century travelogues, and mapping and scientific expeditions reported on what they encountered via comparison. The Siberians' way of life stood in contrast to contemporary European societies and peoples, and the unknown, harsh climate and landscape of Siberia served to distance the edges of Europe, to insist on a separation between their connected histories. Unlike the earlier monsters—the humans with dog heads or mouths on their chests—over time the Siberians became people who were strange and exotic, savage and kind, and clearly different though also increasingly recognizable. As the Siberian native peoples dropped their cloak of invisibility, they stood in for the past, for the ancient customs and the magic that civilization had removed from Europe.

LOOKING AND SEEING: BELIEFS AND CUSTOMS

Following German and French models of research institutes, Peter the Great designed the Imperial Academy of Sciences in Saint Petersburg as a space that would enable the study and collection of all that his empire possessed. Officially established in early 1725, the year of the emperor's death, his plan and worldview nevertheless guided the institution for the next half a century. The whole enterprise had been in motion for almost a decade: scholars were tapped, scientists invited, and expeditions planned. Peter's own private Kunstkamera, his assortment of fabulous oddities and interesting specimens, along with the extensive library for which he had purchased entire collections while traveling through Western Europe, were the foundation of the Academy.[35] The eastern territories were now added to this assorted collection.

Lacking a domestic educated class of scientists, the emperor invited foreigners, largely German and Danish scholars, to set up the institution and serve as physicians, mathematicians, chemists, botanists, astronomers, and natural historians within its scientific community. Their task was to create an empire: to map, measure, describe, and catalog all there was to govern. While many European imperial academies of the time had a markedly utilitarian mission, distinct from the universities, the Imperial Academy in Saint Petersburg bundled multiple roles into one, serving simultaneously as a research institute, a university, a museum, a publishing house, a depositary, and a place for the creation of knowledge about the not-so-distant colonies of the East.[36] Thus, the land of the East became an entity officially known as Siberia, placed on the map and stabilized in the geography of the empire during the eighteenth century.

Having become a defined, delineated object, Siberia and its people could now be examined and described in detail. In contrast with Russia, Siberia was now a far more intriguing space, amenable to scientific classification and description, waiting to be rendered comprehensible. The focus of the geographic lens shifted to the smaller regions—the river valleys, islands, lakes, and mountains—as places occupied by distinct peoples, all described in ethnic terms. The maps produced through scientific exploration, rather than as a result of trade or leisure travel, no longer identified everything east of Moscow as "Tartary." Instead, readers learned about areas occupied by the "Ostiacks," "Samojad," "Tungus," "Yakut," "Yukagir," "Dauri," "Giljaki," or the "Kamchadal"—Russianized names of separate ethnic groups, now recognized to be as distinct as the Chinese or the Mongols.

However, the boundaries of these lands were still fluid, shifting north or south with every new map. Certain groups would appear in far greater detail than others, and consequently take up larger pieces of the geographical canvas. Yet this was no longer a description of a portion of the land standing in for any other region, or even for all of Russia. Boundaries and differences, the goal of the new research, were sharply delin-

Гунгуской Шаманъ при ръкъ Аргуни съ лица.
Ein Tungusischer Schamann am Argun Fluss vorwärts.
Devin toungouse auprès de l'Argoun par devant.

FIGURE 4.2. "Tungus shaman," from Johann Gottlieb Georgi,
1799. One of the early images of a "shaman" based on an
eyewitness account. Unlike the previously circulated image by
Witsen (1692) that seems to have been an imaginary reproduc-
tion, not based on an encounter with a live shaman. An arrow or
a sword piercing the shaman's body without inflicting any visible
harm was a common detail recounted by travellers in Siberia.
Georgi, Johann Gottlieb. 1799. Mandzhurskie narody: Tunguskoi
Shaman pri reke Argune s litsa (Manchurian peoples, Tungus
(Evenk) Shaman, Argun River). Image no. 1241971. Slavic and
Baltic Division, The New York Public Library, Astor, Lenox and
Tilden Foundations. (Reproduced with permission of the New
York Public Library.)

eated among plants, animals, peoples, and continents. Ferns, trees, flowers, and the dense teeming forests were now identified by natural historians as unique species that had never seen before. They were labeled and described, and samples were collected in portable herbaria. The fish acquired Latin names, their likenesses were rendered in exquisite detail, and they were classified in unique families. Just as "natural" boundaries and physical barriers separated the continents of Europe, Asia, and America, the boundaries of difference for Siberian flora and fauna had merely to be discovered then described.

Similarly, natural history and ethnography of the eighteenth century not only made the native peoples of Siberia real and comprehensible but also turned them into objects that could be categorized and then compared to peoples in other parts of the world. Physicians were considered to have appropriate training to carry out this meticulous task, and, as it happened, Peter the Great found the best and most willing in Germany. Michael Gordin convincingly argues that Leibniz's Berlin Academy of Sciences served the czar as an example of an institution of knowledge production. However, just as importantly it was a model of practices and etiquette that the emperor wished to emulate in his court and re-create in Russia.[37] Thus, we meet illustrious German characters in Daniel Gottlieb Messerschmidt, Gerhard Friedrich Müller, and Georg Steller among the many who were discovering, describing, and at times naming after themselves the nature and people that confronted them along the way. They collected minerals and plants, shot and preserved animals, and met the native peoples and recorded their customs, all with a seriousness of purpose and dedication to science.

It was this process that gave birth to the "shaman" as a permanent category, no longer a mere curiosity but an object to be detailed under the heading "Beliefs and Customs," in a chapter often followed by "Eating Habits and Table Manners." Once the learned men of the eighteenth century had discovered a shaman, they then found them everywhere, in every group they encountered. Each displayed quite a wide range of practices and purposes, and they were not the only peculiar characters that fascinated our German scholars.

THE MANY BEGINNINGS OF GERMAN ETHNOGRAPHY

Even in the early eighteenth century, curiosity was not a sensibility abundant in the Russian court, and a utilitarian focus on extracting a few selected resources had been the main driving force of Russian interest in

Siberia for several centuries. However, influenced by the German form of the Enlightenment, particularly via Gottfried Leibniz's influence on Peter the Great, the pursuit of knowledge inspired a new attitude toward the eastern provinces. The Imperial Academy would provide its hired German scientists with considerable resources (even though they constantly complained about the scarcity of funds), and in return they would produce a systematically organized and classified encyclopedia of their world, with facts that could answer some of the most pressing questions of the time: how the continents were related as well as what the distances were between locations in Russia and Europe. They also measured the depth of the lakes, the length of the rivers, and the extremes of the temperatures in winter and summer, as well as descriptions of the customs of the present indigenous peoples of Siberia and speculations about its ancient inhabitants.

The first of these scientists was Daniel Gottlieb Messerschmidt, who had trained as a physician at the University of Halle in Germany at the beginning of the eighteenth century.[38] He was knowledgeable about plants and their uses in medicine, and also had a keen eye for people and their customs and an unmatched, ascetic passion for science. He thus emerged as the perfect man for the job when Peter the Great was seeking someone to collect and catalogue his empire. Starting in 1720, Messerschmidt spent seven long years traveling through Siberia, accompanied for a short period by two Swedish war captives, Philip Johan Tabbert von Strahlenberg and Karl Schulman.[39] He was an expert who could describe nature in all its richness and complexity but with a focus and purpose beyond mere popular entertainment. Messerschmidt received explicit instructions at the court in Saint Petersburg to keep a journal and to build a collection of specimens that he would regularly ship back to the Academy. He was to carry out his duties in the following defined areas:

1. Description of the land.
2. Natural history and its components.
3. Medicine, Materia Medica, epidemic diseases.
4. Description of the Siberian nation and its philology.
5. Monuments and other antiquities.
6. Other strange or interesting items.[40]

This was no longer travel writing about anything remarkable or completely mundane to be dutifully noted and offered to educated readers as

"strange or interesting items." The scientific study of natural history
included nature, people, and history, approached with specific, defined
methods of observation. As Michel Foucault noted in *The Order of
Things: An Archaeology of the Human Sciences*:

> Natural history did not become possible because men looked harder and
> more closely. . . . Hearsay is excluded, that goes without saying; but so are
> taste and smell, because their lack of certainty and their variability render
> impossible any analysis into distinct elements that could be universally ac-
> ceptable. The sense of touch is very narrowly limited to the designation of a
> few fairly evident distinctions (such as that between rough and smooth);
> which leaves sight with an almost exclusive privilege, being the sense by which
> we perceive extent and establish proof, and, in consequence, the means to an
> analysis *partes extra partes* acceptable to everyone: the blind man in the
> eighteenth century can perfectly well be a geometrician, but he cannot be a
> naturalist. . . .
>
> To observe, then, is to be content with seeing—with seeing a few things
> systematically. With seeing what, in the rather confused wealth of represen-
> tation, can be analyzed, recognized by all, and thus given a name that every-
> one will be able to understand.[41]

Natural history involved a shift from looking at the world through
many media to seeing with one's own eyes. No longer was it an accept-
able scientific method to receive reports from travelers and visitors, to
read stories and myths, to cite Herodotus, or to describe the world from
a distance using all these disparate sources while noting all manner
of intriguing detail. In Lorraine Daston's words, a "factual sensibility"
emerged as a central consideration.[42] As the Swedish war captive, and
a brief travel companion to Messerschmidt, Philip Johan Tabbert von
Strahlenberg pointed out, "Others may like a map with more ornaments, which are indeed agreeable to the eye. But it is the accuracy of
the map, which must make it valuable, as the business of geography is
exactly to settle the distance of places, in such a manner, as to be perfectly understood."[43] Scientific facts had acquired their own visibility as
central and necessary.

The scientists employed by the Imperial Academy set off on missions
to see for themselves and to bring back that which was typical and representative as well as unique in the natural world of the empire. Strahlenberg assured the reader in the introduction to his work that everything
he described he had seen with his very own eyes, and that if he relied on
someone else's description, it was the most "credible person" he could
find. In the same vein, Messerschmidt journeyed for seven years as an
eyewitness, collecting and bringing back all the facts he could for every-

one else to see, rather than relying on tales told by returning travelers. Furthermore, the natural historian saw the world around him in a new, bracketed, defined way. Through a scientific lens, he could discern the significant amid the ordinary, the characteristics that stood out, even if they also were common and shared by many.

Stripped of unnecessary baggage, their stories and impressions of the flora, fauna, and people had a new, focused, precise clarity. Messerschmidt traveled to the far corners of the empire with a list of six categories that the world around him had to fit. Following Ides's earlier mercantile journey with "scientific instruments," Messerschmidt's voyage was an explicitly scientific *Forschungsreise durch Sibirien* (Research Journey through Siberia), as his journal was titled, rather than an investigation for resources to exploit or a pleasure trip through fascinating and revolting strange lands. The extensive field notes, drawings, and samples of all manner of natural and cultural life as well as the ensuing maps combined to create the basis of a scientific field. Ethnology—the study of people—emerged as a new domain of research alongside botany and zoology.[44] At the same time, it constructed Siberia for Russia's rulers: giving shape to a vast, impressive empire, and making it available for display and comparison with the overseas possessions of others.

Natural history, regional ethnography, and systematic empire building thus all began in Russia with the odyssey of a thirty-five-year-old, fanatically devoted German scientist. Messerschmidt traveled "alone" with a retinue of servants, a cook, and horse-drawn wagons filled with equipment and boxes for collections. His field notes carefully recorded his observations and measurements but revealed little personal sentiment. He seldom seemed to be tired, sick, bored, or irritated—except by the cost and constant shortage of writing paper, or the periodic need for laxatives, or the occasional encounter with Russian provincial officials or drunken settlers.[45] The German doctor was the first of a cast of eighteenth-century characters who brought Siberia to Europe's consciousness as a new land discovered and created through systematic study. A precursor to Linnaeus, who would travel a decade later among the Sami of northern Sweden to describe the plants, animals, and native people, Messerschmidt set out through Siberia to define its array of natural and social phenomena, peoples and places.[46]

Through Messerschimdt's writing, we meet the Samoyed and the Tungus as distinct ethnic groups, with customs and languages recorded in remarkable detail: he drew their body parts, clothing, and tattoos with as much precision as he devoted to plant leaves, pistils, stamens, petals, or animal hoofs, fins, and antennas.

> Their dress was without any difference with regard to age, social position or gender, it was the same style for a man and a woman; also the hair on the head was merely loosely held together with a string. They had rings in their ears. The skin on the forehead, chin and the sides of the cheeks was marked with blue characters that oftentimes resembled reindeer antlers.[47]

Faithfully following his list of research questions, Messerschimdt paid particular attention to the "description of the Siberian nation and its philology," noting religious beliefs, eating habits, and kin relations, principally those between men and women. From reading his notebooks, it is quite clear that by 1720 there were no "unknown people," no natives who had never met an outsider, a stranger, a trader, or a soldier. Moreover, the different tribes had a clear sense of each other, their differences and similarities. Native geographies mapped Siberia in great detail, if in quite a different manner from the maps generated by the military or travelers. Messerschmidt made note of the nature of the contact between the Russians and the Siberian native people, the degree of hostility between the outsiders and the locals, and the periodic attempts, largely unsuccessful, to encourage conversion either to Russian Orthodox beliefs or to Islam in the southern regions.

Anke te Heesen has suggested that by bringing a set of tools, instruments, and collecting procedures with him, Messerschimdt managed to re-create both a museum and a private study for himself in the field, from which he connected conceptually with the distant European scientific community.[48] As a result, Messerschmidt became the caretaker of a mobile depositary of objects and information, as the natives brought him birds, eggs, pieces of cloth, and items both mundane and special. Messerschmidt's procedures simultaneously carved a social space for him in Siberia, which enabled him to socialize not only with the various Russians he met along the way but also with the local people whose knowledge, history, and material possessions he wanted to collect. Although he was an outsider merely passing through, Messerschmidt was visited daily by Siberian natives, motivated by curiosity, or generosity, or the hope of payment in tobacco, beer, or liquor. *Branntwein*, a liquor distilled from potatoes or grain (or in desperate need, even from wood cellulose), regularly appeared in Messerschmidt's diary as his most common form of currency, and his supply must have been substantial and regularly replenished as he also used it for medicinal purposes, treating both himself and sick patients encountered along the way.[49]

The Language of the Shaman and Spirits: Words and Meanings in Translation

Messerschmidt noted that a vast number of people lived in the different regions of Siberia, and many had distinct tongues that were not mutually intelligible. By the end of his seven-year journey, he had built a voluminous and impressive multilingual dictionary that recorded some thirty-two languages. His linguistic charts and vocabularies formed a set of columns pairing equal linguistic units; every term was recorded in German, Latin, Russian, Hebrew, Tungus, Ostiak, and any local language he encountered. His informants were the people who came to his camp or to outposts or settlements where he had stopped, and the detailed daily account of his journey reveals that the "Siberian native population" came to be represented mainly by the largest groups—the Tungus, the Ostiak, and the Samoyed—who were the most willing (or the least reluctant) to engage newcomers.

During one such meeting, Messerschmidt encountered his first "shaman," who came to visit him just one month after he had departed from Tobolsk, the western capital of Siberia, on March 19, 1721.[50] Messerschmidt's substantial entourage, including the Swedish war captive Captain von Strahelnberg, their servants, and the horse-drawn wagons with all their possessions, had just arrived in a village named Ilcibek. First, they measured their geographic location, latitude, longitude, and altitude; they also estimated their degrees of separation from the Baltic port of Stettin, which was a constant point of reference for both German and Swede, and placed themselves at 72.5 degrees.[51] Their geographic locale established and dutifully recorded, they made themselves at home in a yurt, whereupon they were visited by a man who offered to "schamanen" or divine for them.

> He had with him a Shaman—or a Lapp drum, which was fixed to a wooden Shaitan [carved idol] (dressed with old rags). Before he started his art, he wished to smoke a pipe of schar [a native term] or tobacco. After he had obtained this, he began, sitting, to work with his shaman's spoon (or a drum stick) upon his drum as if he wanted to smear it with fat, he growled a bit gently, softly and murmured. Afterward he got up, he began to beat harder

and harder with the stick on the drum, uttered stronger and stronger cries, jumped up high, jumped around like a great man, grabbed with one hand hot ashes, that were in the fireplace, and in sum the man was quite unhinged/wild. After he had carried on like this for a quarter hour, he suddenly stood still, stared upward and was for a good while completely still. Shortly thereafter he said, almost singing, the following: The doctor left behind four children, of which one would have died ("mentiris Cain!" [you lie, Cain!]), the doctor was to remain here in Siberia for 7 years, also our horse would go lame before we got to Tomsk; in sum the man made up a bunch of lies, and one can see that all his prophecies or fortune-telling were nothing.[52]

Messerschmidt dismissed this personalized fortune—he had no children, and he had a written contract specifying the duration of his travel through Siberia—but he nevertheless interrogated the man in great detail about the performance and the beliefs that had inspired it. The visiting fortune-teller described a multitude of personal deities—"poor Gods," "rich Gods," "nasty Gods," and "kind Gods"—all of which Messerschmidt duly recorded. Messerschmidt was not surprised or even intrigued by the offer of divination by the "schaman," as he knew what to expect. Similarly, in numerous other instances over the years, whenever he had encountered an unfamiliar or incomprehensible event or situation, he made extensive inquiries and noted the responses in his journal.

In his diary entry, Messerschmidt used the term "schaman" as a verb to mean fortune-telling, but he also used it as an adjective to refer to the objects used in the performance. When describing the various forces that the man had claimed helped in telling fortunes, Messerschmidt referred to the wooden carving attached to the drum as "schaitan" or Satan, which had been the most common translation among European travelers since the mid-seventeenth century.

> March 15, 1721, Wednesday: Here we found many schaitans too, among them also a rather large one, set inside a kind of Lapp drum. We asked whether they considered them gods who would bring rain, bread/food or something else. No, they said, these were images of ancestors who lived here on the earth before. Even if they had no writing and no one taught them rules, they did know that there was only one great god who created the Heavens and the Earth. That there was an everlasting soul after this life, whether a good or a bad one, they knew too. But where evil people went, they could not name.[53]

Accordingly, Messerschmidt noted that most of the native languages lacked a word for hell; evil spirits were not said to have a particular home base, but rather occupied a range of places and media, including the air, water, or bodies in human or animal forms.

Further reading of Messerschmidt's field notes and his subsequent linguistic research suggests that the word "schaman" may not have been of native origin.[54] The word as he used it appeared to be more a borrowed "technical" term, a generic word used by travelers rather than a native self-description. As it was not noteworthy to Messerschmidt as a locally specific term, we may infer that "shaman" is a mongrelized word, attributed to a number of languages, that had become part of the lingua franca of travelers since the mid-seventeenth century. It was used to refer to both places and people associated with certain ritual practices, and it would periodically be attached to anyone who engaged in such activities. Similarly, a "schaitan" was a noteworthy ethnographic object, which applied to wooden carvings purchased from various groups or to singular items seen in numerous homes.[55]

A search through the contemporary travel literature of the 1720s reveals other such magicians, conjurers, and their drums. For example, John Bell, a Scottish doctor affiliated with the imperial court who crossed Siberia on the way to China in 1720, wrote in his travel journal of his own observations:

> The Barabintzy, like most of the ancient natives of Siberia, have many conjurers among them; whom they call shamans, and sometimes priests. Many of the female sex also assume this character. The shamans are held in great esteem by the people, they pretend to correspondence with the shaytan, or devil, by whom, they say, they are informed of all past and future events, at any distance of time or place. Our ambassador resolved to inquire strictly into the truth of many strange stories, generally believed, concerning the shamans, and sent for all of same, in that way, in the places through which we passed.[56]

Note that the native words in Bell's dairies are an interesting mix of both well-documented and etymologized terms; some have been traced and documented by later linguists, but others were completely fabricated, "conjured" words for which he had no support, though he stated them with great conviction and certainty (along with assuming the habit of referring to all people of Siberia as "Tartars").[57]

As for Messerschmidt, after seven years of crisscrossing western and central Siberia, he returned to Saint Petersburg in 1728.[58] By that point, he had already shipped hundreds of boxes of birds, mammals, reptiles, insects, dried plants, minerals, native clothing, head gear, and curious items of unclear purpose or origin, along with hundreds of pages of detailed scientific measurements and notes. However, as a result of bitter arguments with members of the Imperial Academy over authorship, property rights, and his travel expenses, which may or may not have been authorized, Messerschmidt was denied membership in the institution. This delayed publication of most of his work, and subsequently he lived a brief, unhappy life in poverty. But Messerschmidt's seven years of bad food, solitude, nasty weather, and uncomfortable beds were not wasted on the Imperial Academy: his work established the foundation in the decades to come for the study of Siberia's natural history and ethnology.

THE EXPEDITION TO FIND EVERYTHING

> In the beginning of the year 1733, I undertook to write the civil history of Siberia, and its antiquities, with the manners and customs of the people, as also was the occurrences of the voyage, which was likewise approved of by the senate. It may be said with truth, that so tedious and long a voyage was never undertaken with more alacrity than this was, by all who had a share in it.[59]

In August 1733, an interpreter, an instrument maker, a drummer, two German landscape artists, three professors, four surveyors, five Russian students, and fourteen guards along with nine wagons filled with scientific instruments, a library of two hundred books, four large telescopes, writing paper, paint, drafting materials, and several kegs of German wine, all hauled by some forty pack horses, began a journey to Tobolsk, then the Siberian capital.[60] This was the research arm of the Great Northern Expedition of Vitus Jonassen Bering, a Danish captain and officer in the Russian navy. The Expedition's task was to explore the eastern parts of the Russian empire and to investigate the possibility of a passage or bridge between Asia and America:

> During the 1733 Second Kamchatka Expedition, sent by the Imperial Order, the aim was to find out all there was along the banks of the Frozen Sea and even more the eastern shores of Kamchatka, America and the ocean of Japan; it was made imperative to obtain, by all means necessary, a description of Siberia, and especially Kamchatka, their exact location, their natural history, and the various nations inhabiting the region; that is to say, to collect all information about the conditions necessary to describe the above mentioned lands. To accomplish this the Imperial Academy of Sciences sent by sea three professors who divided the task among themselves in such a way that one of them was in charge of astronomical and physical observations; the second was to carry out all that is related to natural history; and the third one was to compile a political history, description of the land, the customs of the nations and all ancient history.[61]

Johann Georg Gmelin and Gerhard Friedrich Müller, the two German scientists leading the research expedition, divided the work assigned to them by the Imperial Academy according to their interests and training. Gmelin, a physician and a natural historian, focused on botany, fauna, and geology. Müller, a historian and a geographer, devoted his attention to the people of Siberia and their history, especially their religions, village life, customs, languages, costumes, and political institutions. Not only was the Expedition's geographic focus much narrower than Messerschmidt's had been, limited to one specific region defined as eastern Siberia, but also no single scientist was expected to be a polyglot know-it-all. Rather, each scientist had a defined field of expertise, one dealing with history and culture, the other investigating nature in all its richness. The third scientist on the research team was the young French astronomer Louis de la Croyère, whose competence was regularly questioned by his German colleagues.

However, once the Expedition reached Tobolsk, the two German scientists abandoned the entourage and set off together to conduct a year of fieldwork in central Siberia. At the time, Gmelin was twenty-four, Müller twenty-eight, and prior to being recruited for the Expedition, neither of them had ever traveled far from a university town.

Ten years would pass before Gmelin and Müller were allowed to return to Saint Petersburg in 1743. When they started their journey, their list of research interests had been significantly longer than Messerschmidt's six general questions, and it included land, natural history, medicine and epidemic diseases, and the Siberian nation and its philology, antiquities, and strange or interesting items (although the latter qualification could no longer be used to describe a scientific category or even a research question). They collected and organized archival materials from throughout Siberia, discovered and named new minerals, found never before seen plants and animals, and recorded the customs and religious beliefs of a multitude of native groups in central and eastern Siberia. Müller expanded upon the foundations of Messerschmidt's personal account of the history and customs of central Siberia to transform Siberia into a catalog of places of interest, and an organized system of scientifically worthy curiosities. Although both had periodically pleaded poor health, lack of finances, and obstructions from local Russian officials, they had soldiered on and accumulated sufficient material for more than ten books and several dictionaries.

Botany and minerals were Gmelin's purview, and indeed Müller no longer thought of himself as a natural historian. They separated the social from the natural world; they described them with the same passion and similar methods, but with different eyes. The plants, animals and minerals of Siberia were coveted and collected in all their abundance and beauty, but the people and their history now occupied a separate ontological space.

Earlier travelers had viewed everyone outside Moscow as heathen, and if not a Russian, most likely a Tartar. After Messerschmidt had returned and documented the various groups of people with their different languages and customs, the category of "man" expanded and required many more qualifications: if these people were not Russians, not Christian, and not settled, then how did they come to be whatever it was that they were? The largely unsuccessful efforts to convert the natives to Orthodox Christianity also had led to a major philosophical quandary: if these people agreed to be baptized, would that turn them into Russians? If they learned the language, would they become Russians? If they agreed to settle in the provincial towns that the Russians built, would that turn them into civilized subjects of the emperor? If they married someone from another group, what would become of them and their children? And finally—perhaps most urgently to the traveling party—if they stopped eating fish, would they stop smelling so badly?

Needless to say, these questions were not only of academic interest to the educated scientists but also of visceral concern to the Russians themselves. Intermarriage, precarious lifestyle and eating habits, and questionable faith loomed large in the Siberian frontier towns and outposts. Furthermore, those same questions troubled Russians worried about their place in the history of civilization relative to other European nations. European civilized court society haunted both the Siberian steppes and the Russian educated classes.

Although they were not quite an evolutionary change, the ethnographic questions of the day in the eighteenth century reflected both a notion of progress and a fear of decline. Thus, although Müller wanted to know "everything" about the history and lifestyle of the peoples of Siberia, this "everything" was carefully qualified and focused.

Words and Meanings, Religion and Difference

Language had been of great interest to Messerschmidt, and Müller shared his predecessor's passion for native vocabularies. However, Müller's interest lay less in collecting words than in engaging in comparative linguistics and establishing the geography of languages central to the idea of group identity. Geography of the Siberian ethnic groups and mapping the land went hand in hand, defined by similarities and differences in the languages spoken: "As to their tongue there is some affinity between them and the Crim Tartars, and conformity with the tongues of the Bratti, the Kirgasi and the Sajantzian Tartars; though the last talk pretty commonly the Mungalian and Kalmuchkian tongues, to which countries they are neighbors."[62]

As a historian, Müller tried to trace geographic diffusion as well as linguistic affinities to explain how the different tribes found themselves in their locations. In describing indigenous ownership and husbandry of reindeer, for instance, he noted that each group had a distinctly different word for wild and domestic animals:

Therefore these nations have entirely different words for domestic and wild reindeer, as if these were entirely different kinds of animals. For example:

	Wild reindeer	Domestic reindeer
Tungus	Schókdscho	Óron
Samoyed	Kédere	Týa
Iukagir	Légouf	Áatsche or Ílwe
Koryak	Öllewet or Karngúgui	Chojánga[63]

Müller suggested that in their ancient homeland they must have been accustomed only to wild reindeer, and domestication occurred only after their arrival to their current lands. Any linguistic anthropologist of the early twentieth century would have been impressed by this logic.[64]

Ultimately, Müller's ambition was to establish a sweeping history of Russia that would explain the origins of the Slavic groups as well as the native inhabitants. Besides language, he and his colleagues of the day deemed religion and religious practices central to group identity. Comparing languages and rituals, they puzzled over similarities and differences. If these people were on such a similar level of civilization (low, to be certain), then why did some of them treat their dead differently? "These Jukagiri hang their dead on trees, but the skeletons, or bones of their parents and relations, they afterwards carry along with them when they go hunting. This agrees with what is affirmed of the Samojeds, who never bury the bones of their parents."[65] Was linguistic difference also a sign of different beliefs, or were similar rituals a result of other historical connections?

Thus, Müller's interest in pagan traditions and beliefs was far more systematic than the curiosity that had motivated his predecessors. Müller made extensive inquiries into belief systems, traditions, and practices (at times interjecting his personal opinions). As a result, by the mid-eighteenth century, the knowledge of Siberian native spiritual traditions had expanded sufficiently to delineate a wide range of differences in practitioners, beliefs, and the rituals themselves:

> Each tribe of these people looks upon some particular creature as sacred, e.g. a swan, goose, raven, and such is not eaten by that tribe, though the others may eat it. . . . Korjaki, or Koreki, are a Pagan nation, living on the West and North Side of the country of Kamtschatka. They are naturally good and harmless people, and have no idols of stone, wood, or any other materials, as the Ostjacks have. They use no manner of ceremony in their devotion, but when they go out hunting, they pray to the Supreme Being to bless them with success. However, they have their Schaumanns, or Magicians, and are a very filthy people.[66]

Religion and language had become merged in the discussions of ritual practitioners, complicating the effort to classify and organize even more. The ethnic names that the groups called themselves and how the Russians referred to them did not help in constructing their history. Müller thus hoped that since they were all pagan nations, describing their beliefs and rituals would give some order and would help in constructing the historical path of individual groups. Yet the farther east the Expedition traveled, the greater the variety of words used to describe part-time, situational, or full-time spiritual figures and healers. Increasingly, the scientists also noted that while these may have been "priests," the spiritual practitioners engaged in a wide range of activities that could not easily be classified according to the categories they used—even a decade earlier, Messerschmidt would have considered fortune-telling, healing, and ritual as interconnected.

Thus, Müller treated language and history as separate from customs and faith in an effort to impose some kind of boundaries around categories and give them order. The people of the different ethnic groups, however, did not help, resisting the categories and complicating the histories that Müller hoped to outline. The languages they spoke differed, their pagan beliefs seemed just as distinct, and they referred to their ritual specialists by all kinds of names. The questions of conversion and identity thus grew more complicated, because it appeared the pagan "faith" itself was hardly singular or united.

Gmelin, the natural historian, was also fascinated with the healers and magicians, and he frequently ventured into native settlements on his own to investigate them. He perceptively wrote about a wide range of beliefs and traditions:

> The Votiaks are not entirely without religion. They do believe in some form of God whom they call "loumar," and claim that he is in the sun but they do not pay any special tribute to him. In particularly important moments they have a man whom they call "donna," who serves for them the same function as the "iumasse" does for the Chuvash.[67]

He eventually made such a nuisance of himself—demanding not only to see the ritual specialists but also to watch them perform "tricks"—that his reputation preceded him, and in many villages he was refused entry, even though he offered gifts and payments:

> We wanted to see the Cheremiss magicians but they refused to come. . . . I also learned that the Cheremiss have a kind of 'priest', called 'iougtouch' who is in charge of making the potions, the order of sacrifices, he divines and prays for the future happiness of a family and gives the guests mead and beer whichever he deems appropriate.[68]

Eventually, to coax at least some information from these reluctant informants, one of Gmelin's Russian students, Stepan Krashenninikov, took over the ethnographic interviews. Fortunately, he proved more successful at the task, leaving behind an additionally nuanced perspective on the Siberian natives.[69]

KNOWING THE NATIVES: RUSSIA AND EUROPEAN CIVILIZATION

The new breed of scientifically minded German physicians and natural historians of the eighteenth century created the science of Siberian ethnology. They set the stage for later performances by introducing to the European consciousness the distinctive native peoples of Siberia, along with their cultures and religions. Furthermore, they elevated the indigenous peoples from Kunstkamera curiosities to subjects of study by the Imperial Academy of Sciences. This marked a true change in the way Siberia was perceived, both as a conceptual space and as a country populated by diverse people. Mapped, identified, and classified, the Siberian native population was now a recognizable category of being.

The German scientists scoured the land in pursuit of differences, delineating boundaries between humans, animals, plants, and continents. In the process, they distinguished ethnic groups with distinct religious practices and conjugal arrangements, which reflected back on and contrasted with European customs. Thus, one root of ethnography as a science of difference grew at the eastern edge of Europe. It emerged through a gate guarded by shamans and their tricks, non-European in character and practice.

The appearance of Siberian native groups as recognizable imperial subjects had an immediate impact on the philosophical, and, inevitably, the political discussions of the time as to whether Russia was a European nation (Voltaire[70]) or an Asiatic one (Montesquieu[71]), and whether it possessed the universal human spirit capable of civilization and progress. By producing maps, demographic reports, and detailed descriptions of customs, Russia distinguished itself as a national body separate from Siberia, which was viewed as a place of ancient ways.

With this civilizational chapter of difference in Russian history and geography established, the claim of a "vast empire" grew. When the empress Catherine II submitted a proposal for new code of law in 1767, she introduced the document by an opening statement: "Russia is a European State." Relying solely on the size of the territory, she supported her certainty with exact numbers: "The Possessions of the Russian Empire extend upon the terrestrial Globe to 32 Degrees of Latitude, and to 165 of Longitude." This generously and knowingly incorporated Siberia, all the way to the eastern shores.[72]

Bolstered in her efforts by an extensive correspondence with Voltaire, Catherine refuted any attacks on Russian backwardness and despotic rule by citing extensively from ethnographic accounts, collected through systematic fieldwork by trusted German scientists. All her critics were mere travelers, who never left their fur-lined, enclosed carriages, unable to face the snow unlike the true scientists who informed her rule.[73] Thus, she could defend her Russia with an ode to its experience with religious tolerance:

> It is true, Abbé, that no country contains a greater variety of sects than Russia in general: you will see Mahometans and idolaters in the midst of the habitations of the Greeks, which, though it be the established church, persecutes neither the Jews, Papists, Lutherans, Calivinists, nor Herrenhutters: every one enjoys the liberty of following his own mode of worship. There is,

without a doubt, a great deal of superstition, as well as ignorance, in this diversity of opinions: but we possess a great virtue in Russia, which you are totally unacquainted with; that is toleration: this teaches us to look upon all men as our brothers; and we daily find the necessity of putting this virtue in practice, which you do not chuse to be acquainted with, because it will not fill your pockets.[74]

CHAPTER 5

Sex, Gender, and Encounters with Spirits

He who has intercourse by lying on top commits a great sin.
An Orthodox Itelmen has to do it from the side because the
fish, from which they get the most of their food, do it that
way.

—Georg Wilhelm Steller (1743)[1]

Within the general history of shamanism, the gender and sexuality of its
practitioners has generated particular interest. It regularly comes up in
discussions of shamans far beyond Siberia—specifically, whether men
or women more frequently or naturally performed the role.[2] The subject has spurred many a debate over the centuries, and the debates have
acquired new passion in the last few decades. Some claimed that this
was a role for which only men were selected. Others have argued that
traditionally women were the more "natural sex" to conduct shamanic
rituals, or they have sought to demonstrate that there simply were
many more female or male shamans the world over.[3] And then there
were the accounts of "changed women"—men who became women because the spirits requested it, in order to carry out the difficult tasks of
shamans.[4]

Let us then look at stories of women and men and consider what
role gender may have played in their descriptions. But I wish to broaden
the frame to consider the perceptions and descriptions of women and
men in general, not only the shamans, in early Siberian ethnographies.
When we lift the curtain on stories about women and men, we will see
how shamans were a part of a classificatory process: what is a proper
man, a proper woman, or a proper ritual? In the process, I wish to put
a mirror to the concepts of "gender" and "shaman" in order to ask

what explanatory and genealogical work they have served for anthropologists and archaeologists, especially in discussions of religion and art. When do scholars explicitly evoke sex and gender in relation to an activity? Does the sexual designation of a hunter or a shaman matter more to analysts or to the people they study? Does a sexual designation appear to be the most salient feature of an activity, and if so, how might that activity change once it is gendered in a particular way? The accounts of the sexual lives of native peoples have a long history in anthropology, and Siberia is no exception.

When first reading the materials in German and Russian archives, I expected a progressive narrative in which women shamans took an increasingly prominent role over time. I did not anticipate finding many native women in eighteenth-century accounts, and I awaited the richer cast of characters that would emerge by the early twentieth century. This expectation proved entirely inaccurate. Instead, the history of ethnographic narratives about Siberian natives of all genders turned out to be far more interesting and temporally complex. The stories of shamans, along with the descriptions of their performances and the roles that they supposedly filled, all changed significantly over time. Far from being barren of women, the early ethnographic accounts mentioned them far more often. Diversity appeared at the root, and only dissipated later when the practice became a category.

An early story of a female idol, repeated by every subsequent traveler and located on many maps of Siberia, sets the tone. In 1526, Ambassador Herberstein attempted a scientific explanation for his tale:

> Slata Baba, that is, the Golden Old Woman, is an idol situated on the mouths of the Oby on its further bank, in the province of Obdora. There are many fortresses scattered here and there along the banks of the Oby, and about the neighbouring rivers, the lords of which are all said to be subject to the Prince of Moscow. The story, or I should more correctly call it the fable, runs, that this idol of the Golden Old Woman is a statue, representing an old woman holding her son in her lap, and that recently another infant has been seen, which is said to be her grandson; they also say that she has placed certain instruments upon the spot, which constantly give forth a sound like the trumpets. If this is the case, I think that this must arise from the vehement and constant blowing of the wind through those instruments.[5]

Because early travel narratives took the form of tales, the shamans in them spilled beyond mere descriptive statements. They were extended reflections on myriad topics, ranging from magic, religion, and leadership to the appropriate position of women in a society. Furthermore, a range of characters, not only men and women, appeared even in the earliest dispatches from the distant eastern shores. The accounts evoked women alongside displays of masculinity, same-sex acts, and sodomy with animals, with the narrators alternating among horror, disgust, admiration, and matter-of-fact description of the distant world. The tone over the centuries shifted for a variety reasons, aimed at the moving target of different readers. Ultimately, this broad range of responses makes gender an ideal lens to decipher social facts of the past and the present. Gender provides a viewfinder to some of the reasons these details seemed important to relate. It is hard to evaluate the factual veracity of seventeenth- or eighteenth-century stories of native Siberian women and men, and even more difficult to claim that any of these stories depicts a certain norm. My interest lies in following the changes in emphasis within the contexts of discovery. The personal, professional, and national histories—the science of the remote in the making—from which these narratives emerged are as interesting as the stories told.

SEEING AND BELIEVING

In broad terms, we can frame ethnographies of the Siberian indigenous peoples through two national traditions, German and Russian.[6] Their works may be separated by a little over a century, but they are not entirely separate; rather, they are connected by people and geographies. The German scientific documentation from the eighteenth century marked the beginning of a period of conscious, systematic observation, if not exactly participation. A comparison of these records to the Russian ethnographies from the late nineteenth and early twentieth centuries, however, reveals both similarities and intriguing differences. Amid the wealth of detail about the lives of indigenous peoples, both sets of ethnographies include extensive descriptions of women, and they frequently recognize cultural aspects of gender. Yet the specific details remain diverse, and Siberian men and women play remarkably divergent roles in these stories. The German and Russian ethnographers made very different points and drew almost opposite conclusions about the same people. While looking at the Siberian native groups, each set of observers noticed details that their counterparts did not see at all, and they interpreted their encounters in strikingly different lights.

Reading their accounts, it becomes quite clear that all the travelers arrived with firm expectations. Men, women, power, spirits, and performances were filtered through a language riddled with interpretive claims, representing both the real but also the imagined. Let us begin with the following three descriptions:

> It would disgust the enlightened mind to pursue the detail of all their scenes of magic and enchantments; the ceremonies of which are so egregiously absurd, and so similar to each other, that it will be sufficient to give a succinct account of the most striking and remarkable.[7]

> The branch of shamanism, however, of which I am about to speak, is of a more special character, and refers to that shamanistic transformation of men and women in which they undergo a change of sex in part, or even completely. This is called "soft man being" (yirka´-la´ul-va´irgin); "soft man" (yirka´-la´ul) meaning a man transformed into a being of a softer sex. A man who has changed his sex is also called "similar to a woman" (fie´uchica), and a woman in similar condition, "similar to a man" (qa´cikicheca). Transformation of the first kind is much the more frequent.[8]

> Yirka´-la´ul [is] most probably a Russian pope, who is equivalent here to a "transformed shaman" of the Chukchee, because his upper garment resembles a woman's robe.[9]

In the two hundred years of ethnographic tales by German and Russian ethnographers, both gender and shamans are impressive shape shifters: depending on the historical and cultural contexts in which they were evoked, these anthropological inventions were asked to do quite a few tricks, with a range of effects. Hence, the insistence that male shamans were religious leaders carries the same amount of veracity as the claims that women were more naturally powerful in performing rituals. Yet just because these claims exhibit formal similarity by mirroring each other does not mean that we should treat both the same, or accept them as having equal resonance, standing, and political impact. The claims about male shamans appeared in very different historical and political contexts than those about female shamans, and this does not even address the recognition of transgendered "changed" shamans. Gender factored into all three cases but did very different work, depending on the alliances, theoretical and human, that were being evoked.[10] Ultimately, the details of the history of shamans reveal a great deal about the workings of our own discipline: our modes of thinking, the ways we imagine the past, and the instances when we tie it to or sever it from the present. Our imperfect categories are based on and filled with narratives that reveal many stories about our past and the present.

PICTURES FROM SIBERIAN EXHIBITIONS

Images of women performing shamanic rituals appeared quite frequently in the early accounts of Siberia, and they continued to appear well into the twentieth century in Russian ethnography. However, the commentary on, reception of, and explanatory frame for these female shamans dramatically differed over time. In many initial descriptions, their presence was noted but not the subject of a particular commentary or extensive explanation. For example, in 1763 the Scottish doctor John Bell admired both a particular performance and its comely protagonist, but he implies no general surprise about her gender:

> In Baraba we went to visit a famous woman [shaman] of this character. When we entered her house, she continued busy about her domestic affairs, without almost taking any notice of her guests. . . . Her answers were delivered very artfully, and with as much obscurity and ambiguity, as they could have been given by any oracle. She was a young woman and very handsome.[11]

Georg Wilhelm Steller, who traveled through Kamchatka two decades earlier, depicted shamanism as a veritable free for all: "Like all Asiatic peoples, the Itelmen have shamans, but in their shamanic practices, they are different from all other peoples. The shamans, male and female, are not greatly respected, whoever wants to, shamanizes."[12] Yet the supposed lack of respect or distinction accorded to shamans appears far from uniform; a statement by Steller's contemporary, the Russian student Stepan Krashenninikov, offers a quite different impression in distinctly gendered terms: "The Kamchadales have none who are professed Shamans, or conjurers, as the neighboring nations have, but every old woman is looked upon as a witch and an interpreter of dreams."[13]

Both Steller and Krashenninikov made a strenuous effort to downplay the importance of shamans, at times even denying their very existence. Thus, if anything, their recognition of female practitioners was intended to offer proof of their low status and the limited skill needed for their tasks. It was the suspicious activity they wished to discredit, denying its religious importance and suggesting that it comprised only tricks and deceit. Both were obviously familiar with the person of a "shaman," whom they encountered many times across Siberia, and they provided detailed descriptions in their writing. For example, Krashenninikov professed not to have met any in Kamchatka, only old women who interpreted dreams and practiced witchcraft. Nevertheless, a mere few pages later he described in great detail a "sorcerer" who was so convincing that even some of the Russian Cossacks consulted him on a regular basis for treatment of their ailments:

> Some of the Shamans are reckoned physicians, and are thought, by beating upon the drum, to drive away distempers. In the year 1739 I had an opportunity of seeing, at the lower Kamchatskoi fort, the most famous Shaman Carimalacha, who was not only of great reputation among these wild people, but was also respected by our Cossacks, for the many extraordinary feats that he performed; particularly that of stabbing his belly with a knife, and letting a great quantity of blood run out, which he drank.[14]

Authorial inconsistency aside, the similarities and differences between the native practices, the existence of sorcerers, and their power and influence appeared to be of far greater interest to these early ethnographers than the practitioners' sex. The profusion of *varieties* of shamanism was the dominant theme. The insistence that these people were "not greatly respected" among the Itelmen or alternatively that a man inspired admiration even amid the Cossacks in Kamchatka—a land where any old woman could practice witchcraft—was the most intriguing and simultaneously confusing part of the story. The eighteenth-century scholars sought to draw distinct boundaries between religion, conjuring, and magic, and in this respect, the sex of the shaman remained secondary.

German ethnographers in a Russian colonial setting evaluated the local native practices in light of the failure of the Orthodox church to attract converts. Steller claimed he was told that highly respected shamans were often found in other places, but the accounts from his time seldom contained such stories; rather, the usual rhetorical impulse was to discredit the practice and reveal it as trickery that was obvious to visitors from civilized lands. Krashenninikov noted the great respect the shaman Carimalacha garnered, but then he proceeded to debunk the entire performance. By telling the reader what was behind the screen and how "the trick" was achieved, Krashenninikov implied that he, the educated, scientifically minded scholar could see through the deception. As a scientist with a proper rational detachment, he revealed the deceptive practices while inviting the reader to laugh along with him at the gullible natives, calling to mind Georgi's earlier sentiments that the ceremonies were egregiously absurd. Whether men or women carried out the performance was irrelevant to such an assessment.

Consequently, and inadvertently, we learn that both men and women participated in such tricks and deceptions, that both men and women "shamanized." The consistent theme in the description of the peoples of Siberia in the eighteenth century was their "otherness" as a group, so they lacked any individual identity in the accounts. The famous shaman Carimalacha was one of the few to be identified by name, but then it was only to unmask him as a fraud, a trickster, and not a "real" person. It was his activity that attracted the attention that required explanation; Carimalacha himself remained relatively interchangeable for any other native, man or woman. If his significance derived in part from his gender as well as his fame, it was simply so that his fall would prove greater.

The relative lack of individuality among the indigenous peoples in the early ethnographies was not limited to their names or personal stories. Masculinity and femininity in the eighteenth century served to mark distinct groups, a feature of their collective ethnic character as a sign of variation within it. In the circulating images of Siberian natives—the Tungus, the Ostyak, the Samoyed, or the Koryak—the men and women were remarkable in their gender sameness. The men in particular lacked any signs of masculinity; only the inscriptions below the picture gave a hint that the reader was looking at an illustration of a man (figures 5.1 and 5.2). Beginning with clothing that lacked obvious gender specificity and continuing with childlike facial features provided for Siberian men and women alike, the generic depictions of Siberians finished by adding passive postures, palms helplessly held upward.

The period illustrations portrayed people who were unlike men and women in the contemporary European classificatory schema of gender. At the same time, these images and their descriptions expressed the frustrations of the traveling men—scholars, scientists, missionaries, or military personnel—who could not tell the men apart from the women—or, more importantly, the women from the men. Anxiety over potential confusion in matters of sexuality permeated most of the writings of the time. Cornelius de Bruyn, a Dutch traveler in the early 1700s, provides a typical example:

> The women are incurious, and wear their hair loose and disheveled, [they] are scarcely to be distinguished from the men, who are for the most part beardless, or at most have only some few hairs upon their upper lips. . . . Some of them wear, moreover, waistcoats and breeches made of the same skins, with white boots, and the only difference in the last particular between men and women is this, that the latter add slips, or lists of black upon theirs.[15]

Самоедъ
Ein Samojede
Un Samoiede

FIGURE 5.1. "Samoyed man," from Johann Gottlieb Georgi, 1799. A Samoyed man on a hunt, yet resembling a Renaissance courtier in his colorful smock and stockings more than an indigenous hunter. Georgi, Johann Gottlieb. 1799. Samoiadskie narody: Samoed. (Samoyed peoples: A Samoyed) Image no. 1241965. Slavic and Baltic Division, The New York Public Library, Astor, Lenox and Tilden Foundations. (Reproduced with permission of the New York Public Library.)

Самоѣдка спереди.
Eine Samojedin vorwärts
Femme Samojede par devant.

FIGURE 5.2. "Samoyed woman," from Johann Gottlieb Georgi, 1799. A Samoyed woman who is indistinguishable from the earlier illustration of a Samoyed man, almost more masculine, except for her downcast eyes. Georgi, Johann Gottlieb. 1799. Samoiadskie narody: Samoiadka speredi. (Samoyed peoples: A Samoyed woman) Image no. 1241966. Slavic and Baltic Division, The New York Public Library, Astor, Lenox and Tilden Foundations. (Reproduced with permission of the New York Public Library.)

The lack of beards on the men particularly troubled Europeans. As Londa Schiebinger has noted, Carl Linnaeus declared in his lectures at Uppsala University in 1740 that "God gave men beards for ornaments and to distinguish them from women."[16] The beard served not only to differentiate men from women in fundamental terms, but also to delineate the types of men. Men who lacked this important eighteenth-century symbol of virility and leadership stood lower on the scale of masculinity and also humanity. Such gender characteristics served as civilizational markers in the classification of native peoples of Siberia.

Russia remained a border territory between European civilized appearance versus Asian conflation of men and women. The full beards of Russian men suggested an overdose of masculinity, an untamed virility that called out for a heavy dose of civilizing influence. Thus, Peter the Great early on in his reign introduced the "beard tax" so as to change the wild, untamed, or overly Orthodox Russian image.[17] West European men were the ideal, a model of the ability to keep facial hair in check with the tools of civilization—razor blades and shaving mirrors. At the other extreme, native men with only "a few hairs upon their upper lips" destabilized the gender regimen of masculinity, veering dangerously closely to the possibility of becoming women.

Despite the persistent European anxiety about the lack of difference between Siberian men and women—or possibly because of it—the native women received plenty of attention from the visiting scientists. As they were considered the embodiment of Nature, Siberian women's sexual behavior merited extensive description. When reading the travelogues and scientific reports, it pays to recall that all the early European travelers and explorers to Siberia were men: Messerschmidt traveled with male servants, as did the members of the Great Northern Expedition, Gerhard Friedrich Müller, Johann Georg Gmelin, and Steller. These scholars' teams included male students, male assistants, male drivers, and even male cooks. The first women to write personal accounts of travel across Siberia were missionary wives, who arrived only at the beginning of the nineteenth century.[18] Moreover, much of the information in the travelogues was secondhand or even thirdhand, conveyed to the male visitors by other men living in the settlements, including Russian Cossacks, military personnel, fugitives, and migrating settlers. These accounts then reveal multiple layers of colonial relationships, particularly when it comes to dealing with women.

The German ethnographers frequently noted the exploitation of the natives by the Russian settlers, missionaries, and Cossacks: "The inhabitants constantly have military personnel billeted in their houses, who do them more harm than good because the host and his neighbors are not only being exploited, but also cannot object to their 'guests' seducing their wives and children."[19] Yet even as they condemned the brutal, heavy handed, and largely unsuccessful civilizing attempts by the Russians, the German scientists easily divulged their own participation in the exploitation of these same native women, as one "scientific experiment" by Steller illustrates:

> What makes these people so lecherous and prone to venery is probably the consumption of so many fish eggs and bulbs, as well as moldy fish . . . for semen is frequently generated and the blood vessels are stimulated by the stinking fish fat. I myself have found that an Itelmen woman who, as an experiment, ate at my table for half a year and was totally kept from the usual food became much more moderate and modest.[20]

As Anne McClintock has noted, colonial adventures the world over were imbricated with desire, disgust, and power over others.[21] The reader may return the gaze and wonder about the experience of the Itelmen woman who was kept in a stranger's house, fed with unfamiliar food, and continuously watched. How did she find herself in that situation in first place? And how did the experiment end? We are never told, except for the finding that the woman became "more moderate and modest."

Despite their claims that the natives' gender appearance was indistinguishable, eighteenth-century ethnographers paid close attention to the women, and they had plenty to say about them. Descriptions of relationships between men and women, and their different roles and local customs appear throughout discussions of marriage, birthing, child rearing, and kinship. Sexual modesty was a topic of great fascination, one that revealed as much about the newcomers and the scientists as it did about the Russian colonizers and the native subjects. Thus, Stepan Krashenninikov, one of the small number of Russian students traveling with Müller, described Koryak marital and sexual relationships in considerable detail:

> The Wandering Koreki are extremely jealous, and sometimes kill their wives upon suspicion only; but when any are caught in adultery, both parties are certainly condemned to death. For this reason the women seem to take pains to make themselves disagreeable; for they never wash their faces or hands, nor comb their hair, and their upper garments are dirty, ragged, and torn, the best being worn underneath. This they are obliged to do on account of the jealousy of their husbands, who say, that a woman has no occasion to adorn herself unless to gain the affections of a stranger, for her husband loves her without that. On the contrary, the Fixed Koreki, and Tchukotskoi, look

upon it as the truest mark of friendship, when they entertain a friend, to put him to bed with their wife or daughter; and a refusal of this civility they consider as the greatest affront; and are even capable of murdering a man for such a contempt. This happened to several Russian Cossacks before they were acquainted with the customs of the people. The wives of the Fixed Koreki endeavour to adorn themselves as much as possible, painting their faces, wearing fine cloaths, and using various means to set off their persons. In their huts they sit quite naked, even in the company of strangers.[22]

By the eighteenth century, native groups in many parts of the world were identified by their economic and subsistence behavior, such as the nomadic "wandering" and settled "fixed" Koryak. However, in Krashenninikov's description the similarity in male control of women's sexuality erased such essential differences. The nomadic Koryak were supposedly jealous, guarding women as private property of individual men. The settled Koryak, while generous and friendly, treated women's sexuality as personal property as well, subject to sharing and exchange. Furthermore, whether nomadic or settled, this observer perceived both groups to be threatening when it came to sex. When a traveler became too friendly with a nomadic woman—or not friendly enough with a woman from a settled group—the inevitable outcome was death. The native men decided upon the degree of sexual freedom or restraint, not the woman herself, but also not the visiting stranger. In Krashenninikov's rendering, women's sexuality was a life-threatening test of knowledge of local culture, controlled by native men and consequently feared by outsiders.

Yet the women appeared simultaneously desirable and disturbing to visitors, Russian Cossack and scientist alike. In these stories, it was never the foreign self that precipitated these particular social relations, whether a participant in a jealous husband's pursuit or a generous father's offer. It was not desire or the sexual act itself that proved unfamiliar, confusing, and potentially life-threatening, but rather its local context. By not knowing or ignoring the unfamiliar rules, traveling European men confronted danger, giving rise to intense speculation about how deeply such difference ran. In Steller's words, the greatest sin to an Orthodox Itelmen was to behave like a European man when it came to sex; fish were the closest behavior they wished to emulate. As in many colonial settings, claims of coercive native sexual advances, unwanted intimacies, and their inevitable outcomes were all too familiar tropes.

Krashenninikov, a student from Saint Petersburg, carried on through Kamchatka alone when his German superiors, Müller and Gmelin, would not continue any farther. By the time the expedition had reached this eastern edge of the Russian empire, after years of travel among native Siberians with an occasional detour to visit local Russian officials, the professors wished nothing more than to return to the comforts of their offices and libraries in Saint Petersburg.[23] The young Russian student, on the other hand, combined youthful energy with a lower status in the academic hierarchy. When ordered, he pressed on to Kamchatka to meet the Koryak, the Kamchadal, the Itelmen, and a German scientist named Georg Steller.[24]

Whether or not Krashenninikov actually acted out his desires, risking his life while navigating the web of local customs, he wrote about such potential encounters most persuasively, and left behind voluble descriptions of encounters with women. Later designated as the "father of Russian ethnography,"[25] young Krashenninikov serves as a perfect guide to eighteenth-century Siberian mores regarding gender and sexuality, understood to be salient characteristics of native societies. To him, women shamans were not a particular anomaly; he noted them without taking them seriously. Rather, the central theme was the foreignness of the native people as a whole, with women serving as attendants to this larger unknown world. His descriptions are first and foremost a mirror of science, its themes and methods of the time.

While outlining the range of dangerous liaisons awaiting foreigners, Krashenninikov provides a snapshot of eighteenth-century European sensibilities. This grows particularly apparent when we compare his descriptions of the Koryak with later accounts of the same region and people written by others. Some one hundred years after Krashenninikov in 1864, George Kennan, an American explorer and telegraph company employee, visited the Wandering Koryak and wrote about the treatment of women (and children) with a very different eye and a sense of chivalry transcending civilization:

> The natural disposition of the Wandering Koraks is thoroughly good. They treat their women and children with great kindness; and during all my intercourse with them, extending over two years, I never saw a woman or child struck. Cruel and barbarous they may be, according to our ideas of cruelty and barbarity; but they have never been known to commit an act of treachery, and I would trust my life as unreservedly in their hands as I would in the hands of any other uncivilized people whom I have ever known.[26]

That an American traveler might perceive the Koryak differently one hundred years later is not by itself a surprise, but, in addition to Kennan's appreciation of the Koryak men's character and treatment of women, his view of their appearance and gender attributes is a dramatic change. He saw the Koryak men of the nineteenth century as gentle, kind, and honest; their masculinity was unquestioned—tall, with handsome features apparent to anyone who met them, their gender identity no longer puzzled the traveler. "Cruel and barbarous" as the Koryak may still have been for Kennan, their kind attitude toward women and children laudably suggested a common humanity to him. Furthermore, in travel writing from the Victorian era, sexuality was hidden from the sight of the readers, unmentionable in the text in any overt way; thus, the eighteenth-century focus on gender and sexuality stands out as noteworthy, appearing almost relentless.

Finally, the larger frame of comparison shifted as well. By the time of Kennan's journey, Russia's colonial conquest was complete: the country had acquired the status of a formidable empire, and its relation to Europe was little questioned, especially not by an American visitor seeking business opportunities. At the same time, the wide circulation of accounts of native North Americans by the end of the nineteenth century provided a ready comparative case for their Siberian equivalents:

> The wandering natives of Siberia, *contrary to all our preconceived ideas,* we found to be tall, athletic, well-formed men, often more than six feet in height, with bold dark features which reminded us of our own North American Indians. They have not, however, a single trait in common with them nor with the Esquimaux of Labrador and Greenland. Physically, morally and intellectually they are a much finer race of men than the latter, and their honesty and generosity distinguish them sufficiently from the former.[27]

As it seems unlikely that the Koryak men had changed dramatically in physical appearance over the course of a few generations, the lens that refracted their relative masculinity clearly had shifted with the centuries and observers. Rather than perceiving gender confusion between the men and women, the American visitor saw the Siberian native peoples as graceful, noble savages, the embodiment of "well-formed men." The Eskimo of Labrador and Greenland now seemed further below the Siberian indigenous peoples on the scale of civilization and the measure of morality.

NATURE BEFORE CULTURE: THE "INSATIABLE" SIBERIAN WOMEN

In the case of eighteenth-century ethnographers, it is important to consider audience: the readers for whom such vivid descriptions were

written. Russian and German accounts that were composed during the
same period, particularly when addressing topics of gender and sex, oftentimes hardly seemed to describe the same native people. As editor
Marvin Falk noted in his introduction to the twenty-first-century English
translation of Steller's 1763 work on Kamchatka, "Scientific knowledge
of the biology, botany, and ethnography of Kamchatka has been based
upon the research of two scientists working during the 1730's and 1740's
under the auspices of the Russian Academy of Sciences: Georg Steller
and Stepan Krashenninikov. Krashenninikov arrived in Kamchatka with
the rank of student in 1737, Steller with the rank of adjunct professor in
1740."[28] Nationality, educational background, social rank, and age all
played a role in these ethnographers' perspectives. Steller and Krashenninikov provided remarkably differing accounts of Kamchatka.

If Krashenninikov warned of the Kamchadal husbands, alternately
jealous or overly benevolent, Steller viewed the native women as fear-
some. The latter's portrait of the Siberians contrasted remarkably with
earlier accounts, even though he remained equally focused on sexual
behavior. Although Steller's greatest contribution to science may have
involved the flora and fauna of Kamchatka, he also had a keen eye and
a vivid imagination when writing about local customs. In his view, the
Itelmen women were assertive, dominating, and a true force of nature:
"The woman is in command of everything and holds everything that
is worth anything in safekeeping; the man is her cook and worker and
if he does anything wrong, she withholds her favor and his tobacco,
which he then has to coax out of her with many pleas, caresses and
compliments."[29]

Like his contemporaries, Steller was intrigued by the sexual practices
of the natives; he not only observed them but also designed experiments
involving them, such as the previously described six-month project on
the impact of food on the sexual appetite of a local woman. For Steller,
the Kamchadal represented the true, unspoiled human condition before
influence of civilization; "natural" was the most frequent label he applied to their customs, character, and physical features:

Their food predisposes their bodies to certain inclinations, which in the
natural state are the most important and sensible. They tend toward con-
tentment and naturally, like animals towards lust. They consider nothing a
shame or sin except what harms them. One can pretty clearly see from these
people's simplicity how human beings living in natural freedom without
any mental cultivation or moral code would have to be temperamentally
constituted.[30]

Steller, like other eighteenth century ethnographers, explored the history of native groups at some length, speculating on their migratory paths from farther away in Asia based on the linguistic similarities between different native languages. Any possibility that these people could have been related to European civilization was a completely foreign notion. The divide between Europe and Siberia remained an immense civilizational chasm. The Kamchadal were an example of humans *before* civilization, lacking the benefits of culture in the German sense of *Kultur*: literature, the arts, law, and formal religion. Native technology, or lack thereof, was yet another clear measure of the historical distance between the indigenous Kamchadal and civilized European peoples, and Germans in particular: "The chopped-down trees, as I came across them here and there were miscut with many dull blows in such a way that in all likelihood the cutting of trees must be done by these savages, as in Kamchatka, with stone or bone axes similar to those used by the Germans of old and known today as 'thunderbolts.'"[31]

The copious notes that Steller recorded for the Imperial Academy were intended to serve a larger scientific purpose. The natives, as he saw them, were a living example of a fundamental philosophical question of his time about the relationship between civilization and morality, a question as relevant to European societies as were the native Siberians themselves. Philosophers of the day posed this query in terms of the social and political implications of a state of nature: In the absence of civilization, is there a natural basis for moral behavior? They defined civilization as a system of formal laws and regulations, with morality expressed through religious practices. As Steller put it,

> Those who consider these people, or the Samoyeds and Laplanders because of their differences, more virtuous than others are sadly mistaken. The single sentence 'I desire nothing that is unknown or useless to me' refutes the opinion, which is so prejudicial against civilized people. . . . With the example of the Kamchadals, the questions of the theologians and moralists 'Are there perfect moral actions, or are there any actions which are good or bad before there is law?' can be decided. The Kamchadals blaspheme God when they think that he has done something wrong and consider nothing shameful other than what does harm.[32]

To round out his case, Steller added a claim that women were much closer to instinctive, "natural" behavior than men. Where other earlier travelers could not tell the difference between men and women, Steller recorded a remarkable list of distinguishing characteristics supposedly displayed by the native women he observed. His account thus gives us the sense of gender that the eighteenth century envisioned as belonging to a "pristine stage." Furthermore, the description also stood as a counter to the proper, civilized behavior of Western European women. The stories of native women present their behavior as a relic of the past, a reminder of ancient female animality, haunting the edges of civilization. As the historian Jennifer Morgan, writing about perceptions of indigenous women in the Americas and Africa by English travelers, noted:

> Travel accounts produced in Europe and available in England provided a corpus from which subsequent writers borrowed freely, reproducing images of Native American and African women that resonated with readers. . . . The struggle with perceptions of beauty and assertions of monstrosity . . . exemplified a much larger process through which the familiar became unfamiliar as beauty became beastliness and mothers became monstrous.[33]

Native women's bodies and behaviors served as the perfect canvas upon which to write the narrative of civilized womanhood. As an addition to his mission to collect plants and describe the animal world, Steller produced a detailed account, contradictory and confusing as at times it may be, of sexual practices among Siberian natives.[34]

> Although the Itelmen love their wives so very tenderly and dearly, they are all nevertheless great lovers of variety. When they fall in love with another woman, they immediately leave the previous one, and some have women along all paths and trails. No one calls a whore in Kamchatka anything but "Miss," even if she has borne ten children. . . . Thus it is never said of a person in Kamchatka "he fornicates," and to this day, fornicating is neither a shame or a sin. Nonetheless, the men are not jealous, living on the sly with many other women and young girls, which they like a lot, but the men have to guard their secret carefully because their women are very jealous, although the latter demand freedom in everything, covet the love of other men, and are insatiable and above all so conceited that she who can list the most lovers is considered the happiest woman, and they try to outdo each other in bragging. No Cossack lives with his wife alone, but with all women he encounters, and the women in turn with all men.[35]

Morality in sex, measured by a Protestant sense of proper conjugal arrangements—and the label "whore" for women outside such unions—expressed a standard of civilized behavior in which the natives were clearly deficient.

Steller, like all scientists of his time, used European customs to assess the world, and the world repeatedly failed to measure up. For him, as for his student Krashenninikov, jealousy represented a question of dominance, but in this story the women held the upper hand. Men might have many affairs, even with very young girls, yet they lived in fear of losing the favors of women. Unlike Krashenninikov, who seemed mortified of making mistakes through not knowing the proper local customs for sexual liaisons, Steller presents himself as an outside observer with a scientist's detachment. Nonetheless, in reading his lengthy chapter on "The Character and Disposition of the Natives," one cannot fail to notice his obsession with fornication and sexual activities, which he portrays as the central preoccupation of the Itelmen. He reports that untamed sexuality and excessive fecundity are not only common but tolerated: a "whore" might have ten children without any sanctions or even a reprimand. For Steller, this was a perfect example of nature without civilization, the feverish social chaos to which a society would sink into in the absence of laws and regulations, particularly the regulation of women's behavior.

Women may have appeared dominant by Steller's account, but they were also "insatiable," lacking in self-control, and entirely devoid of civilized proper manners. They represented the familiar dangers of sexual appetite, grown monstrous if left unchecked and undomesticated. Steller's work resonates with the wider swath of European literature that used distant lands for discourses on morality, self-discipline, religious faith, and the rule of law. Such works defined societies from Africa to the native Americas by their condition of absence and lack. In this respect, Siberian native women were just another piece of the mosaic that reflected the urgency of maintaining a proper, civilized world. For, in Steller's view, desire ran rampant across the northern wasteland:

> They not only carry on like this among the Itelmen but also in the Russian villages, because the Cossack wives who were taken from this nation still consider it a great honor to be loved by many, and in this regard, things were no better recently on Kamchatka than in Sodom and among the Quaker.[36] On Kamchatka women also commit adultery with women, by the way of the clitoris, called *netshich* on the Bolshaya River. These people also have male lovers whom the men, in addition to their wives, make use of through the behind without any jealousy. In the past, the women also committed sodomy with dogs a lot..[37]

Ethnographic accounts of same-sex relations among native peoples were not entirely uncommon during the eighteenth century. Müller, for example, described this sexual behavior of some indigenous Kamchadal in 1730:

132 | Chapter 5

> There are personages of male gender in Kamchatka who act against nature and in perversion choose to practice the position from behind. They have a native term for such people—*Tschupan*. But all men of the village hate them and do not want to associate with them. They live among the women, they carry out all the work that women do and they dress in women's clothes.[38]

Both Krashenninikov and Steller devoted several pages to such social arrangements, providing remarkable detail. The differences between their accounts, however, are noteworthy. Krashenninikov described men who dressed as women, the "koekchuch," who performed women's work, particularly sewing, and were considered feminine; however, he was noncommittal as to their sexuality, claiming that these men "have no relations with men, either because they are disgusted by men or chose to abstain" (although he included descriptions that suggest otherwise).[39] Krashenninikov's claims would seem to reflect his own preference for framing gender in a traditional mold of dominant, possessive men and submissive, reticent women. He had precious little to say about the native women's intimate lives, having had only limited contact with them; instead, he frequently referred to his older mentors' observations:

> Steller was present at the delivery of one of these women, who went out of the hut about her ordinary business, and in a quarter of an hour afterwards was carrying her child in her arms, without any change in her countenance. He likewise relates that he saw another woman who was in labour for three days, and to his great surprise was at last happily delivered of a child.[40]

Emphasizing the native women's ease of birthing, which had been a common theme among travelers since at least the sixteenth century, served two purposes.[41] It was at once a critique of European women's weakness and a dismissal of any feelings of pain among the native people, the women in particular. Such narratives present the natives as alien, different from Europeans not only in their emotional makeup but also in physiological terms, as evidenced by their inability to feel even such basic tactile sensations.

Steller's account of assertive, dominant native women tells us a great deal about his views on sexuality in general and women's desires in particular. Steller also was clearly aware of the possibility of female same-sex acts, and he went into the trouble of inquiring about a specific native terms. It is noteworthy that he never provides native terms for any body parts but the clitoris (*netshich*). The question arises: did these sex acts actually occur, or was this merely a colonial fantasy (as with his claims about sodomy with dogs).

Again, in these vivid accounts of abandon and debauchery, as well as in Krashenninikov's more modest descriptions, we should recall the historical context and the intended audience. The biblical reference to the Sodom, which was the only time that Steller evoked the scripture in his ethnographic writings, connected the Kamchadal women with a familiar place of sin. Moreover, sodomy in the eighteenth century did not denote a particular physical act or homoeroticism but rather was a specific legal term. "According to a mid-eighteenth-century German dictionary, the Zedler lexicon, sodomy was 'every unnatural use of the genital organs, either with humans or animals,' albeit done 'with lustful intentions.' Sodomy might even include masturbation as another unnatural use of the genitals."[42]

Steller was writing at a time of significant changes in the Protestant church in Germany, when some branches (such as the Brüdergemeine or the Moravian Brethren, referred here as Quakers) appeared particularly radical. These religious societies gave far more prominent roles to women in the church than any other denomination. They spoke of sexual acts within the context of their religious ceremonies, and some went so far as to question the permanence of gender entirely, suggesting that single brothers of the church were male only provisionally on earth and would become sisters after death.[43] Such claims generated the strongest criticism and condemnation from mainstream Pietists in Germany. Steller was familiar with those discussions—some of the harshest rhetoric came from his own home institution in Halle.[44] Encountering men dressed as women, or men and women engaging in acts of "sodomy," on the far eastern edges of Siberia would have seemed to him not so much new or foreign but familiarly blasphemous. We should not be surprised, then, that Steller's reaction to Kamchadal behavior proved far stronger and more verbose than Krashenninikov's. Steller was reminding his own readers at home of the excesses that might follow if a society did not maintain its moral principles and instead gave in to the desires of the flesh.

The moral warnings written into the ethnographies grow particularly apparent in the depictions of clever, cunning, at times even beautiful native women who are so dangerous in their degenerate behavior. Overall, Steller portrayed the Kamchatka natives, and women in particular, in a favorable light, but their sexuality, left unguarded and uncivilized, posed a grave danger. As in other colonial narratives from the eighteenth century, he warned of the need for laws and government, cautioning the reader about the dangers of natural excesses:

The Itelmen are equipped with an excellent intellect, a lively imagination, and a prodigious memory, but lack of judgment. Their intellect is apparent from their amazing and amusing ideas, reasoning and inventions, and their lively melodies; their memory from a thousand superstitions; their poor judgment from their theology, morals, and understanding of nature. But in all these respects the women far surpass the men, who are much more morose, stupid, and slow. In general, I can say of the Itelmen that their minds surpass those of all other Siberians heathen peoples because they are so far away from them.[45]

At times the behavior of native women—never the men—invited comparison to a European sense of proper public and private demeanor, and contrasted with the Russian lack of such comportment. In numerous accounts from the eighteenth century, when a Siberian native woman's physical appearance inspired admiration, she was considered as "almost capable" of fitting into a European or Chinese court society. An offspring of mixed race could be particularly attractive but also dangerously seductive:

The Cossack children, born of Russian fathers and Itelmen mothers, are so good looking that one finds perfect beauties among them. Their faces commonly become elongated and European, to which the Itelmen's black hair, eyes and eyebrows, the white, soft smooth skin together with rosy-red cheeks add special attraction. On top of that, they are very ambitious, cunning, secretive, and amorous, enchanting even those who between Moscow and here did not succumb to an illicit love affair.[46]

"Immorality run rampant" in a frontier setting was a popular theme in colonial narratives.[47] Anxiety in new social settings and destabilization of traditional hierarchy translated into concerns over customs, particularly those related to food and sex. In Siberia, the early focus of such European suspicion settled as much on the Russians as it did on the natives, and the ease with which the former succumbed to the savage, lawless ways of the latter. The German scientists regaled their readers with tales of Russian Cossacks ruined by the lustful native women, condemning both in the process. They warned about the dangers of the absence of moral laws. Native women served as the perfect lesson on the pitfalls of pure nature, even while they embodied the potential of transition from uncivilized to civilized in the form of their beautiful mixed-race offspring. The women exemplified the obvious need for laws and rules if civilization were to succeed "between Moscow and here," the edge of the empire.

However, these particular scientists emphasized that this was not a German colonial expansion. They deemed the Russians' attempts to be brutal, unsuccessful, and driven by greed. In Steller's summation, the empress—who was of German origin—was poorly served by her own uncivilized subjects:

> Before being baptized, the Itelmen were free subjects; nowadays they have become godsons and slaves of the Cossacks. Before they paid their tribute; nowadays, since they have been excused from paying it into the governmental coffers, they have to pay four or fivefold tribute for their children's baptism, for marrying and for visits from the greedy clerics.... Not only are God and religion thereby disgraced before ignorant and uninstructed people, but there also rises the false prejudice that all their conversion has been undertaken for private interest's sake, whereby all Her Majesty's best intentions fall in a heap and become unfruitful.[48]

THE ABSENCE OF TRUE RELIGION AND THE NATURE OF SHAMANS

Considering the attention that eighteenth-century narratives paid to native women, we should ask what they might tell us about the gender of shamanic practice. How do we reconcile these stories of strong-willed but insatiable and deceitful women, at times controlled as property, at times reviled as polluting characters? The answer is surprisingly simple. In the seventeenth- and eighteenth-century ethnographies of Siberia, women appeared quite frequently as shamans. In this respect, Georgi, Müller, Gmelin, Krashenninikov, and Steller all told a common tale. They did not consider shamanic rituals or beliefs to be a true "religion" according to their classificatory schema, so they displayed little surprise when women figured in these activities.

Although all these writers were intrigued by the performances themselves, they judged the underlying concepts to be silly, ignorant, deceitful, and lacking any scientific validity. The observers deemed "shamanizing" to be mere trickery, magic of the amusing kind. Shamanism was placed on a par with jugglers, and was nothing comparable to the dominant world religions of Christian or Judaism, or even "Mahomedan" or Buddhism, as Johann Gottlieb Georgi made clear:

> The schamans have certain forms which they repeat at the solemn festivals and sacrifices, with variations adapted to particular circumstances. They consist of invocations addressed to the gods, and incantations, threats and promises made to the devils. But it often happens that these ignorant priests are so unskilled in their function, that they confound and perplex the whole

rite by jumbling together names, allegories and objects. It happens frequently to them likewise, as well as to the rest of this sect, to take one god for another, to address a devil instead of a god or a saint, and to ask of one what belongs to the province of another. The ceremonies relative to the devils are absurd, puerile, frantic, and contemptible; and the priests are fanatics and abominable cheats. Fraud and fanaticism are not incompatible in the human mind.[49]

Thus, in this context, they were not surprised by women shamans, as they did not consider these serious religious rituals. To the contrary, "shamanizing" went hand in hand with the other observed feminine behaviors: manipulation and cunning. Sherry Ortner's analogy of 'male is to female as culture is to nature' fits this particular historical case quite well: religion was masculine and civilized, shamanism was feminine and primitive.[50] Thus, we find numerous descriptions of female shamans being casually presented as a natural phenomenon, which suggests that it probably was a common enough practice among the indigenous Siberian populations.

Yet their observations about female or male shamans were more complicated than simple notes on popular local entertainments, as their descriptions inevitably appeared in chapters on the religious customs of the natives. The circumstances in which these scholars acquired their information about shamans were themselves highly incongruous; the details were often obtained through coercion, or collected in the process of missionary conversions, or recorded after attending rituals that puzzled or bewildered the observers. Gmelin's complaint about uncooperative natives who had refused to perform tricks or divine for him captured the general ethos of this research.[51] Consequently, the heterogeneity of gender roles and relationships appeared in the language of colonists, and only partially and imperfectly mapped onto the more familiar gender patterns of Europe. The fact that women could also serve as shamans among some peoples was not, in and of itself, the most surprising thing about them. Steller, after all, repeatedly stressed this while pointing out the complete inversion of European norms: "the Itelmen maidens and women always surpass the men in intelligence and cunning."[52] However, when these travelers reported on such inverted hierarchies, they remained unclear about the extent of power that these native women had. They observed women performing most domestic duties, yet among some groups they also were heads of their households and performed shamanic rituals. The result contributed to an unclear understanding of what shamans did in these communities, while con-

FIGURE 5.3. "Krasnoiarsk shamanka," from Johann Gottlieb Georgi, 1799. A female shaman in a long coat with a drum. Tatarskie narody: Shamanka v Krasnoiarskom uezde. (Tatar peoples, Shaman (female) in Krasnoiarsk district) Image no. 1241953. Slavic and Baltic Division, The New York Public Library, Astor, Lenox and Tilden Foundations. (Reproduced with permission of the New York Public Library.)

veying a strong sense of the natural hierarchy between men and women. Yet despite Steller's claims of women's superior intellect and his stories about magical women, the illustrations of shamans that accompanied his work always portrayed the practitioners as men (figures 5.3 and 5.4).

Тунгуской Шаманъ при рѣкѣ Аргунѣ сзади.
Ein Tungusischer Schamann am Argun Fluß rückwärts.
Devin toungouse auprès de l'Argoun par derrière.

FIGURE 5.4. "Tungus shaman," from Johann Gottlieb Georgi,
1799. A male shaman in a decorated coat, about to stab himself
with an arrow (compare with Figure 4.2). Georgi, Johann
Gottlieb. 1799. Mandzhurskie narody: Tunguskoi Shaman pri
reke Argune s zadi (Manchurian peoples, Tungus (Evenk)
Shaman, Argun River, back view). Image no. 1241972. Slavic and
Baltic Division, The New York Public Library, Astor, Lenox and
Tilden Foundations. (Reproduced with permission of the New
York Public Library.)

Thus, the seventeenth- and eighteenth-century ethnographers inadvertently attested to a rich mosaic of behaviors among native men and women that defy the simple categories we may wish to impose on them. These scientists who were otherwise devoted to describing unusual plants and animals often found the people bewildering and lacking in "true religion," and thus they dismissed their customs as magic or trickery. Yet their excessive detail, despite its judgmental presentation, remains to trouble our own categories and perspectives. These early narratives provide a small window into the formation of anthropology in the eighteenth century, into colonial societies on the edge of Europe, and into the categories we use today to classify the world of the past and present.

In Georgi, Gmelin, Müller, Krashenninikov, or Steller, we certainly encounter both male and female shamans as well as those who resist a gender category, be they men dressed as women or women who looked too much like men. The answer to the question of women shamans is, then, a cautionary tale about what might escape the categories into which we organize the world. The early scientists recorded tales of women conjuring, telling fortunes, interpreting dreams, healing, and chasing away storms. They also recorded tales of respected magicians and of old women doing whatever people asked of them to alleviate their woes. But their view of the shamans of their time was also distorted by the lens of prospective conversion and potential civilization:

> In a word, the gods of all these nations are in general such contemptible things, that no child in Europe would accept of them for toys. . . . But it should be found possible in some future period to remove the chief of them, these people, of whom many are of an excellent disposition, may be persuaded to forsake their errors, and to adopt a reasonable worship and the true religion.[53]

When we study women shamans, we risk a similar optical illusion, forcing these shape shifters into the singular reality of what we want to see or not see when it comes to gender.

CHAPTER 6

Changed Men and Changed Women

Choices and desires make actions before actions can make
"history." But predefined social relations and language forms,
as well as the body's materiality, shape the person to whom
"normal" desires and choices can be attributed. That is why
questions about what is possible for agents to do must also
address the process by which "normal persons" are
constituted.

—Talal Asad (1993)

One particular aspect of Siberian shamanism fascinated and repelled
the early ethnographers: the apparent ability and willingness of men to
change into women in order to perform ritual functions. Descriptions
of this phenomenon varied widely across the sources, ranging from ap-
prehensive denial to detailed accounts. Explanations, however, were
harder to come by. Neither a German nor a Russian scientific background during the eighteenth or nineteenth centuries provided a conceptual framework that could accommodate such behavior. The early
travelers found the Siberian connections between sexuality, religious
ritual, performance, healing, and everyday existence confusing at best
and at worst utterly incomprehensible. Although the scientists recorded
gender crossing, they did not venture far in analyzing it. By contrast, the
end of the nineteenth century offered a momentary opportunity for
gender analysis, courtesy political exiles infused with Russian revolutionary spirit and a willingness to imagine social difference in radical
new forms. In the midst of their own forced marginal existence in Siberia, these urban exiles-turned-ethnographers could well imagine that a
spirit might order a Koryak man to change into a woman. This chapter

details their history as well as the sense of alternative lives and experiences that their work suggests.

Revolutionary fervor created a space that allowed for difference, and the native Siberian shamans, changed men, questionable women, and their spirits walked right in. But this moment passed quickly. Freudian theory would supersede revolutionary zeal, only to be discarded in turn when the new communist order deemed that sex and gender were no longer salient to social progress. Thus, the idea that shamanism might involve questionable men disappeared into history, only to be resurrected at the end of the twentieth century in very different contexts.[2]

The historical arc of attention to shamans is a travelogue of scholarly ancestors and intellectual paths. All the researchers referenced their predecessors' work, but they judged those efforts in the light of different interests, as seen in the late nineteenth-century Russian ethnographer Vladimir Jochelson's assessment of earlier research:

> The science of ethnography in the eighteenth century i.e. at the time when those scientists were making a study of the tribes of northeastern Asia was in a rudimentary state, and the methods applied by them can no longer be regarded as satisfactory. Steller, for instance, in his book on the Kamchadal, says that there are no special shamans, and that they have no special shamanistic garb and no drums; and at the same time his book contains three illustrations representing front, back, and side views of a shaman dressed in ceremonial garb, beating the drum and performing shamanistic rites. The illustrations are clearly those of a Tungus shaman dressed in a coat with tassels, and other paraphernalia characteristic of Tungus shamanism.[3]

Jochelson's comments reflect a shift in emphasis as well as method. Whereas travelers and missionaries early on may have had difficulty explaining strange social arrangements, entranced as they were by magic that resembled witchcraft, by the late nineteenth century the topic had become a matter for systemic analysis. As anthropologists began to travel the world alongside colonial missions and merchants, they collected copious information about marriage customs, dowries, and bride price, wife exchange and polygamy, and kinship patterns and lines of decent. Native peoples the world around found their way into specialized journals and scholarly meetings as well as public presentations. This systematic analysis yielded considerable results, but its categories and sensibilities produced their own sort of alchemy when it came to combining religion and gender.

The previous chapter illustrated how the earlier writings presented an explicit tableau of believers and true faith, but also frank accounts and active speculation about sexual behavior. By contrast, in nineteenth-century ethnography, religion acquired a sedately omnipresent status, even as the natives' flesh modestly disappeared beneath a heavy drape of metaphors. Scholars either carefully avoided sex altogether or treated it as a separate subject matter related to reproduction and kinship. The proposition that all societies had some form of religion, no matter how low they stood on civilization's ladder, had become a topic of active, if contentious discussion.[4] Gender and sex, on the other hand, receded into the background. Framed by patterns of marriage and family most common in the Western world, Victorian moral condemnations also often involved opaque language: "The system of polyandry . . . , which, next to promiscuity, is the most revolting form of family existence, finds defenders only among nations so immature as not to have developed a belief in possible female chastity; it is a form always attended by a manhood submerged in unnatural crimes."[5]

Yet any monolithic image of modest Victorians, buttoned up to their starched collars, sipping tea and discussing religious ritual among distant natives, would be misleading. The turn of the same century saw considerable social upheaval across much of Europe, which included a fascination with sex and psychological repression.[6] To see the broader picture, we need only return to the corners that shamans inhabited when ethnographers first met them. Siberian ethnography marched in its own direction, aware of the philosophical trends in Western Europe and America yet shaped by distinct political, social, and personal histories. Its marginal location at the edge of continents allowed for a different trajectory of ethnographic observation and an alternative imagination about social relations. In Siberia, we find modalities that did not quite fit the common sense of a universal human experience of the world, let alone Victorian mores.

However, I should also note that the authors of this alternative view had themselves "changed" by virtue of their own political experiences and their condition as exiles. Complex threads of action and desire linked and revealed changed men, both natives and scholars. Thus, the shamans of this chapter remained local, even as they re-entered a larger historical narrative, one that sought difference and alternatives to modernity. Exiled to Siberia, the Russian political prisoners became ethnographers and subsequently encountered lives, bodies, and social customs in forms that they previously had only imagined.

RELIGIOUS LEADERS AND THE TROUBLE WITH SEX

In January 1908, Roland B. Dixon, a student of Franz Boas, a member of the 1897 Jesup North Pacific Expedition, and a true Harvard man, delivered the presidential address to the nineteenth annual meeting of the American Folklore Society. For the title of his address, he chose "Some Aspects of the American Shaman," and his sweeping style suggests that he hoped to make an impact on the conference attendees:

> In any study of religious beliefs and ceremonials of savage or semi-civilized peoples, either special or comparative, the shaman stands easily as one of the foremost figures. On almost every side of their religious life his influence makes itself felt, and his importance reaches out beyond the limits of religion into the domain of social life and organization and governmental control.[7]

Dixon then approached the delicate issue of gender, framing it with early twentieth-century notions of clearly delineated, universal roles. His emphatic statement did not expect a response; he was merely pointing out what he took to be obvious:

> One of the broadest distinctions which may be made, in connection with the making of shamans, is that of sex,—whether the practice of shamanism is open freely to both sexes, or is more or less restricted to one or the other. In this particular, America is at one with most of the rest of the world in that, predominantly, shamans are male.[8]

Dixon acknowledged the existence of female shamans among some groups, particularly in northern California where he ascribed greater numbers and social importance to such female practitioners. He also noted the "curious custom" in Patagonia of male shamans wearing female clothing. Nonetheless, he concluded that male shamans constituted the general pattern, and hence were defined as the universal norm. By the beginning of the twentieth century, the shaman was an accepted anthropological category of "religious life," one that needed little explanation, only refinement and evidence of presence in a specific instance. Moreover, in contrast to earlier ethnographic renderings, this social category now stood clearly marked at a theoretical level as being masculine.[9]

By the late nineteenth century, sex, gender, and religion had intertwined into a sacred bundle of seemingly inseparable—and, as Dixon suggested, universal—traits. Relying on stabilized modern categories, influential writers rallied evidence to stress the gendered nature of the beliefs and practices that connected religion, art, and sex. Two texts proved particularly instrumental in making these connections real, substantial, and credible. In his only significant publication, *Mother Right: An Investigation of the Religious and Juridical Character of Matriarchy in the Ancient World* (1861), the Swiss jurist Johann Jakob Bachofen wrote with great conviction that motherhood was the essential, primary social force of the earliest societies.[10] He further concluded that sex in early matriarchal societies involved mystical cults, prior to the natural, if unfortunate, development of patriarchy and religion. In *Primitive Marriage* (1865), John Ferguson McLennan argued in a similar vein that promiscuity and sexual anarchy had been the natural state of existence in early societies but were superseded by civilization's step forward toward family, kinship, and patriarchal hierarchy.[11] Both texts remained immensely popular among the general readership for decades afterward, evoking a Victorian fantasy of a different ancient world where sin was rampant, family rules were nonexistent, and women were in charge. Eventually these assertions became accepted as "historical facts" by scholars of the stature of Lewis Henry Morgan and Friedrich Engels, thereby gaining citation widely in the scholarly literature and haunting twentieth-century discussions of the topic.[12] Matriarchy and mystery cults, the reader learned, developed into male-dominated societies, patriarchies with organized religion and male priests. Some might profess regret at the disappearance of the idyllic if anarchic societies where women had enjoyed high status tied to their procreative powers—their "mother right"—but the wheel of social evolution had rolled on, leaving cults and women's leadership positions behind.

For ethnologists of Dixon's generation, any continuing existence of "savage or semi-civilized" societies with powerful female shamans would clutter their sequential analysis. The possibility of gender transformation or unsettled natural categories would upend the whole schema. Rather, the dilemma was whether female shamans, if they indeed existed, were common. If this were shown to be the case, how could such practices still be called religion, given that women and religious leadership were theoretically incompatible? The research question of the day then, as Dixon presented it to his gathered scientific peers in 1908, was whether shamans were truly religious leaders, as the term was understood at the time: that is, men of great influence over "social life and governmental control." To him, gender was a secondary issue of little scholarly interest, an obstacle amid a grander theory. As many of his fellow scholars argued, as they provided plenty of ethnographic evidence from distant places, shamans served as the equivalent of priests in semi-civilized settings. Based on this anthropological "fact," it was only a logical next step that a religious leader was inevitably, naturally male. Female leaders were rare, exceptions to the rule, and possibly relics of the matriarchal past.

For anthropologists of the day, gender was indistinguishable from sex, a natural and fixed trait, untroubled by physical or genetic ambiguity. As the expert on things sexual and universal Ernest A. Crawley proclaimed in his seminal and widely cited article "Sexual Taboo: A Study in the Relations of the Sexes," "The social relations of the sexes have rarely followed the lines marked out by natural laws. At an early stage of culture man seems to have exerted his physical advantages and to have thus readjusted the balance in his own way. The subjection of the female sex is a general law of human history."[13] To support that contention, Crawley provided an overwhelming, two-page list of ethnographic cases gathered from distant corners of the world, all familiar to anthropologists of the time. For him, the universality of women's subjugation was solid and unquestioned, as given as women's absence in leadership roles in the European nation states of the period.

By the middle of the nineteenth century, the social position of women and their participation in political life had become topics of heated public debate. Anthropology stood at the ready to provide numerous cultural examples and to espouse theories about the centrality of the status quo. Scholars of the time enthusiastically engaged in scientific studies of the size of women's brains relative to men's, then subsequent comparisons with brains of the lower races. The threatening possibility of women's voting rights became couched in a discussion of the role of the newly emergent science of man, and "public anthropology" was prepared to weigh in:

> It is no uncommon event to hear the question "What is the aim of Anthropology?" To that question I do not presume to attempt any complete answer . . . but I hold that the science, in order to be worthy of the name, must deal with practical as well as speculative difficulties, and I know of no subject upon which it ought to give a more authoritative decision than upon the claims of women to political power. Let it not be supposed that I wish to trespass on the domain of the statesman; he is the judge of times and seasons, of present expediency or inexpediency, with which the mere anthropologist has no concern; but if the science of mankind is unable to throw some light upon the proper relative position of the two sexes in matters of government, there can be but little hope that it will ever fulfill the expectations of its votaries.[14]

Pronouncements like these now appear anachronistic enough to be considered amusing moments of disciplinary history, but before condemning all early anthropologists with a broad brushstroke as participants, supporters, or beneficiaries of such sentiments, we should recognize those who stood on other sides of the argument.

Some students of distant societies found in them an example of either what was lost or what could have been, and hence viewed them as a source of potential solutions to the social ills of the times. Indeed, looking to the East, in Russia we find scholars, radicals, and idealists for whom native societies became an intellectual refuge, even if living among them was not of their own choosing. Most of these Russian scholars were accidental ethnographers, exiled to remote places where lawyers, accountants, or teachers of mathematics were not in high demand. Yet these places removed from the so-called universal human order and hierarchy offered the tantalizing prospect of a different configuration. It is at this moment that Siberia became a historical anomaly within anthropology, a reputed location of female shamans and "changed women"—men who became women. It was also a space where ethnographers and scholars whose political marginalization had opened them up to considering possibilities of an alternative human existence could write their unconventional histories. In them, Russia's eastern frontier departed from the predictable path in the evolution of societies.

NATIVE MARRIAGE AS REVOLUTIONARY THEORY AND LIVED REALITY

From the seventeenth century to the recent past, Siberia has had a long history as the site of Russian exile.[15] At the end of the nineteenth century, a particularly notable group arrived: the members of the socialist antimonarchist organization People's Will (*Narodnaya Volya*), who had been sentenced to exile for the group's assassination of the czar Alexander II in 1881.[16] Thus, urban Russian Jewish intellectuals encountered the Koryak, Chukchi, Yakut, Gilyak, and Kamchadal of Eastern Siberia for the first time. For the next decade, Vladimir Bogoras, Vladimir Jochelson, and Lev Shternberg found themselves living among people whose lives and social order they had previously only imagined as history or as prehistory. Here, they met the embodiment of what they took to be primitive communism in a pristine form: the living, breathing proof of the accuracy of the writings of their intellectual guides Lewis Henry Morgan, Friedrich Engels, and Karl Marx.[17] The native Siberian

FIGURE 6.1. Jochelson in a Yakut house. Vladimir Jochelson writing notes in a Yakut house during his exile/ethnographic fieldwork. Image taken between 1895 and 1900. Image no. 11016, Jesup North Pacific Expedition Archives, American Museum of Natural History Library. (Reproduced with permission from the American Museum of Natural History Library.)

groups were thus not only a historical ideal, but also a real, living political imaginary for these socialist thinkers who were seeking an alternative to their own historical condition. The exiles took to studying their hosts with all the earnest zeal of newly minted ethnographers.

Ignoring the hardship of his life in eastern Siberia, and neglecting to mention the involuntary nature of his stay, Vladimir Bogoras recalled his lengthy prisoner's exile as a fieldwork experience: "The following account of the Chukchee tribe contains chiefly the results of my own observations, made during a protracted stay in the Kolyma district from 1890 to 1898."[18] With impressive diligence and perseverance Vladimir Jochelson, his wife Dina Brodsky Jochelson, Lev Shternberg, his wife Sarra Ratner-Shternberg, and their colleague Vladimir Bogoras learned multiple indigenous languages as they moved from region to region.[19] Unable to leave—exiled "in the field"—they traveled for close to a decade (between 1889 and 1899), crossing vast distances through unfamiliar landscape in difficult conditions, especially so for urban revolutionaries who had never lived outside a city. They recorded in exhaustive detail the lives of the various groups of native people, redefining fieldwork, observation, and participation in the process.

With an eye to Siberian indigenous populations as an example of the original form of society as well as its potential political future, the revolutionary exiles detailed an impressive variety of behaviors and customs. As the anthropologist Bruce Grant noted in his discussion of Shternberg's theoretical formation, "Gilyak group marriage provided a living illustration of where mankind had been at the very time when Russia was debating where to go."[20] These societies permitted a vision of the future in reverse: the road from the past suggested what might still lie ahead. But however idealistic, these revolutionaries were not blind. To the contrary, they were fully aware of the decimation of the native populations by the brutal colonial regime of the Russian empire:

> It began with extermination during the bloody wars of the early conquest by the Cossacks, and in subsequent mutinies, which were subdued by wholesale murder. After that came severe oppression; demand of tribute (hitherto wholly unknown); exactions from the officials and Cossacks, who succeeded in enslaving a number of the strongest men and women; and the fraudulent acts of the merchants, who imposed on all those that remained free the burden of interminable debts. Then came contagious diseases.[21]

Their initial ethnographic descriptions display an explicit interest in the material conditions of these societies as well as a hope for continued social equality:

> The Chukchee camp knows hardly any other social position than the master, his nearest relatives and his assistants.... Elements of population of different character; for instance, very poor families, consisting mostly of widows and orphans, who have no near relatives, and who depend for their support wholly on their neighbors. The Chukchee camp rarely knows such categories of people. All families of the Reindeer Chukchee are connected among themselves by ties of relationship. Thus a poor family without relatives is almost impossible.[22]

The exiles produced lengthy, detailed accounts of the indigenous groups relying on their social networks, and in these accounts they were clearly reflecting on their years of devoted revolutionary work among the workers and peasants of western Russia. Their field studies in Siberia were simultaneously a political proclamation about the essential role of society in taking care of its poor.

Nonetheless, these revolutionaries-turned-anthropologists were not so enthralled by their socialist convictions that they overlooked uncomfortable facts. Signs of inequality amid this happy tableau of indigenous life—particularly between men and women—troubled them. Both Bogoras and Jochelson devoted lengthy passages to the topic. Because revolutionaries of the time centered their analyses on the division of labor and access to means of production, these newly minted ethnographers described in impressive detail the disproportionate share of labor that women carried out without receiving any commensurate benefit in social standing:

> Among the Reindeer Chukchee, women work much harder than men, especially the younger ones. . . . The care of the house, which in the nomadic life of an arctic climate requires almost uninterrupted hard toil, falls wholly to the share of the women, also skinning and butchering, gathering roots, preparing food, dressing skins, making garments, and much more, not to speak of the duties of the mother. Moreover, man almost never shares in the woman's part of the work; he does not even know how it is performed.[23]

In the early writings of these exiles, women represented the working class: oppressed, exploited, and frequently abused—their descriptions of rape and violence were graphic and all too numerous. At the same time, in an attempt to document the earlier history of matriarchy, and out of a conviction that women deserved equal social status in the future communist society, they devoted more pages to women's roles and gender issues than any other ethnographer either in Siberia or anywhere else in the world at the time.

That Bogoras, Jochelson, and Shternberg wrote so extensively about the plight of women was remarkable given the ethnography of their time, but it was not coincidental as they drew inspiration directly from the Russian revolutionary movement of the late nineteenth century. The educated urban activists Vera Figner, Sofia Perovskaya, and Anna Yakimova had been their comrades in arms, equal leaders of the organization, who actively participated in both group discussions and the actual

FIGURE 6.2. Two Koryak women wearing grass masks, 1900.
The image reveals nothing about the persons under the masks, the
occasion for the disguise, or the meaning of the costumes, leaving
the viewer to guess. Photo: Vladimir Jochelson, 1900. Image no.
1428, Jesup North Pacific Expedition Archives, American
Museum of Natural History Library. (Reproduced with permission from the American Museum of Natural History Library.)

insurgency to its bitter end—including the executions and prison
sentences.[24] Furthermore, Shternberg's and Jochelson's wives, Sarra
Ratner-Shternberg and Dina Brodskaya Jochelson, accompanied their
exiled husbands to Siberia, and stayed on not merely as obliging spouses
but as equal partners in the ethnographic research.[25] They became the
only source of information about women's lives, in a precursor to a
common tradition later in twentieth-century anthropology of wives with
their own academic credentials participating in their husband's field-

work.[26] In the interests of physical anthropology, Dina Brodskaya took measurements and hundreds of photos of native bodies.[27] Brodskaya then analyzed the gathered data as part of her doctoral dissertation at the University of Zürich, where she was awarded a medical degree in 1906.

The photographs capture the unbridled enthusiasm for the newly discovered science of ethnography on the part of the Russian exiles. Yet those images simultaneously suggest ambivalence and discomfort on the part of the subjects.[28] Well meaning as they may have been, and sensitive to gender and aware of the class struggles in the empire and relationships between the Russian administrators and the native peoples, the political exiles remained uncritically enamored with scientific understanding and explanation when it came to documenting the lives of the Kamchadal, Koryak, and Gilyak in Siberia. The resulting detailed ethnographic accounts combined socialist idealism with an admiration for the clan based "primitive organization" and the family. Writing to a friend in 1891, Shternberg enthusiastically described his observation of the Gilyak group marriage as if it came straight out of the work of his favorite authors: "I found among their (Gilyak) kinship terminology and family-kin rules identical to those of the Iroquois and the well-known Sandwich Island groups, literally, remnants of the form of marriage upon which Morgan based his theory and which also served as the starting point for Marx and Engels."[29]

Publishing their work in Russian anthropological journals after their return from exile, Shternberg and his companions were determined to show the existence of social evolutionary processes among native peoples of Siberia. Initially, predictable change seemed quite easy to demonstrate in many indigenous institutions, including kinship patterns or shamanism. Female shamans in particular provided a useful illustration for this endeavor. Once they had been described through the lens of early matriarchal societies, they could appear as an older form of religious life and social structure. Explaining the prevalence of women shamans among some groups, and their simultaneous "simpler forms of ritual," Bogoras asserted: "Ordinary women shamans, besides changed women [*pre-vrashchennyie zhenshchiny*] (men who changed their gender, and resemble women in all respects), do not have spirits 'inkubov,' because women's shamanism is simpler than men's. Women's shamanism is simpler and more ancient than male shamanism."[30] While recognizing the significance of gender, the perspective of social evolution relied on such a concept mainly to establish sequential order.

Yet as much as these ethnographies took their inspiration from the writings of Morgan or Engels, framing their questions in terms of historical materialism and material conditions of existence, they were hardly mechanical reflections of the social theory of the day. Bogoras, Jochelson, and Shterneberg displayed an acute awareness of the inherent conflicts between theory and lived reality. They also had sufficient distance from European centers of knowledge to display the tensions and changes within early twentieth-century Western European social theory. Fieldwork experience significantly modified their initial enthusiasm for historical materialism and socialist ideals. Amid his description of the institution of the family in Siberia, Jochelson went so far as to note self-critically the dangers of theoretical attachment:

> When I began to study the family relations existing among the tribes of the extreme northeast of Siberia, among them those of the Yukaghir, I was still influenced by prevailing theories, and looked, first of all, for survivals of the past which should exist according to these theories, such as survivals of promiscuity, group-marriages, matriarchate, marriage by capture; but I soon came to the conclusion that such a preconceived way might only obscure the investigation, and that in collecting facts concerning the family organization of a tribe one should certainly apply, so far as feasible, the historical method to distinguish diverse strata, and that one should free one's self of the idea of a uniform evolution of the family relations of all mankind.[31]

One aspect of native Siberian societies, proved even harder to fit into a social evolutionary framework than the family. Ubiquitous and highly diverse, shamanism eluded the materialist expectations of Morgan, Marx, and Engels.

> It is interesting to note that traces of the change of a shaman's sex into that of a woman may be found among many Siberian tribes. During shamanistic exercises, Tungus and Yukaghir shamans put on, not a man's, but a woman's apron, with tassels. In the absence of a shamanistic dress, or in cases of the so-called "small" shamanism, the Yakut shaman will put on a woman's jacket of foal-skins and a woman's white ermine fur cap. I myself was once present at a shamanistic ceremony of this kind in the Kolyma district. Shamans part their hair in the middle, and braid it like women, but wear it loose during the shamanistic performances. Some shamans have two iron circles representing breasts sewed to their aprons. The right side of a horse-skin is considered to be tabooed for women, and shamans are not permitted to lie on it. During the first three days after confinement, when Ayisi't, the deity of fecundity, is supposed to be near the lying-in woman, access to the house where she is confined is forbidden to men, but not to shamans. Troshchansky ... thinks that among the Yakut, who have two categories of shamans, the "white" ones representing creative forces, and the "black" ones repre-

FIGURE 6.3. Yakut shaman in a ceremonial dress, 1902. A young shaman with a drum posing for a photo against a white screen. Photo: Vladimir Jochelson,1902. Image no. 1829, Jesup North Pacific Expedition Archives, American Museum of Natural History Library. (Reproduced with permission from the American Museum of Natural History Library.)

senting destructive forces, the latter have a tendency to become like women, for the reason that they derive their origin from women shamans.[32]

THE MYSTERIOUS WAYS OF THE SPIRIT: RELIGION, DESIRE, AND THE NERVOUS CONDITION

Once the Russian revolutionaries had spoken to real, living, and (as far as they could tell) effective shamans, they realized that the phenomenon was far more complicated than any evolutionary schema would allow. Part of this insight derived from their own passionate engagement with experience, which stretched their imaginations beyond the scope of many of their contemporaries. By and large, the earlier eighteenth-century travelers had taken shamanism to be mere trickery or darker magic, masquerading as serious ritual and in conflict with true faith. They had described it as superstition, confident in setting it apart from recognized, official religions. To them, natives in remote corners of the world remained devoid of the institution of religion and were plagued by profound misconceptions about the nature of the sacred and spiritual and the difference between reality and fantasy. Furthermore, the eighteenth-century ethnographers thought of themselves as religious men, who lived in a world of wonder, so shamanism was less foreign to them yet more threatening than it would be for their successors.

By the late nineteenth century, however, anthropology had become an established scientific framework for pronouncements about native peoples, and religion itself had expanded into a universal category. From the perspective of materialist social science, all religion was "true" enough without being real, and, as E. B. Tylor put it; all societies were deemed to have had some form of religion:

> Here arises a profoundly interesting question, "Are there, or have there been human tribes so low in culture as to have no religious conceptions whatever?" This is an old question, and has been affirmed and denied for thousands of years with a confidence that may seem surprising to us, who see on what imperfect evidence both affirmation and denial were based. Ethnographers, if looking to a theory of development to explain civilization, regarding its successive stages as rising from low grades upwards, would receive with great interest accounts of tribes devoid of all religion. I fail to find the existence of tribes in this state proved by sufficient evidence. . . . The savage's poor shy gods hide in holes and corners before the white man's mightier Deity.[33]

While discussions whether polytheism had preceded monotheism continued to rage among anthropologists, the basic premise that religion existed among even the most "savage tribes" had moved beyond the circle of active dispute. Instead, the prehistoric origin and emergence of religious sentiment became a focus of much greater interest.

The adoption of an explicitly scientific approach had profound consequences for work in the field. While the formation of categories bracketed and defined human experience and enabled comparisons of societies in evolutionary stages, it also created dilemmas of classification. Shamanism eluded a simple place in the established ethnographic categories. Shamans appeared as a part of native myths or in descriptions of ritual celebrations that focused on song and music. Although they were included in discussions of religion, they stood at its edge, foiling efforts to squeeze them fully into the conceptual box. Shamanism, as observed throughout Siberia by the end of the nineteenth century, was a worldview more than a "religion" in the sense that it permeated everyday experience.[34] It framed attitudes and relationships with animals and the natural world, and created ties and differences between men and women, friend and foe. Shamans influenced and directed mundane tasks and elaborate rituals. They narrated stories, sang songs, and mumbled indistinctly. They were not always predictable, and were sometimes feared even as people consulted them in search of order. They were the conduits to disparate worlds inhabited by spirits; they could reach into other realms and return without suffering major harm. At once simple and strikingly complex, shamanism was everywhere and in no one specific place, floating beyond social categories of religion, ritual, artistic expression, or even folklore.

The Russian exiles dutifully recorded the many forms that shamanism took, gradually recognizing that it confounded easy explanation. On the one hand, they could fit the gendered nature of the phenomena, particularly the sexual relations with the spirits and the specific demands that the spirits made on their human interlocutors, into their revolutionary visions of social relations. However, the phenomena they observed did not address in any simple way the division of labor, social hierarchy, or materialist history. Native shamans defied any easy class analysis: they were powerful without always being wealthy, and they were indispensable for negotiating life. The exiles' intellectual guides, Morgan, Marx, and Engels, proved of little help in understanding a world that exceeded the expectations of "primitive communism."

The question of gender played a central and evolving role in the exiles' analysis of shamans. Jochelson and Shternberg found increasing appeal in Freud's new theories of the human psyche, the role of the subconscious and its gendered manifestations, and sexual relations as a social force. Yet even when equipped with Freud, they struggled to explain why shamans might adopt an inferior feminine role, given the power of traditional patriarchal hierarchy. Jochelson approached the subject by recognizing social hierarchy and the subordinate position of women among the Kamchadal natives. He described the inferior position that changed men placed themselves into by becoming women, admitting the possibility that sexual drive may have played a role. Yet even after years of ethnographic study—an experience that had taught him to think differently about spirits, souls, beliefs, the imaginary worlds, and the material existence—Jochelson remained puzzled as to why a woman shaman would be more powerful:

> "Every *koe'kchuch*," says Krasheninnikoff, "is regarded as a magician and interpreter of dreams" but, judging from his confused description, it may be inferred that the most important feature of the institution of the *koe'kchuch* lay not in their shamanistic power, but in their position with regard to the satisfaction of the unnatural inclinations of the Kamchadal. The *koe'kchuch* wore women's clothes; they did women's work, and were in the position of wives or concubines. They did not enjoy respect: they held a social position similar to that of woman. They could enter the house through the draught-channel, which corresponds to the opening in the roof of the porch of the Koryak underground house, just like all the women; while men would consider it a humiliation to do so. The Koryak told me the same with reference to their *qava'u*. But, setting aside the question of the perversion of the sexual instinct connected with this so-called "change of sex," the interesting question remains, "Why is a shaman believed to become more powerful when he is changed into a woman?"[35]

Gender presented the revolutionaries with a stubborn obstacle. They could recognize different social relations, and even worldviews, celebrating equality and disapproving of hierarchy. They could describe gender inversions, even contemplate their sexual possibilities, but ultimately they found them puzzling.

Freud did offer a potential resource through his study of hysteria. Several ethnographers suggested that the preponderance and the power of female shamans might derive from the highly performative and unpredictable nature of the shamanic event.[36] When engaged in their art, shamans behaved in an erratic fashion—they leaped, danced, fell down motionless, shrieked, talked to invisible others, or sat silently for far too long, listening. These traits contradicted notions of rational behavior as understood by Western educated observers, especially the sort of behavior expected of religious leaders. Observed in close detail in various settings and contexts, shamanic ritual exceeded tame understandings of folklore or set cultural performances. Rather, it gradually turned into a public display of erratic emotional responses to external stimuli. Shamans' peculiar conduct, the earlier gimmicks and tricks, now appeared as symptoms of a medical condition, one thought to be common in various guises among primitive peoples the world over. Under the growing influence of Freud's work, women in remote Siberian villages seemed to have been as prone to neuroses and traumatic dreams as the Viennese bourgeois patients who visited the psychoanalyst's clinic.[37]

In the early decades of the twentieth century, established scientific wisdom held that women had the weaker nervous system; hence, they were far more susceptible to the influence of emotions. Shamanic dances, drumming, and the occasional trance, whether practiced by women or men, resonated with the case studies of women discussed in the new crop of psychiatric textbooks. Freud's famous patient Dora suddenly had many distant cousins, even in the far reaches of eastern Siberia. The revolutionary ethnographers found this interpretation appealing:

> Shamans were neurotic, afflicted people and women much more commonly suffer from "nerve pain." These nervous inflictions start among girls around puberty and lead to fits when they pull their hair and wish to kill themselves. Nervous afflictions are very common among the Tungus and Yakuts, overwhelmingly among women, and take various forms. Even among educated Russians hysterics are only women, so clearly the roots are biological. Among cultured peoples such form of expression has no more place.[38]

The emergence of this medical angle on the belief system held sway during the early decades of the twentieth century, and it found its strongest expression in the so-called Arctic hysteria that all shamans, but women in particular, supposedly suffered. Bogoras popularized the term in his discussion of the general health of the Chukchi in 1901: "The Chukchi are the healthiest of the tribes of the Kolyma country. Their women are free from that form of arctic hysteria which besets almost all Yukagir and Lamut women."[39]

The reference to hysteria began circulating among Danish researchers studying native populations of Greenland at the turn of the century, and at first it was never seen in descriptions of populations in Siberia.[40] However, less than a decade later, claims of a near epidemic of hysteria among the Yukagir or the Yakut in the northeastern regions of Asia percolated through the literature. When the Polish geographer and an early ecologist Stanislaus Novakovsky asserted that mental illness was linked to specific races and was far more common among the "primitives," he argued for the environmental basis of Arctic hysteria, suggesting that it should be medically labeled "Hysteria Siberica" and restricted to the Siberian native peoples.[41] When ethnography embraced this psychological turn, a fertile new field of medical and scientific approaches to the study of native peoples developed. It also prefigured the later neurobiological view of shamanism that became popular later in the century.

However, it was Maria Czaplicka, a lone female anthropologist in the early decades of the century, who applied the term most specifically to shamans.[42] Although her thesis *Aboriginal Siberia: A Study in Social Anthropology* (1914) was based on exhaustive literature review rather than fieldwork, it picked up a thread in the intellectual climate of the time. Her focus on hysteria even extended to her etymology of the term *shaman* itself: "Saman is a Manchu word, meaning the one who is excited."[43] After it was published by Oxford University in 1914, her manuscript acquired a remarkable degree of circulation, and it became the standard reference text for everyone who wished to write about shamans and their neuroses anywhere in the world.

Although the Russian exiles had ultimately stopped short of extending Freud into a grand analysis, instead insisting on the unique qualities of Siberia and remaining puzzled by its aspects of gender, Czaplicka's later readers felt no such qualms. The growing centrality of British social anthropology easily trumped the decade of fieldwork that Bogoras, Jochelson, and Shternberg had performed. Most of Siberian ethnography entered British and subsequently American intellectual circles through Czaplicka's modest text, even if its author herself was soon forgotten. Thus, readers subsequently encountered Siberian shamans in such distant comparative contexts as Indonesia or the Pacific Islands. For example, in 1929, Edwin M. Loeb, an early twentieth-century ethnographer, made a distinction between a noninspirational seer and an inspirational shaman in Indonesia by citing the "common knowledge" of the prevalence of mental illness in Siberia:

> If the people who have true shamanism in its most elaborate form were the originators, then Siberia must have been the birthplace of the art. This is certainly the region where people suffer more from nervous diseases, including "arctic hysteria," than any other known region of the world. According to Miss Czaplicka, it would be difficult to draw a dividing line between these diseases and inspiration.[44]

Even more striking was the wholesale adoption of Czaplicka's work by the Cambridge-trained social anthropologist John Layard, one of the central figures in Melanesian studies. Anthropologists had agreed earlier that shamanism was a predominantly male domain akin to religious leadership, but the new psychological direction embraced enthusiastically the "changed women" in Siberian ethnographies. Moreover, Layard made direct connections between hysteria, neuroses, shamanism, and homosexuality, citing Czaplicka's *Aboriginal Siberia* as the authoritative text on the subject:

> In discussing this phenomenon, it is important to note in the first place that the "change of sex" is found chiefly among Paleo-Siberians, namely, the Chukchee, Koryak, Kamchadal and Asiatic Eskimo, that is to say, among those tribes least affected by later infiltrations of culture. Thus, far from dealing with a decadent phase, we have here to do with one of the fundamental aspects of shamanic practice.[45]

The low status of women and their hysterical nature might not itself explain the influential position of female shamans, but it opened a door for discussing homosexuality and gender changing among male shamans. Although female shamans were mentioned, they were increasingly shunted aside in a rush to discuss men dressed as women, men changed into women, and men asked by spirits to become women so they could be human lovers. As Shterneberg illustrates, the mystery of changed shamans having children with their spirit husbands proved irresistible to ethnographers:

> South Tungus, Buryat, Yakut all have both male and female shamans, chosen by a spirit for "marriage." . . . Among the Chukchi, Kamchadal, and the Koryaks, this phenomenon takes the form of transvestism—or gender change of the shaman. The male shaman changes into a woman—he dresses like a woman, he talks like a woman; the Chukchi even have a special women's language—a special phonetics for women's pronunciation. The shaman has to stop doing any kind of men's work, and perform only women's tasks, and even if he remains married, he considers himself to be a woman. This could be a case of latent homosexuality, but it could also be the case of female spirits choosing the male body to settle into and changing it to serve their purposes. This sex/gender change occurs not only among the north Asian peoples but also among the Dayaks, and the Kadyaks.[46]

At the same time Layard brought shamans to bear on contemporary problems: "The tendency towards homosexuality among epileptics . . . doubtless also exists among those shamans who are genuinely pathological, as well as among those of the lay community suffering from similar though less controlled nervous affections."[47]

Class analysis, community service, prehistoric matriarchy, primitive communism, and social evolution all vanished, eclipsed by the psychiatric/medical paradigm. Siberia yet again served as an imagined place of origin, this time for the mental pathologies of societies. Shamans willing to change gender under the pressure of the spirit world became a prime case study of the nervous condition. The actual women shamans faded from interest, gradually disappearing in the archived notes of forgotten ethnographers. The diversity of the ethnographic record, full of difference, gave way to the neurotic state, which could easily then be reapplied to a transcendental, biologically constituted human.

CODA

In this work I do not to follow all the many paths shamans have taken in the twentieth century farther than the early 1920s because my central concern is the adoption of Siberian shamans into archaeological stories about universal prehistory. The early twentieth century was when archaeology emerged as a fully scientific discipline, linking the ethnographic record to the material past. By then shamans were familiar, almost domesticated. The range of their practices had achieved some categorical acceptance within ethnology, muting questions of gender. The next chapter will guide us through this prehistoric terrain and into the deep past as well as addressing one of the iconic figures who defined shamanic studies within religion, Mircea Eliade.

Female shamans did reappear in postrevolutionary Russian writings.[48] Yet by that point they had changed; they were no longer the exploited laborers from the accounts of the revolutionary exiles or the neurotic moderns of the early twentieth century. Rather, Russian scholars in the 1930s, obligatory members of the Communist Party, evoked the inspiration of Marx and Engels anew to document them as earlier, primitive social forms.[49] Unlike their revolutionary predecessors, these shamans had a clearly defined future—they would no longer be needed in the communist society under construction. As the linguist and ethnographer Dimitrii Zelenin[50] wrote with all the zeal of the new Russian scientist in 1935, "During matriarchy the most important social functions were filled by women. At that time even the healing function of shamans was done by women. . . . Thus we can say that the ideal, normal shaman was a woman, and male shamans adopted women's clothes and resembled women. A woman is a shaman by nature—say the Chukchi."[51]

Nature notwithstanding, when read through the Soviet version of Marxism, religion could only represent false ideology, one that contributed to the exploitation of the working classes. Hence, shamanism ultimately signaled a survival of feudal relationships, leaving little room for any discussion of gender, desire, or neuroses:

> We distinguish two stages of shamanism as religion: shamanism of primitive communist societies; and shamanism that reflects social relations of a class society. Shamanism of the nineteenth and twentieth centuries belongs to the second stage. Many of these tribes did not have their own feudal lords but they suffered at the hands of feudal lords of other nations whom they fought with. This class structure is reflected in the hierarchy of the spirits that nineteenth century ethnographers noted.[52]

As suppression of any religious expression became an official policy, shamans disappeared from most Soviet ethnographies, mentioned mainly as remnants of the long-vanished past. Only with the arrival of new post-Soviet ethnographers, frequently Westerners allowed again into the far edges of the Russian empire, would shamans return to the prominence they had briefly enjoyed among the revolutionary exiles.[53]

CHAPTER 7

French Connections and the Spirits of Prehistory

In its aim religion does not differ from science. Of course their ways and methods are different, but religion as well as science strives to comprehend the external world and to subjugate it.

—Waldemar Jochelson (1924)[1]

ARCHAEOLOGY AND THE SCIENCE OF ART AND RELIGION

How and when did shamans and their magic become a part of stories about the very remote past? The eighteenth-century scientists who roamed the far edges of Siberia regularly pondered whether the Scythians, the earliest ancestors they could conjure, came from these regions.[2] But how did the stories of shamans make it all the way to the earliest human creations such as the Ice Age cave paintings or rock art?[3] In this chapter, I seek to highlight the tangled relationship of religion, science, and art in the formation of archaeology during the nineteenth and early twentieth centuries. My focus will be on the early scholarship and speculative analogy about prehistoric forms of religiosity, magic, and art.

Archaeology touches the past through material remains, pieces of "things" left behind. Yet as archaeologists we wish to show how people lived, what they felt and dreamed of, how they thought about death, and what they feared. Stone tools may be the most abundant archaeological materials from this early stage of human society, yet it is the paintings, carved objects, and figurines that capture the attention and give substance to imagination. Nevertheless, the leap from the material to the imagined has been the contested, the moving terrain over which archaeologists have built the prehistoric past. Here, I wish to guide the reader from the stories about shamans to stories about the earliest paintings and spiritual quests. In the process, I will show how historical threads that weave these narratives together solidified and became enforced, how shamans and scientists became a good match, and the settings in which this took place.

Rather than a detailed chronological marathon through the early years of archaeology, I offer two figures from this early period who represent divergent ways of studying and interpreting the past. They were both French, an affiliation that tied them to one of the most influential centers of archaeology as a scientific discipline at the turn of the twentieth century. France presents a singularly significant case, given that the major periodization of human prehistory became standardized here.[4] At the same time, wealthy amateurs and Catholic priests played a significant role in mediating the question of religion and art within scientific archaeology, establishing important precedents during a tumultuous period of social, cultural, and historical upheaval.[5]

Archaeology emerged as a recognizable scholarly discipline in Europe by the late nineteenth century. At the time, attention focused primarily on the rise of civilizations and the origins of the present. Deep prehistoric times in particular drew attention, as the emergence of humans from caves offered an apt metaphor for modernist understandings of culture emerging from nature. However, Darwin's evolutionary theory and historical materialism did not simply displace theology in theoretical discussions of "man's place in nature."[6] The relations among evolutionary theory, an essential building block in prehistoric archaeology, religious views, and the practices of scientists in the nineteenth and early twentieth century were complex, and were far more intertwined than most histories of archaeology credit.

From the secular, academic perspective of disciplinary memory, the victory of reason and science over faith and superstition may seem obvious. But the role of religious scientists, especially the Catholic priests of France, deserves careful scrutiny and close attention when it comes to shamanism. Discussions of the origins of art, spirituality, religion, and social life provided a testing ground where one could merge scientific and religious views and project them onto the past. France was a particularly fertile ground because, unlike in the English- and German-speaking worlds, Darwin's theory was met with a mixed reception at best, encountering fierce competition from Lamarck's version of evolution. At the same time, given the critical French role in defining prehistory, it would be a mistake to position France as an anomaly in the establishment of the study of human antiquity. Rather, French archaeology exemplified a complex terrain for the early twentieth-century emergence of the science of prehistory, one that included local, regional, and international networks of scientists, amateurs, politicians, and religious figures.[7]

At the turn of the twentieth century, France stood divided into rival political and cultural camps, defined by traditions of revolutionary republicanism and the Catholic church. This tension extended beyond contemporary politics into the scholarly perception of prehistory. On one side of the debate, firmly rooted in nineteenth-century discussions of science and religion, we find Gabriel de Mortillet, a French socialist freethinker, rabid materialist, and "father of French prehistory." Describing him, Elie de Cyon, a vocal and passionate defender of Catholic views in science, captured the company that de Mortillet kept:

> The 19th century was mainly a militant century. The men of science could not or did not remain indifferent spectators to political, social, religious and philosophical battles, which subsequently divided the spiritual domain. Armed with their positive knowledge, they engaged in the war against ignorance and lies, the scholars-naturalists were able to take part in these struggles with all the necessary authority.[8]

Across the millennial boundary, at the beginning of the twentieth century, we find Abbé Henri Breuil, a Catholic priest, prehistorian par excellence, and the other father of French prehistory.[9] Both men pursued the common project of imagining human origins but from opposite perspectives, blending the scientific analysis of material remains with politically and religiously inflected accounts of the emergence of humans as sentient beings. Gabriel de Mortillet laid the foundation of the earliest time divisions, and his chronology is still used today, albeit in modified form.[10] Abbé Breuil, on the other hand, combined evolutionary chronology with discussions of the emergence of higher thoughts expressed in art. Paleolithic symbolic representation in the form of cave paintings, engravings, and portable carved items became a chronological marker of human capacity for religious ritual and thought.

Although frequently presented as polar opposites, I suggest that the relationship between these two men—and the groups they represented—actually stands in for more than opposing contradictions within the new science of the past. Nineteenth-century materialism grounded the early twentieth-century discussions of early magic, spirit, and religion and provided the necessary scientific context for their study. Between them, both de Mortillet and Breuil—oftentimes through their collaborators and surrogates—constructed an essential framework for archaeology as the new science of the past, one that we still follow to this day. In so doing, they redefined what it means to be human relative to deep history, describing the emergence of humans who were not only *anatomically* modern, but also spiritual, religious, and artistic beings.[11]

REMEMBRANCES AND GENEALOGIES

On June 9, 1900, Henri Edouard Prosper Breuil took religious vows in the Cathedral of St. Gervais et St. Protais. He was one of several priests ordained that day, and there was nothing unusual about the ceremony, a traditional Catholic ritual in a small French town at the turn of the twentieth century. Nonetheless, Abbé Breuil, as he came to be known in his well-documented and productive life, is conspicuously absent from the list of memorable, historically influential figures of the diocese. The list, proudly posted by the official historian of the parish, is quite short and would certainly benefit from a famous personage. Well known throughout France, Europe, and as far away as South Africa, Breuil's name would surely add luster. Yet his renown echoes primarily through different circles than those recognized and proudly displayed by a Catholic diocese: for scientists and lay readers alike, Abbé Breuil is known as an archaeologist not a priest, as the acknowledged "father" of French prehistory in the twentieth century.[12]

There is an obvious reason why the Catholic diocese of Soissons may feel ambivalent about one of their own being the foremost prehistorian of the country. Tensions and conflicts between religion and the science of human evolution appeared throughout the mid-nineteenth century. Even before the introduction of Darwin's ideas, Lamarck and Geoffrey Saint-Hilaire had public arguments with Georges Cuvier in the early decades of the century. Following the publication of Darwin's *On the Origin of Species* (1859) and its translation into numerous languages, including French, the arguments acquired an international scale and continued for decades. Yet the story of the relationship between religion and science, particularly the science of human origins in France, is far more complex and nuanced. It is not a simple story of the church opposing the teachings of human evolution and a battle of two camps, scientists and priests, over the souls of ordinary people. Many official members of the church were equally dedicated and devout scientists, whose alliances were complicated and far from one-sided. At the same time, many scientists were not atheists, but rather professed a range of ambivalent views as wavering agnostics, deists, or even practicing Christians, which they sometimes expressed indirectly through research questions.

The story of Abbé Breuil allows us to examine how an ordained priest managed to work as a scientist of early human prehistory and even more to become one of its seminal figures. Did his position as a religious man conflict with his profession, and, if so, how did he resolve such an obvious dilemma? As an archaeologist, Breuil never explicitly argued for prehistoric religion. However, he did assert his views on spirituality through discussions of the emergence of art, symbolism, and magic. I suggest that he, and others who perceived religion as a universal phenomenon, got around potentially irreconcilable views of human nature by speaking about the question of spirituality indirectly, and focusing on art, creativity, and magic.

In order to outline such a nonlinear history of French prehistory, it is essential to treat Breuil less as a singular figure worthy of hagiography—impressive and intriguing a prehistorian as he may have been—and more as a representative of a larger social historical position, that of religious scientists, who were common through France and much of Europe at the time. We thus have to situate his activities and views in their social context and examine them as a response to debates within archaeology at the end of the previous century. To this end, I will contrast Breuil's work and writing specifically with that of Gabriel de Mortillet, his mid-nineteenth century predecessor, the so-called father of French prehistory. De Mortillet's adamant insistence on the nonexistence of prehistoric religion and his unwavering anticlericalism was the baseline from which every prehistorian in France operated at the end of the nineteenth century. Abbé Breuil succeeded in shifting the conversation around this potential impasse, moving the science of prehistory in France forward by effectively side-stepping the question of religion altogether. Thus, the version of prehistoric archaeology that ultimately consolidated in early twentieth-century France stood less directly in opposition to religion, instead redefining spirituality as a domain of human creativity and imagination.[13]

RELIGIOUS SCIENTISTS

The fact that many priests, particularly Jesuits, have been involved in education and scientific research is hardly a subject of controversy, but the involvement of Catholic priests in human origins research, particularly in France, has received little critical analysis.[14] Most archaeologists who work in Paleolithic Europe "know" that Henri Breuil was a priest, as he is referred to in the literature as Abbé Breuil. Yet this aspect of his identity has received scant attention in discussions of his work. If mentioned at all in histories of archaeology, his religious background is usually explained away by stating that he was a "non-practicing" priest. For example, when writing about Breuil in 1964, the American physical anthropologist Carleton Coon stated adamantly, "He performed no parochial work at all, nor did he receive any pay ... Broderick reports two occasions only on which the Abbé said mass and one when he gave the last rites. The physician attending him at his death was a Muslim. Unlike his friend Teilhard de Chardin, Breuil had little to say about religion."[15]

Technically this is all true. Henri Breuil did not occupy a parish, did not serve any parishioners for pay, and did not attend services in an open, public fashion. Yet all the images and photographs of the Abbé routinely show him in a priestly outfit, overtly signaling his affiliation, making him instantly recognizable.

Breuil never severed his ties with the Catholic church and in all outward signs remained a celibate priest all his life. Furthermore, throughout his life he moved in a wide network of priest-scientists, starting with his seminary mentor Abbé Guibert and continuing with many other collaborators and companions, such as the abbé brothers Bouyssonie or the Austrian priest and founder of Spanish prehistoric archaeology Hugo Obermaier. He benefitted from this circle tremendously in his personal and professional life. Rather than the facts of his biography, I would submit, it is the insistence of those who later wished to make him profoundly secular—and thus scientifically more credible—that suggests an inherently oppositional tension between science and religion in the history of the field.

Stories of priests walking the fields of their parishes collecting archaeological materials during the nineteenth and twentieth centuries are well known throughout Europe. However, unlike most priests who were involved in prehistoric research at the time, Breuil's archaeology was not a hobby or taken up well after his religious vocation. Rather, he went through his ordination even as he became a respected prehistorian, the two transformations occurring simultaneously. Walking along parallel paths his entire life, Breuil described his vision in the following terms:

We must not confound religious truths with the symbolic forms by which they are passed on from generation to generation. These forms must be adapted and purified in accordance with the development of the human spirit. On the other hand, scientific truth founded on fact must not be confounded with provisional theories constituting working hypotheses.[16]

The case of Henri Breuil thus offers something more than a biographical oddity or a compartmentalized life balanced between science and religion. Rather, it also illustrates a generative moment in the institutionalization of European prehistory, where "the human spirit" might be another grounds of truth, reducible to neither science nor religion. By looking more closely at early twentieth-century archaeology through the figure of Henri Breuil, we can perceive the conflicting social currents that surrounded it, and the degree to which religion and science were co-constitutive in the formation of interest in prehistoric art, shamanism, and creativity. At the same time, Breuil represents a continuation of the ambivalence about the relationship between science and the spiritual realm. The same ambivalence enveloped and accompanied the German ethnographers who observed and classified native peoples in the distant geographies of their imagination in Siberia. Uncertain whether shamanic rituals should be labeled as religion or as magic, they provided ethnographic detail that many turned to later on. Science, ritual, magic, and religion have long ancestral lines across wide spaces.

THE BEGINNINGS OF ARCHAEOLOGY AND THE ORIGINS OF HUMANITY

French scientists played a central role in the birth of European archaeology as well as in its extension to universal human prehistory.[17] Some of the earliest formative statements about the stages of human evolution and the sequence of these projected stages as well as the eponymic sites with archaeological remains that illustrate these cultural sequences have their home in France. Indeed, one can trace much of the intellectual history of "anatomically modern" humans during the Paleolithic period site by site, simply by following a network of archaeological sites through central and southern France. The same region also produced some of the earliest examples of prehistoric symbolic representation, particularly portable carved objects and the famous cave paintings. All these finds increased the general awareness of human antiquity by the turn of the twentieth century.

However, during the first formative period of discovery, stone tools defined the essential element of human progress, not symbolic expression in the form of paintings or carved objects. The accepted range of prehistoric human capabilities, their cognitive wherewithal, and especially their expression of symbolic needs remained deeply contentious. An impassioned debate about the emergence of human spirituality raged relentlessly from the 1850s and continued well into the early twentieth century. In early moments, the discussion focused on mortuary practices and the presence (or even more the absence) of burials; only later did it shift to include the broader question of symbolic abilities, such as the creation of art or the expression of human emotions such as laughter.[18] Thus, in order to talk about Henri Breuil and the science of prehistory in the early twentieth century, we need to back up some fifty years to consider the milieu in which archaeology transformed from a pleasurable outdoor activity for interested amateurs into the serious pursuit of an educated scholarly elite pursuing a specific intellectual agenda.[19]

French prehistory emerged as a scholarly field in a context framed by the dramatic relationship between the church and the state after the French Revolution. Prior to 1905, the official separation of church and state, fierce arguments between the clericals and anticlericals counted as among the most significant political events of the last three decades of the nineteenth century.[20] In retrospective accounts, the ultimate rejection of church influence by members of the educated elite frequently appears as a victory of science. This is particularly the case for research related to human antiquity, capped by the eventual, triumphant acceptance of Darwinian evolution. However, the path leading to this outcome was hardly that simple or straightforward. To illustrate this, I turn to the point when the radical feminist Clémence Royer, the first female member of the Society of Anthropology (Société d'Anthropologie), translated Darwin's *On the Origin of Species* (1859) into French. This was also the moment when a sometime socialist engineer named Gabriel de Mortillet returned from exile in Italy and embraced materialism as the definitive explanation for human progress from antiquity to his own time.

POSITIVISM, MATERIALISM, AND THE SOUL IN ANCIENT TIMES

In at least one key detail, Gabriel de Mortillet's trajectory exemplifies the life of a man of knowledge in the second half of the nineteenth century: his deep belief in the possibility of a new kind of society profoundly informed his practice of science.[21] In this respect, he is a perfect parallel to the Russian revolutionary intellectuals we met in the previous chapter, Bogoras, Jochelson, and Shternberg. They, too, devoted their lives to the creation of a new society by any means necessary, and anthropology appeared a very good tool indeed.

Alongside fellow freethinkers such as André Lefèvre, Eugene Veron, Charles Letourneau, Abel Hovelacque, and Henri Thulé, de Mortillet actively promoted the political agenda of the materialist Left through anthropology.[22] A common perspective rather than occupation united these men. Except for de Mortillet, who was already working as an archaeologist, all these men were lawyers, doctors, writers, or fellow travelers of independent means. In anthropology, they found a science through which to express their views on the past, present, and future of human society. Using journals, laboratories, the museum, and the Société d'Anthropologie to define a new science rooted in rationalism, this group of "angry young men" actively worked to pursue social change.

Louis Laurent Gabriel de Mortillet was born in Meylan (Isere) in 1821. After receiving an education at a Jesuit college in Chambery and a conservatoire in Paris, he became a geological engineer. As a student, he became involved in radical politics, and he remained dedicated to socialism throughout his life. As the new owner of *La revue independent* (1847), and hence a publisher of controversial pamphlets, de Mortillet was quickly forced into exile in Italy after 1848. He worked as an engineer and geologist in Savoy, returning to France only in 1864. While in exile, de Mortillet participated in several prehistory projects, including the excavation of the submerged Lake Varese dwellings in Italy, during which he developed an interest in antiquity. Upon his return to France, de Mortillet settled in Paris and began the publication of a new journal: *Matériaux pour l'histoire positive et philosophique de l'homme*. It was in this journal that he laid out his views on the human path from antiquity to the present, tying every progressive stage firmly to material evidence, and representing the overall trajectory as the "history of labor and struggle for existence." The journal was the first ever to be devoted entirely to prehistory, although it was "not so much a learned review as a combat journal."[23] De Mortillet waged this combat on two simultaneous fronts: opposing the Catholic church in an attempt to confront its political and cultural influence, while also seeking to promote an evolutionary paradigm as the dominant scientific view.

In terms of simple primacy, Gabriel de Mortillet cannot be credited for the invention of prehistory in France. He was not the first prehistorian in the country, let alone in Europe.[24] The antiquity of humans and their long history had interested a notable collection of scientists and thinkers since at least the end of the eighteenth century. The catastrophist Georges Cuvier, the customs officer (one of many memorable customs officers in French history) Boucher de Perthes, and the deist Geoffroy Saint-Hilaire were all instrumental in establishing the possibility and acceptance of human antiquity. By the time de Mortillet and his collective intervened in the debate in the 1860s, the main conceptual battle had been won—the "antediluvian" man of Boucher de Perthes was now referred to as a "prehistoric" ancestor, and the Biblical flood no longer figured for scientists as a chronological marker of distant time. Rather, the past now revolved around geological markers and references to natural events unmentioned in the Bible.

Although this linguistic turn was significant, prehistory only became a discipline in France when institutions, societies, and journals gave a tangible, material form to the discussion of human antiquity through collections, circulated publications, brick buildings, and a world exhibition. In this sense, the institutional birth of prehistory in France occurred in the early 1860s starting with the establishment of the Museum of National Antiquities in St. Germain-en-Laye in 1857. The publication of *Matériaux pour l'histoire positive et philosophique de l'homme* as a specialized publication devoted solely to prehistory followed in 1864. This journal eventually found an institutional base in the École d'Anthropologie, as the Muséum National d'Histoire Naturelle was closed to radical supporters of evolutionary theory. In 1867, Paris hosted a colossal "Exposition Universelle" on the Champs de Mars with over 9 million visitors, and de Mortillet played a leading role, personally organizing and supervising the *Promenade Préhistorique* at the exhibition, giving the newly emerging science of prehistory unprecedented public exposure and inspiring long-lasting interest. The establishment of permanent university lectures at the École d'Anthropologie in 1875 constituted the final building block. Scientific materialists had succeeded in building an institutional home for their prehistoric science in the *métropole* Paris, a place from which to influence science and society through research, publications, and teaching. De Mortillet's small band had now claimed the entire human past.

CLASSIFICATION, CHRONOLOGY, AND STAGES
OF PROGRESS

For prehistorians of de Mortillet's generation, the main research question was to determine the process of human cultural and physical development by determining its prehistoric steps. They hoped thereby to map out a progressive path that would be both comparative and universally applicable. Edouard Lartet, who excavated one of the first cave sites in France, the rock shelter at Aurignac, drafted a tentative model in 1861 that claimed not only a coexistence of ancient people and extinct mammals but also an evolutionary sequence. Lartet suggested a sequence that was based on the typology of animals that roamed the land with ancient humans, labeling the periods as the Age of the Cave Bear (*l'Age du Grand Ours*), associated with the Aurignac site, the Age of the Elephant and Rhinoceros, the Age of the Reindeer, and the Age of the Auroch.[25] The major innovation of Lartet's scheme was the establishment of a contemporaneity between people and ancient mammals that no longer lived in Europe. Even more daring was his merging of human and natural history, naming the periods not by the inhabitants of ancient Gaul, or their suggested prehistoric cultural activities, but by the animals that they may have eaten (or were eaten by).

Following in Lartet's footsteps, de Mortillet took upon himself to create a systematic linear developmental scheme, one based on strictly materialist philosophy. In it, he described prehistoric physical and cultural developments as a steady march through unwaveringly progressive stages, and he assumed universal applicability. De Mortillet used French archaeological sites as eponyms when creating this cultural and evolutionary sequence. Thus, he described the culture of the "Époque de Saint-Acheul" (named after the stone tools found at the gravel site Saint-Acheul, near Paris), the Mousterian culture of the Ice Age (named after the site Le Moustier in the Dordogne valley), the Solutrean (named after the site of Solutré in the Loire valley), and finally the Magdalenian culture (named after La Madeleine in the Dordogne valley).

By using French archaeological sites rather than Lartet's large animals, de Mortillet established the centrality of both western Europe and France in the evolution of human culture. The juxtaposition of an evolutionary stage with stone tools from a location in France achieved several goals at once. De Mortillet asserted the materialist perspective as primary in the investigation of human antiquity while at the same time making labor and technology central to human progress. Locating this central argument geographically in France, he placed French prehistoric archaeology at the forefront of a new discipline. By taking this particular direction, de Mortillet addressed multiple audiences. On one side was the greater international scientific community, as prehistory research was also emerging as a vibrant and dominant field in Britain, Belgium, Germany, and Denmark. The new archaeologists deemed the older generation, with their rationalist and positivist philosophy, to have been "excessive admirers" of Germany.[26] Making France the home base of scientific materialism gave the new philosophical approach a national genealogy. In 1879, André Lefèvre expressed sentiments felt by this anthropological community: "When an independent group, unaided and committed to no sort of compromises, raised the banner of *Free Thought* towards the close of the empire, it did not walk in the footsteps of Virchow, Moleschott, Büchner, Vogt, though still encouraged by the alliance of such men; it resumed a possession of its own inheritance, which had well-nigh passed into the hands of strangers."[27]

By rejecting German genealogy, the French materialist philosophers were ready to take the stage. Equally central was de Mortillet's engagement with natural philosophers in his homeland. In the French context, his new schema offered a radical contrast to anything preceding it, including the most popular version of transformative changes posited by Georges Cuvier. A founder of vertebrate paleontology, Cuvier was a functionalist who believed that all similarity in form is the result of similar function rather than genealogical descent. He remained steadfast in his scientific opposition to evolutionary theory as well as his adherence to conservative politics. At stake was the fundamental question of evolution: can nature change without divine intervention? De Mortillet's version of materialist philosophy tied human culture and its development directly to the evolution of stone tools, technology, and thereby labor.[28] As a geologist, de Mortillet was well positioned to make his case in terms of stone tools, and to connect human ancestors with the natural world through the medium of lithic technology. At the same time, the new classificatory schema of stone tools and prehistoric cultures proved eminently practical, allowing for the direct application of the theory on site at field excavations. Any practicing prehistorian could now collect his archaeological materials and compare them to the master typologies. The stone tool types were organized in the display cases of the museum in St. Germain-en-Laye for everyone to see, offering a visual guide to the philosophy that de Mortillet espoused. By implication, human progress appeared not only possible and tangible but over the long run inevitable, as reflected in the tools of labor left in the archaeological record. Nature changed, de Mortillet asserted, through the intervention of human labor and control of the natural environment. With the establishment of an age-system defined through artifacts and a triumphant public display, the ascendancy of the materialist vision of prehistory seemed assured.

BRING OUT YOUR DEAD

Having established tool making and labor as the central forces of human evolution, de Mortillet and his supporters pressed on about the absence of religion during the earliest period of antiquity. According to their interpretation of the archaeological evidence, which relied on a distinctly materialist view of evolutionary theory, a daily struggle for food and shelter and animal-like life marked the beginning of human society. Only in much later stages, they asserted, did any sense of symbolic behavior and social life appear. This interpretation of the archaeological materials suggested that human spirituality was a secondary social development and had played no role in the early emergence of human society. Given sufficient satisfaction of basic needs, later forms of society might develop complex rituals in relation to human productive forces, but judging from stone tools, religion or a belief in an afterlife was unnecessary in the early stages of prehistory.

Because the archaeological record of the Quaternary period remained quite sparse—consisting solely of tools used in daily lives of the "troglodytes" (as their makers were then known)—everyday life during the period seemed ultimately mundane. Thus, the topic of death and the possible attitudes toward it among these ancient peoples became a focus of attention in discussions of prehistory. Alongside, anthropologists, philosophers, writers, and even poets chimed in. The initial writings focused on the possibility of human burials and the rituals associated with them as a reflection of a belief system. The great majority of Paleolithic sites found at the time lacked any human remains. This may well be due to the poor preservation of skeletal materials, although later archaeologists have also considered the possibility of funerary alternatives to burials. In the absence of preserved human skeletons, any discussion of ancient burial practices remained a hypothetical argument driven by abstract views of prehistoric life.[29] The standard image of the evolutionary path suggested that prehistoric people emerged out of dark caves into the "light of history."[30] According to the materialist, anticlerical view of anthropologists of the time, the darker portion of that path out of a cave resembled animal life, devoid of any spiritual capacity.

In discussions about the origins of funerary ritual, Clémence Royer proved particularly adamant in denying any possible religious sentiments in the early stages of human evolution, and she described attitudes toward death in as animalistic terms as possible. Now best remembered as the official translator of Darwin's work into French, Royer was perhaps better known at the time for her own evolutionary views, presented in a spirited—and unauthorized—preface to *On the Origin of Species:*

> Yes, I believe in revelation, but a permanent revelation of man to himself and by himself, a rational revelation that is nothing but the result of the progress of science and of the contemporary conscience, a revelation that is always only partial and relative and that is effectuated by the acquisition of new truths and even more by the elimination of ancient errors.[31]

Running full thirty-seven pages, this preface presented a discourse on religion and science and a vigorous espousal of materialism as the revelation. Although generally considered a philosopher and not a prehistorian, Royer frequently wrote on anthropological topics, particularly prehistory. Constructing her arguments on the basis of political adherence to anticlericalism, progressive politics, and the conviction that evolutionary theory was the only possible path toward truth in science, she focused on one aspect of religious life that remained a vexing issue even for the freethinkers: the question of death. For the former Catholics among the anthropologists, the ritual of the funeral and concern for an afterlife seemed to have retained a strong grip on their imagination, judging from the emphasis they placed on its denial. Royer explained human behavior the same way as animal behavior: a process of adaptation through progressive, evolutionary stages. She interpreted the absence of human remains as a clear indication of the absence of any spirituality, and a sign that in Quaternary times humans abandoned their dead as any animal would.

De Mortillet was just as certain as Royer about the absence of any funerary rites during the Paleolithic. However, he addressed the issue through a discussion of specific archaeological sites and their excavated materials. Convinced that ritual behavior (which he equated with religious sentiments) was not an innate human characteristic, he suggested that it had arrived late in Europe, appearing only with the invasion of

Neolithic people from the East. The conflation of geographic location and human consciousness resulted in a claim that religion could not have possibly originated in France; rather, it had to be a foreign element brought from outside. Assuming that Paleolithic graves were nonexistent, when human skeletons did appear in some caves, such as in Aurignac, de Mortillet explained the remains as being invasive to the time period in question. Relying on his expertise as a geologist, he accounted for these materials as intrusive elements either moved by geological forces into lower, Paleolithic layers, or directly buried by the more recent populations into greater depths: "During the Neolithic era the dead were very frequently buried in the caves and consequently placed very often in Paleolithic deposits. It is one of the great causes of error. It is thus necessary to be very circumspect in the determination of the age of the human bones."[32]

Related discussions offered another explanation for the meager skeletal remains in the archaeological sites: perhaps the surviving group members had eaten the dead. Although the anthropologists of this circle worked very hard to make every connection between the animal and human world, here they eventually balked. However, they rejected the cannibal hypothesis not because they ascribed any moral sentiment to the ancient populations, but rather because they considered it to be a rare custom among closely related animals. De Mortillet's general conclusion remained that spirituality had played no role in early prehistory:

> Death was nothing for the man of these remote times. There was not thus belief in the existence of a spirit. There was not either belief in a god protector or one punishing his creatures. A concept of a spiritual being did not exist. Everything seems to indicate that the Paleolithic man was completely devoid of any feeling of religiosity.[33]

ART, SYMBOLS, AND THE SPECTER OF RELIGION

In 1922, Marcellin Boule, a professor at the Museum of Natural History and the director of the Institute of Human Paleontology in Paris, delivered the Huxley Memorial Lecture at the Royal Anthropological Institute in London. This was the highest honor bestowed by the institute on an anthropologist at the time. Boule dedicated his lecture on recent progress in "human paleontology" to Prince Albert I of Monaco, who had just passed away in 1922, and who had been the founder and financial supporter of a research initiative known as *L'Institut de*

Paléontologie Humain (Institute of Human Paleontology). Half a century after de Mortillet arrived on the scene, Boule's presentation recognized a significant turn in the public face and presentation of prehistoric archaeology. It was a shift away from the materialist foundation set in the previous century and a public rejection of its founding father. Evoking many of the famous British geologists and prehistorians, Boule outlined a genealogy that differed strikingly from the French scientific materialism and evolutionary thought that had been dominant since the 1860s. After listing the numerous major contributions of Gabriel de Mortillet to prehistoric archaeology, Boule continued: "Gabriel de Mortillet rendered great service to prehistoric archaeology but he was frequently an obstacle to the progress of the same science due to his preconceived ideas and his anti-religious preoccupation."[34]

The issue at stake was the Grimaldi cave, discovered and excavated on the property of the Monaco royal family in the 1870s. The site contained prehistoric figurines as well as skeletal remains of some fifteen individuals, including several children who showed distinct signs of burial rather than abandonment. De Mortillet publicly attacked the scientific methods in use, questioned the stratigraphy of the caves, and suggested that the carved objects were obvious fakes.[35] The dispute was one of many involving de Mortillet, who grew increasingly combative toward the end of his life. Still opposed to any possibility of burials and funerary rites during the Paleolithic times, he fought relentlessly against the idea of prehistoric art on the same grounds. Creativity was too close to spirituality and abstract thought, and difficult to separate on the basis of evidence alone.

However, the topic proved harder to explain away on theoretical terms alone. The discovery of carved objects and a growing number of painted caves left a powerful impression, and attracted many new scientists to prehistoric archaeology. When scholars initially brought to light evidence of symbolic representation in prehistoric contexts, they encountered strong resistance and rejection of their evidence. De Mortillet and his fellow materialists continued to argue that religion and spirituality had been absent in the early stages of human evolution. With the earliest finds of small carved mammoths on pieces of ivory at La Madeleine by Lartet and Christy in 1864, they sought to prove a different but related point: the primal coexistence of ancient humans and large prehistoric mammals. The materialist prehistorians interpreted the depiction of animals as an adaptive response, an imitation of surrounding nature—the later basis for the "art for art's sake" explanation of prehistoric symbolic behavior. De Mortillet did not dispute the existence of the carved objects and decorative pendants and shells found at many sites in France, but he insisted on treating them the same as stone tools and other objects of technology, items admired for their simple adaptive value.[36]

In 1879, however, the painted caves of Altamira were discovered in northern Spain by an amateur archaeologist named Marcelino Sanz de Sautuola. These new finds posed a dilemma of a different order to that of the portable carvings and objects recovered before then. The large, colorful, and magnificently executed paintings could not be dismissed as too simple or lacking in imagination. Instead, the French skeptics called their authenticity and age into question. De Mortillet and his colleague Emile Cartailhac were particularly adamant in rejecting de Sautuola's hypothesis that the paintings dated from the Paleolithic, and they loudly ridiculed even the suggestion at the 1880 Prehistoric Congress in Lisbon. Moreover, they stated that art was solely a French domain, a rather ironic stance given earlier suggestions about Neolithic importation of religion to their country with the onset of agriculture. It was the lawyer Edouard Piette, not associated with the freethinkers and materialists of Paris, who took on the prehistoric art mission from the provinces of southern France and fought de Mortillet for decades.

Only after de Mortillet's death did Emile Cartailhac publish a retraction of his position on Altamira in *L'Anthropologie* under the title "La grotte d'Altamira, Espagne. Mea culpa d'un sceptique."[37] In reality, by 1922 Boule was not saying anything new or that revelatory. Rather, he made public thoughts that had circulated privately for a number of years. De Mortillet at the time of his death was an established icon of prehistoric archaeology, but his strongly held anticlerical views led him to promote throughout his life an uncompromising theoretical approach and to publicly scorn all dissent. As a consequence, he not only discouraged research into questions of prehistoric art, religion, and origins of spirituality but even actively suppressed and attacked it. He was a promoter of a particular doctrine, a church of materialism that found a devout following in French archaeology. The interesting point about Boule's speech for us then is the extent to which de Mortillet had apparently held sway. As long as archaeologists perceived prehistoric humans devoid of spiritual nature, they had no particular use for shamans. Once cracks appeared in the materialist paradigm, however, then the figure of the shaman offered a form of mediation, one that still connected humans to an animal world. It was left to Abbé Breuil and his companions to turn the page on art in the new century, and through it on the question of religion and spirituality in prehistoric times.

By the late nineteenth century, cracks had indeed started to appear. If at first isolated, Piette remained relentless, and after de Mortillet's death in 1898 the gates opened for a surge of interest in prehistoric art and religion in the new century. With it came one of the most interesting twists of French prehistoric research: the activities and accomplishments of Catholic priest-scientists, who succeeded in advancing the goals of modernism. Through their very public clashes with the materialists, they helped shape the research agenda of prehistory for the twentieth century. They ultimately laid the groundwork for the general acceptance of the antiquity of art and religion. However, the struggle was not about the acceptance or rejection of Darwinian theory; rather, because the materialists favored alternative forms of evolution, each side had a mixed reaction to it. The conflict was about the role of art, imagination, spirituality, and magic in the origins of human societies, and ultimately about what it meant to be human. Through their work, the religious scientists institutionalized and popularized prehistory as the new science of the past, and identified the core of humanity in spirituality and art.

RELIGION, SCIENCE, AND THE IMPORTANCE OF A PLACE

Here we return to Abbé Henri Breuil. In 1904, Albert of Monaco, the royal from the tiny Mediterranean principality who was known for his passion for the natural sciences, received Breuil's reproductions of the cave paintings from Altamira, Font-de-Gaume, and Marsoulas. Although he may have recognized their scientific value, Prince Albert was captivated first and foremost by the artistic representations, and he immediately committed to financing all of Breuil's research, reproductions, and publications.[38] In one fell swoop, Breuil acquired full-time support for his prehistory research throughout the Mediterranean region and a patron who regularly visited his excavations and accompanied him on numerous occasions in the field. But the most lasting and influential impact of Prince Albert's support would be the establishment of Institute of Human Paleontology. The new institute placed Breuil's version of prehistory permanently on the map of scientific institutions while permitting him to continue to amass evidence of prehistoric art.

Connecting fieldwork in the provinces with knowledge, affirmed and reproduced through metropolitan teaching and publications, the prehistorians of Breuil's circle had been patiently and effectively redirected the emerging science of the past, but until then, there had been something missing. All that changed once the new institutional setting anchored their accomplishment. The Institute of Human Paleontology, established in Paris in 1910 with sufficient financial backing to permit independence from existing organizations, it left its members free to chart their own course. With new energy, Breuil and his collaborators occupied themselves with Quaternary art and wrote at length about art and magic, adroitly maneuvering between the edicts of religious doctrine and the dogma of materialist philosophy.

Fieldwork was Breuil's trademark. Pictures of him in fields, caves, and rock shelters all over the world—inevitably equipped with a hat and a walking cane—accompanied many publications in the scholarly and popular press. His collection of data was extensive, detailed, and not based on museum depositories. Unlike Mortillet and the many gentlemen of science who resided in Paris and only occasionally made excursions to the countryside, Breuil was a passionate field archaeologist. His fieldwork gave him a certain monopoly on a view of the universe, a window that allowed a glance that could not be replicated in a museum or a laboratory. Breuil certainly capitalized on this aspect of the science and became a master of it. At the same time, his field focus left him with relatively attenuated means for the dispersal and circulation of the knowledge of the past that his work generated. Early in his career, his invited lectures, public discussions, and even publications and printed exchanges were infrequent. Consequently, his network of fellow scientists remained relatively restricted, as the main circulation of knowledge was concentrated in a few Parisian institutions, not all of which were receptive to his interests. The construction of a new building for the Institute of Human Paleontology, however, changed all that. Decorated with engravings of prehistoric scenes from selected archaeological sites that Breuil personally chose and commissioned (figure 7.1), the Institute provided prehistoric art with a new permanent and visible structure.

The institute, an imposing structure taking up an entire city block, was built just around the corner from the venerable Museum of Natural History, until then one of the main spaces for the production of knowledge about prehistory. Yet this new institute was quite expressly *not* a museum. It was a research laboratory, a new invention that combined fieldwork and a laboratory space to encourage innovation. It presented knowledge about the past as actively scientific, in contrast to

FIGURE 7.1. Bas relief of cave artist, Institute of Human Paleontology, Paris. In this commissioned representation of the Paleolithic artist, the figure is clearly male, engraving a bison onto a cave wall. The entire circumference of the Institute of Human Paleontology was decorated with these images, in the public eye of every passerby, reinforcing the message of the research conducted inside. (Personal photo by the author.)

the speculative and less demonstrative manner in which museums displayed their wares. Breuil and his collaborators gained a space that allowed them to investigate the kind of past that they considered central to human development. At the same time, Quaternary Man and his artistic evolution could be studied without the interference of the Catholic church. Thus, Breuil's group could increasingly avoid the battles over materialism that embroiled de Mortillet and his supporters, either ignoring them or responding in their own terms through regular publications, lectures, and events hosted in the new edifice.

With Marcellin Boule as a director, Henri Breuil was named a professor of "prehistoric ethnography" in the new institution, while Hugo Obermaier, the Austrian priest and prehistorian, his inseparable companion, became "professor of geology and prehistory." The supporters of de Mortillet perceived this as an official endorsement of an antimaterialist line of research and denounced the new venture loudly and angrily. Writing in *La Grande Revue* in 1911, Adrien Guébhard, the former president of the Prehistoric Society, labeled the newly established institute a modern "*château des papes*," a court reserved for "priest prehistorians," and accused the pope of having thus acquired a firm grip on the science of prehistory.[39] Given the Catholic church's opposition to prehistoric research within its own walls, the accusation held some irony. However, it reflected the deep conviction among de Mortillet's supporters that the clerical wing of archaeology and its interest in prehistoric art could only represent a cabal driven by religious sentiment. The political and intellectual reality was too complex to permit simple refutation. Breuil had to tread his path carefully, and by remaining beyond the bounds of the official priesthood, he quietly avoided the religious question. The building that Albert of Monaco built, and the finances he provided, enabled Breuil and his circle to find a space between the polarized discussions for their work. Avoiding both the religious dogma of the church and the embrace of devout materialism, they produced a new vision of prehistory focused on creativity, and the human spirit they took it to embody.

Over the next three decades, Breuil continued to pursue his vocation in ever-wider circles, expanding his involvement in prehistory to South Africa and China and authoring highly influential books. Throughout the Abbé's rise to prominence, his calling card remained prehistoric art. However, from his entrance into the setting of the Institute of Human Paleontology, he increasingly connected art to magic. Magic was the spiritual motivation, origin, and force for art throughout time. Rather than entering debates over prehistoric religiosity directly, he focused on evidence of prehistoric creativity, and by extension spiritual life. His own public views on religion remained relatively muted but open and apparently untroubled.[40] Breuil clearly regarded himself as a man of science, fully committed to the work of reason. At the same time, his vision diverged sharply from de Mortillet's materialism: the true work of prehistory was not illustrating human progress through increasing stages of ingenious labor, but rather ultimately tracing "the history of the human spirit."[41] For Breuil and his generation, art was the portal through which claims to spiritual life could re-enter discussions of the human past.

THE SCIENCE OF ART AND MAGIC

One of the supporters who stood by Breuil in the fight over his appointment at the Institute of Human Paleontology was Salomon Reinach.[42]

A classicist, an expert on Greek and Roman pottery, and the chief curator at de Mortillet's creation, the Museum of National Antiquities in St. Germain-en-Laye, Reinach and played a central role in the emerging discussion of prehistoric art. His seminal article "L'art et la magie" appeared in the journal *L'Anthropologie* in 1903.[43] Reinach's work opened the door—or we should say the gates, considering the amount of research and publications that flooded the space—to discussions of Ice Age art. As an expert on religion in the classical world, he came to the topic from a different professional place and made connections to literature beyond the shelves of prehistoric archaeologists.

In particular, Reinach drew on the influence of Ernst Grosse, who emerged at the end of the nineteenth century as a leading German authority on "primitive art" (*Kunst der Naturvölker*). Grosse suggested an "ethnological method" to art history: a cross-cultural comparison of art drew on non-Western ethnographies and avoided a progressive model.[44] Reinach was inspired by this revolutionary theoretical idea, and proposed that just like the Hyperborean, Australian, or North American natives, or the Bushmen of South Africa, surely the "troglodytes of the Reindeer Age" had created art in an effort to influence their daily struggles with magic:

> It is, indeed, this mystical idea of *evocation* through drawing or a relief, similar to *invocation* by word, where we should look at the origin of the development of art in the Reindeer Age. This art was not what is art for civilized people, a luxury or a game; it was an expression of a religion, very coarse, but very intense, made of magic practices whose single purpose was the conquest of daily food.[45]

The idea of "hunting magic" was thus born.[46] Moreover, Reinach brought the materialist view of the previous century to a very public close by explicitly rejecting de Mortillet's claim about the absence of prehistoric religion: "I believe it is quite legitimate, contrary to de Mortillet, to attribute to cavemen a developed *religiosity*."[47] Reinach elaborated the point in greater depth in a multipart volume *Cultes, mythes et religions* published two years later, providing a critical lead for his contemporaries.[48]

Despite this moment of influence over prehistory, Salomon Reinach hardly features in histories of archaeology, beyond those of classicists interested in Greek myths. However, for our purposes, Reinach provides a direct tie back to Siberian shamans. Being a classicist, a field firmly steeped in the traditions of German scholarship, he drew theoretical inspiration from German academics in Halle, a historical center of classical and philosophical research.[49] These scholars in turn relied on their own predecessors, ethnographers sent from Halle just a century or two ago to map the peoples of the far eastern edges of the Europe. The Hyperboreans of Reinach's text are the very same indigenous people of the mythical, northern land described by Herodotus, the floating Siberians discussed in Chapter 1: "Ethnography has for a long time informed us about the artistic tastes of some contemporary peoples living in a wild or barbarous state. Bone engravings and bone sculpture flourished among the Hyperboreans, the Eskimo in particular."[50]

The magic places over the Ural Mountains, by then well documented in German ethnographies of Siberia, served Reinach, and everyone else after him who cited the text, as an exemplary connection between art and magic in the Age of Reindeer. "The power that these men claim that the animated images have, others expect from a carved or a painted effigy; in such a fashion among the Goldyak of eastern Siberia sculpted fish are used as 'charms' to attract fish."[51] The Hyperboreans played a starring role when classical scholars engaged in discussions of art and religion. The classicists may have questioned Herodotus as a source, yet they continued to turn to him when speaking of the distant cold places in the North. The establishment of prehistoric archaeology as a scientific discipline and its subsequent separation from classical disciplines removed the legendary Hyperboreans from archaeological texts by the second half of the twentieth century.[52] Nonetheless, their influence lingered. Herodotus might no longer serve as a verifiable source, but he became an illustration of other beliefs in the past, now recast in the figure of the prehistoric sorcerer. In turn a "real," well-documented image of a shaman replaced the tales from mythical people in distant lands.

An image carved and drawn in a French cave Les Trois-Frères, and subsequently rendered by Henri Breuil (figure 7.2), offered scientific proof of a prehistoric shaman's existence. While Salomon Reinach provided the vocabulary and framed the discussion of art and magic, it was Breuil who offered the visual proof with an incontrovertible image of the being who would personify their union. In the words of Comte Henri Bégouën, the man who took the baton of art and magic from Salomon Reinach while Breuil collected archaeological evidence:

Two years ago I had the honor of showing you a series of photographs of prehistoric sketches engraved on the walls of the cave Trois-Frères à

FIGURE 7.2. *"Le sorcier,"* Les Trois-Frères cave, Montesquieu-Avantès, France. Reproductions of the "sorcerer" image from the cave, intially made by Breuil, subsequently reproduced in every text about prehistoric art. (Image by Vicky Herring, reproduced courtesy of Dr. John Robb, Leverhulme Trust "Changing Beliefs of the Human Body" project, Cambridge University, UK.)

Montesquiueu-Avantès (Ariège). One of them represented a strange human figure, its high location of more than three meters above, in a nook of a rock allowed only an imperfect photographic reproduction. So as to see all the details, a sketch was necessary. Abbé Breuil was willing to spend several weeks identifying and studying the cave engravings.[53]

Bégouën met Breuil in 1911 while visiting decorated caves near his property. He was an educated landowner from the south of France, whose sons Max, Louis, and Jacques were the "three brothers" of Les Trois-Frères cave, which they discovered in 1914. One of the last of the generation of wealthy amateur archaeologists, Bégouën invested all his energy, time, and financial support into prehistoric research. After Cartailhac's death in 1921, Bégouën became a lecturer in prehistory and a director of the Museum of Natural History in Toulouse. It was from this position that he tirelessly worked for the recognition of prehistoric art as a spiritual expression, a connection between a view of the world, artistic effort, and magic once performed by powerful shamans, sorcerers, and priests in the depths of the caves.

> It appears that the artist was the sorcerer himself, who traced with attention to detail and fidelity his own portrait dressed in his ritual garb. He placed it in the most secluded corner of the lower cave, but on a wall overlooking hundreds of depictions of animals that he or his comrades have for many generations, drawn as premonitions. Because everything in this cave speaks of magic.[54]

In 1920, Bégouën sketched out the details of the hunting magic hypothesis that Reinach initiated. By then, a shaman or a sorcerer was not just an illustration of an idea about how art may have originated. There were very few human representations among the thousands of painted or carved animals, to be sure, but the odd hybrid from Les Trois-Frères cave offered potential proof—an image of the artist himself. Moreover, by then the image of this creator had stabilized as a male form. The sorcerer and *his comrades* ("ses confrères"), Bégouën claimed, had been practicing magic for generations. Any doubt about the origin of art, religiosity of prehistoric peoples, or the gender of the performer should now be considered settled. The short piece from 1920 contained only two images: the "sorcerers" from Les Trois-Frères cave. Nonetheless, it presented them as crucial visual evidence of hunting magic. Replicated for decades afterward around the globe, the images circulated well beyond their original context. They too became wayward shamans.

In 1927, Henri Bégouën delivered a longer treatise on the topic of art and magic entitled "L'art préhistorique est d'origine magique," by then a well-developed and respected theoretical approach to the interpretation of prehistoric symbolic representation. Reflecting on the impact of Reinach's original piece from the turn of the century, Bégouën considered the last thirty years of research, particularly the explosion of discoveries since Altamira. Given the previous struggle over the acceptance of the material reality of cave paintings, carved objects, their authenticity and meaning, he took this body of material as a clear refutation of de Mortillet's strict materialist vision of the past. Magic, spirituality, sorcerers, and shamans were now a permanent part of the prehistoric past. Thus, Bégouën, returning to the image from Les Trois-Frères cave, concluded his lecture:

> Is this a representation of a higher being, a *great spirit* of certain primitive peoples? Is it not rather a *sorcerer,* a master, when he wants to be, of animal nature, having taken the attributes of those he wants to dominate through his magical powers? Such a concept is common among primitive peoples and the Siberian *shaman* is a striking example of this.[55]

SHAMANS AND THE UNIVERSAL SPIRIT OF ART

For all that prehistoric archaeology remains firmly locked in an embrace with material analysis and evolutionary theory, it also carries with it a trace of something else: the haunting images of ancient animals. Once painted deep inside dark caves, they came to light when artfully reproduced by archaeologists in the early twentieth century. Amid the hundreds of reindeer or bison, one of the best-known images of all remains that of Breuil's "sorcerer," an ancient figure who supposedly mediated the worlds of humans and animals by means of magic. This sorcerer carried his magic into modern times. He brought together disparate characters—classicists, religious scientists, wealthy landowners, university professors, revolutionaries, even a prince. Through the stories they told, they made the science of the past real, tangible and material, closing the circle between the present and the past. Through the figure of this magician, the Siberian shaman, as an ethnographically redefined indigenous category, could now extend into prehistory. As it did so, however, it lost its historical diversity, including all traces of gender variability and subversive sexuality. All the things that had once troubled early travelers to Siberia vanished amid early twentieth-century norms. When later archaeologists followed Brueil's interest in prehistoric art and took up the shaman motif to explain it, they did so without realizing what had been left behind alongside what was gained.

In the first three decades of the twentieth century, French prehistoric archaeology developed a solid scientific reputation and international prominence. Salomon Reinach, Comte Henri Bégouën, Emile Cartailhac, and Abbé Henri Breuil, together with their extensive network of collaborators and comfortable institutional backing, laid a solid foundation for the interpretation of prehistoric symbolic representation. Prehistoric art now served as a confirmation of ancient spirituality, religiosity, and the creative spirit. The theoretical frame —hunting magic—captured public and scholarly imagination, and consequently gathered more support and evidence with each new archaeological discovery.

The idea of magic and transcendental spirits in prehistory only gained in appeal after World War II. It was at that point that Mircea Eliade stepped in and provided more detail about shamanism and flights to other worlds than any single ethnographer ever could. Archaeologists were as eager as everyone else to listen. Eliade stands as a major, controversial landmark in the much longer history of the search for the origins of art and religion. A Romanian émigré living in France and writing amid the traumatic aftermath of World War II, he offered a powerfully seductive story of spirits transcending history rather than being burdened by it, set in a primordial world that appealed to universal qualities of humanity.[56] As a historian of religion, Eliade collected the long, varied historical and ethnographic record of Siberian indigenous groups. But he also reworked it into a new, synthetic whole, one shaped amid an atmosphere of postwar nostalgia and attraction to Eastern transcendental philosophy.[57] While he may have towered as an emblematic figure for twentieth-century religious studies and served as a font of inspiration for a generation of scholars in the 1960s, his work was a point of translation rather than origin. Nor, as should be clear by this point in the text, was he always the most reliable source of information about Siberian shamans.[58]

Several theoretical models displaced hunting magic in the interpretation of prehistoric art in the 1960s: structuralism, social models, practice theory, and gendered approaches. Nonetheless, the shamanic hypothesis rebounded with renewed energy and enthusiasm in the 1980s. Having taken a detour through South Africa, it shed the cloak of the sorcerer and found new anchorage in biological functions of a universal human brain. Strangely ahistorical, genderless, and all-powerful, these new, transcendent shamans found their way into every corner of the world without even trying. As we shall see in the final chapter, however, they would still remain ultimately elusive—true to their nature as wayward spirits.

Conclusion

On my very first day in Siberia in Akademgorodok, a town built for scientists in a bucolic setting near a lake, about 30 kilometers from the capitol Novosibirsk, I got hopelessly lost in the woods around the complex in which I was staying. My usually reliable sense of direction failed, and I truly did not know where I was. Even less did I know how to find my new home. On my arrival, I had briefly seen an old woman—a classic Russian "babushka"—who, from her entrance hutch, seemed to watch the comings and goings of everyone residing in the dormitory in the woods. At a loss about what else to do and finding myself again at her doorstep, I knocked on the window. She already knew all about me and where I belonged. I asked her in the Russian of my childhood tales, "Where am I?" She answered, "Here. But I will take you where you ought to be." She then led me through the woods, pointing the way to my room.

I will end my story of traveling spirits and wayward shamans in the recent past, far to the South rather than the North. At the end of the twentieth century, shamans reemerged prominently in discussions of rock art, creativity, and spirituality in South African archaeological circles. This region boasts a spectacular archaeological heritage, including a remarkable trove of rock art. In the late 1970s, a major change in the study of this legacy began to shift the way scholars perceived prehistoric imagery worldwide. Up to that point, the most common approach had been to view the South African finds as unique artifacts without discernible context, an aesthetic expression that, however admired, was difficult to interpret or understand. Moreover, the depictions of animals, people, and abstract shapes had very little to say to archaeologists of the 1950s or 1960s, who remained focused on broader questions of human adaptation to a range of ecosystems.[1] The makers of the paintings and engravings had long vanished, and the dating techniques available at the time were not suitable for the materials at hand. Statistical and structuralist analyses thus appeared to be the most creative ways to analyze the images beyond mere description.[2]

South Africa, however, offered a unique resource: ethnographic accounts of the indigenous peoples known as San (called historically by various other names such as the Bushmen, Hottentot, or Soaqua). The San were not only the presumed descendants of the ancient image-makers, but they also continued to produce similar art into the colonial era, providing a potential link between prehistoric and historic forms. Both historical archives from the late nineteenth and early twentieth centuries, and Kalahari ethnographies from the 1960s and 1970s contained a wealth of information on the everyday lives, rituals, and mythologies of these peoples. Two collections merit particular mention. The Bleek and Lloyd ethnographic and linguistic archive became one of the central sources of information for understanding rock art in southern Africa.[3] Wilhelm Bleek met the /Xam men from the Karoo region in the Breakwater prison in Cape Town in 1863, where they were being held on accusations of cattle theft and violence against local farmers. Eventually he managed to get them released into the custody of his household, as the conditions for linguistic and anthropological work were not ideal in the prison. After Bleek's death, his daughter Dorothea and his sister-in-law Lucy Lloyd took on the task, contributing to the archives and rock art collections through the 1940s.[4] Because the /Xam language is now extinct, the Bleek and Lloyd collection survives as a unique record, registered with UNESCO in 1997 as a part of the Memory of the World heritage collections.

An additional ethnographic resource from the same time period is the oral history recorded by Joseph Millerd Orpen. An Irish immigrant to the Cape colony, a sheep farmer, a land surveyor, and a part-time politician, Orpen was guided through Lesotho in 1873 by a man named Qing, one of the last Maluti San.[5] Qing's stories about his people and his thoughts on the rock art of the Drakensberg region as recorded by Orpen remain one of the central sources of ethnographic analogy in

interpretations of the rock paintings. In the early 1970s, Patricia Vinnicombe, a major figure in twentieth-century South African archaeology,
drew on this source to suggest a potential breakthrough in the study of
rock art. In her seminal publication about the prehistoric images of the
region, *People of the Eland: Rock Paintings of the Drakensburg Bushmen as a Reflection of Their Life and Thought* (1976), she treated the
paintings as an archaeological resource in their own right.[6] In the first
systematic statistical analysis of a vast number of images, Vinnicombe
suggested that they depicted San rituals and religion: "My own intensive
field-work on the eastern borders of Lesotho and the Republic of South
Africa, and subsequent analyses of rock art samples in different regions
of southern Africa, has led me to believe that religion, and there is no
need to qualify or apologize for the term, was one of the prime motives
which prompted the art."[7]

The stage was now set for scholars to connect prehistoric art with
the ethnographic record in South Africa. Vinnicombe's successor, David
Lewis-Williams, would make this task his life's work. A graduate of the
University of Cape Town who had majored in English and geography,
Lewis-Williams's longstanding interest in rock art was the basis of his
becoming an international authority on the subject. He gradually developed a general theory about the production of prehistoric imagery by
shamans under trance, a perspective that came to be known as the "shamanic hypothesis." Following Vinnecombe's lead, Lewis-Williams first
turned to the Bleek and Lloyd archives and subsequently to San ethnographies of Megan Biesele and Lorna Marshall.[8] In an effort to find a
way out of the descriptive impasse that had been reached by rock art
researchers, he emphasized the social context in which the prehistoric
images may have emerged: "I now see two experiences as crucial in determining the path that I took. The first was the uncanny experience of
paging through the numinous notebooks that Wilhelm Bleek and Lucy
Lloyd had compiled in the 1870s; the other was time spent in the northern Kalahari Desert with Megan Biesele, the American anthropologist
and friend of the Ju/'hoansi (!Kung) San."[9]

Lewis-Williams initially focused on several central rituals—girls' pu-
berty rites, boys' first-kill rites, and marriage observances—and interpreted the paintings accordingly. However, over time, larger themes
emerged within his work, all built on key elements of southern San
thought: the crucial role of shamanic dance, the place of the eland as a
potency-filled animal, and the transformation of shamans into partial or
entire animals, represented by therianthropic figures in art.[10]

It is essential to recognize the significance of this ethnographic turn in the study of rock art, given the South African intellectual and political context of the time. Until then, most paintings had been interpreted as either simple hunting magic or art for art's sake, ostensibly simple renditions of life in prehistoric communities. In the early twentieth century, scholars tended to assume that hunting and gathering people had little or no sense of the past or the future, that they painted merely for entertainment or to satisfy some immediate need. This fit both the larger evolutionary assumptions about civilization and the particular racial prejudices of South Africa's apartheid regime. By contrast, Lewis-Williams opened a door to a richer understanding of magic, ritual, and dance, a world of meaning that emerged from out-of-body experiences and vision quests and expressed itself through art. Suddenly almost every site with paintings could reveal new detail in previously unnoticed figures that lurked in the margins. For example, the eland no longer appeared merely as a favorite hunted animal but rather as a polysemic symbol full of power, central to the shamanic transformation, rain making, healing. As Lewis-Williams explained,

> The eland's potency is one of the reasons why it is the most frequently depicted antelope in many parts of southern Africa. It is also the antelope on which the artists lavished the most care: it is painted in shaded polychrome and in variety of postures more frequently than any other antelope. . . . shamans believed they actually became eland. Transformation into an animal seems to have been an essential part of /Xam shamanism.[11]

Reading rock art in terms of historical and contemporary San folklore proved the beginning of a major paradigm shift. In the 1980s, Lewis-Williams, together with his followers and students, increasingly emphasized the figure of the shaman and shamanic performances as the central themes of all South African rock art:

> Ethnographic evidence shows that whatever associations or connotations the art may have had, it was essentially shamanistic. It comprises symbols of the supernatural potency shamans harnessed to enter trance, depictions of hallucinations and activities associated with San shamanism, and metaphors of trance experience. Moreover, the detail of numerous hallucinatory depictions as well as ethnographic data suggest that at least in many instances, the artists were themselves shamans and they were depicting—for whatever reason—their own spiritual experiences and insights.[12]

The interpretation of rock art gradually shifted from efforts to understand a range of rituals as social experiences of a community, commemorating and marking particular events or rites of passage, to expressions of "altered states of consciousness." Shamans had relied on such states as a source of power and "potency," and subsequently illustrated their experience in the numerous rock shelters and caves. Rock art sites thus represented a rich record of shamanic practice, and hence the spiritual legacy of the San peoples.

For the research group led by Lewis-Williams, the story of art became the story of shamans, and the story of shamans became the story of trance. Despite occasional claims that many individuals could have served in this role, there was a distinct shift toward perceiving them as specialists with particular powers, skills, and agency. Nonetheless, the emphasis clearly rested on ritual practice and the experience of altered states:

> We emphasize what we believe to be the most important and overriding feature of shamanism and the one with which . . . [we are] principally concerned—altered states of consciousness. This emphasis is echoed by San words for "shaman." The modern !Kung of the northern Kalahari Desert use *n/um k"au,* which means "owner of the *n/um." N/um* is supernatural potency that . . . likens to electricity: harnessed it is beneficial, uncontrolled it is dangerous.[13]

One could not adequately explain prehistoric art simply through social analysis or ecological model building of subsistence strategies. Art derived directly from the world of human experience.

The shamanic hypothesis found fertile ground far beyond South Africa. In reaction to the hypothesis testing, pattern recognition, and statistical analyses of the "new" processual archaeology of the 1960s through 1980s, some archaeologists began to move away from studying populations to investigating the dynamics of singular households, individuals, and their agency.[14] These "post-processualists" objected to an impersonal view of the past, devoid of any sense of real people. Thus, attention to shamans and ritual performances in the past found an eager audience among a new generation of archaeologists, attuned to more modulated expressions of social power. Yet the shift away from processual approaches was never seamless or unidirectional, and post-processualists were hardly the only potential heirs. The New Archaeology had made a valiant effort to turn archaeology into a science of the past, calling for a standardization of methods, systematic use of terms, rigorous testing, and if not prediction, then at least verifiable proofs. Even if some post-processual archaeologists seriously questioned the status of Western science, for the majority of archaeologists, particularly in North America, scientific tools, methods, and efforts toward objective narratives retained a powerful allure.[15]

In this conceptual milieu, "cognitive archaeology" emerged. The cognitive approach recognized the desire for individual agency, yet attached it to a universal human cognitive apparatus, fusing biology and culture into one.[16] Thus, researchers of rock art added a new strand of evidence to the previously explored ethnographic records and the rock art itself: the science of the mind, in the form of medical, neuropsychological studies of altered states of consciousness.[17] Following this body of research, Lewis-Williams emphasized the importance of "entoptic phenomena"—geometric hallucinations often experienced in early trance states induced by drugs and hyperventilation.[18] He suggested that researchers might interpret abstract patterns found in art, such as zigzags or dots, as evidence of ancient hallucinations:

> Because the human nervous system is a universal, all people, no matter what their cultural background, are likely to "see" these geometric mental images. Consequently, the largely shamanic context of San rock art suggests, simply on a priori grounds, that we should expect to find rock art images that, in some way, depict entoptic phenomena. . . . The input of individuals is clearly evident in what may be seen as a second, or deeper, stage of altered consciousness. During this stage, subjects try to make sense of entoptic phenomena by elaborating them into iconic forms of people, animals, and important or emotionally charged objects. The brain attempts to recognize, or decode, geometric entoptic forms by matching them against a store of experiences, as it does normal sense impressions.[19]

Highly specialized, late-twentieth-century findings of Western science of the brain promised to decode the rock art of long-vanished African hunters and gatherers. According to this interpretation, shaman artists painted culturally specific images, which they experienced during ritual dances. These performances involved rhythm-induced hallucinations that drew on personal experiences yet were processed through a universal neurological system. Amid the interlinked components of this hypothesis—universal human neurology, locally specific culture, and innate artistic expression—biology reigned supreme. If the cognitive approach held true, then one might identify traces of shaman artists in any time period without cultural context, no matter how distant in prehistory, no matter where on the globe.

The shamanic hypothesis rapidly expanded in scope. Although it started modestly in South Africa in the context of San rock art, speculation on shamans soon migrated into other parts of the world where painted caves or rock art had been a long-standing enigma. Writing in 1988, David Lewis-Williams and Thomas Dowson suggested that shamans most likely produced the paintings in French Paleolithic caves as well. This leap into neurological unity left most of history behind. Henri Breuil became the background figure for French prehistoric archaeology with this new interpretation of the painted caves, and his contemporaries such as Comte Bégouën and Salomon Reinach were never mentioned. The Russian or German ethnographers vanished entirely. Eliade, on the other hand, was seen as a founding authority on shamans, which was now understood as a pan-human category.

Although direct ethnographic accounts might be absent for Ice Age Europe (unlike for South Africa), the investigators viewed neuropsychological research as robust enough to overcome this shortcoming. Shamanic hallucinations were ultimately a biological rather than a social fact:

> We develop a model for classifying and addressing Upper Paleolithic signs that avoids simplistic ethnographic analogy . . . and the impasse of induction from internal analysis. This approach derives from current research on San (Bushman) rock art in southern Africa, where the shamanistic nature of the art has turned attention to altered states of consciousness. Southern Africa is a particularly favoured area because shamanistic images can be approached simultaneously from two directions. In the first place, neuropsychological research explains the forms of certain depictions, and, secondly, the meanings of some of these depictions can be established from directly relevant ethnography.[20]

Once the shamanic interpretation of Paleolithic paintings in western Europe had been made, it did not take very long to consider the Neolithic mind as well, and to incorporate the Near East as well as northern Europe. This interpretive move allowed researchers to find the universal human mind, as framed by the shared biological structure of the brain in all places and all times.[21]

However, most stories, no matter how well told, eventually come to a conclusion. By the end of the twentieth century, a growing number of critics raised objections to several issues central to the shamanic hypothesis. Its lack of attention to diversity in many artistic depictions, critics suggested, risked overlooking distinct cultural and historical settings when stressing similarities between patterns.[22] Others noted the problematic nature of "altered states of consciousness," given that what it means to be in a "normal state of consciousness" remains a contentious issue among philosophers and medical professionals. The presumed centrality of trance remained a concern with scholars working among present-day shamans in many parts of the world.[23] Literary scholars and historians pointed out the problematic nature of ethnographies written during the Victorian era, permeated as it was by the profound racism and inequality of colonial settings. Such ethnographies, these scholars noted, relied on extinct languages and historically situated translations.[24] Finally, recent neurological research itself has begun to emphasize the "plasticity" of the human brain, complicating any attempt to simply translate phenomena across time via fixed neurological structures.[25]

In 2007, Thomas Dowson, who had been one of the most eloquent defenders of shamanic origins of art, suggested that it was time to move on. In explaining his change of heart, he cited concerns with art as a Western category and the argument's replication of the Cartesian dualism of humans and nature:

> The narrative of the history of art from Lascaux to the Louvre is then flawed from the outset. The differences between Upper Palaeolithic cave art and any creative tradition since, are not one of the realization of innate potential, but of skilful human beings engaging with their diverse environments in different ways. There is, therefore, no such thing as the origin of art; and shamanism has long since been used to provide a reality to this fiction I have just outlined.[26]

A similar case of an ahistorical transcendental category that awaits archaeologists' critical eye is "religion," the other component of the shamanic package projected into Paleolithic prehistory. Despite its unwavering popularity in nonacademic settings, particularly in North America and Europe, the shamanic hypothesis appears to have run into increasing resistance among scholars as a singular explanatory device for prehistoric art and its origins.

THE BLIND MAN, A WOMAN'S CAP: CONTAMINATED HISTORY AND THE GEOGRAPHY OF IMAGINATION

> On the Kolyma river I met such a shaman, by the name of Konon. Konon is blind. He was often called in to cure the sick and was regarded as a powerful shaman. But he told me himself that he did not have the main emege´t. Instead of a shaman's coat he dressed in a woman's coat sañiya´x, while instead of a drum, he used as a horse for his journey to the subterranean world a willow with three branches. This willow is called jalbi´r. On his head Konon used to wear a woman's cap made of ermine skins.[27]

South African rock art may or may not have been created by ritual specialists while hallucinating. I did not set out to evaluate such claims in this text. Rather, my interest in shamans has always been in their history and geography—their invention as an idea and their global travels on the wings of imagination. The guise under which this category appears has varied significantly over the past several hundred years. It entered popular and scholarly consciousness along Europe's northern and eastern edges, amid multiple encounters with the indigenous people of the Russian empire. When I anchor the circuitous travels of this category in its Siberian origins, I do not mean to argue for purity or a singular meaning of a term. To the contrary, I wish to suggest that the history of shamans reveals both the power and the limitations of conceptual categories in seeking to encompass cultural and temporal diversity. When taken seriously, the concept of the shaman proves a useful guide to the past and the present precisely because of its variability. By examining several episodes of the larger shamanic story, we glimpse ways in which people have imagined alternate ways of being for several centuries. Placing this historical travelogue alongside the shamanic hypothesis, we might then better recognize the changing contours of our own collective imagination.

Rather than trying to argue "against shamans," as I have occasionally found myself accused, I hope to impress a simple point: history matters when considering categories. However remote or unknown the other regions may be, traces of the past can linger in later perceptions. Some fade, others reemerge in accordance with times and interests. Both facts and fictions are social creatures, born into contexts that either nurture or ignore them. Taking a longer view reminds us that any current certainty has unsettling horizons. Beneath the popularity of shamans in the last several decades lies a more varied, patchwork history spanning centuries and continents and involving many characters. Several centuries of ethnographic accounts of Siberian shamans present us with an intriguing range of practitioners. Men and women, people who have changed genders, and shamans of various ages, abilities, and social standing have filled roles in households and in larger communities and performed all kinds of rituals, small and major. Some ingested mushrooms, others did not. Yet the archaeological appropriation of the figure has for the most part imagined a public, male religious leader as the standard representation of the origins of human spirituality, creativity, and knowing.[28]

The category of shaman has achieved remarkable currency in prehistory, but it generally appears in a monochromatic tone, with little hint of color. Largely oblivious to the complexity of history and unaware of the diverse forms recorded over the centuries, archaeologists continue to cast the shaman a stock player. Only rarely do they reflect on the origins of this convenient character, or consider the extent to which our collective history might prove multiple and varied. Shamans appear in archaeological interpretations through the remnants of mysterious traces from the past, emerging dimly behind a cave wall or a rock shelter, or hovering over odd artifacts left behind. They are more often known than explained, and when explained often shrink into universal functions of human biology.[29] In either case, the sense of particularity that history can recall for us—a man's blindness, a woman's hat—vanish into the vague smoothness of a general category. However smooth, this category rarely remains blank; like a mirror, it reflects our assumptions.

Why, then, should those studying prehistory care about all the historical particularities of a concept, especially when in search of a simple analogy? The reason is precisely to recall that analogies are never simple and knowledge never timeless. Rather than settling on one transcendent ancestral figure, we might then again glimpse a far more varied, confusing, and colorful array of possibilities. In the early twentieth century, diffusion enjoyed great popularity as an explanatory model in anthropology and archaeology. The idea that groups of people passed traits along to each other held a particularly powerful grip on the German tradition.[30] While scholars may no longer subscribe to that simple notion of diffusion when it comes to agriculture or sedentism, on a theoretical level we continue to happily practice it. Concepts seem to spread the way domesticated plants or animals used to, moving from region to region, slowly adapting to local conditions. For all that shamans may be even harder than domestic sheep to demonstrate in the archaeological record, they have proven remarkably resilient and persuasive in the fields of ritual theory. Called into existence time and time again by a range of historical realities and imaginaries, their history points at multiple moments of origin. They appeared at the margins of empires in the early days of colonial expansion, rooted in a scholarly fascination with magic, which led to an eager acceptance of tricksters and magicians. Later, shamans stood in for ancient human forms, men and women of indistinguishable gender who became the target of the classificatory impulse of the early scientific expeditions of the eighteenth century.

Scholars in the nineteenth century discovered shamans anew, this time as a general type that was increasingly common in many distant places. Their peculiar ways of life provided a reversed mirror for modern Europe, one that could either confirm the rightfulness of the civilized manners and distinctions in European societies or offer an alternative for its political ills. On the eastern frontier of Russia, political exiles perceived shamans and their communities as living a life of primitive communism, and so embodying a possible alternative to oppressive political and social conventions. By willing their bodies and spirits to change, humans might travel and transform, representing both the past and the potential future. Academics in the twentieth century embraced shamans with unprecedented vigor, adjusting their skills, abilities, roles, and significance with every new context. Under the influence of psychoanalysis, ethnographers even rediscovered the varying gender of Siberian practitioners, while expanding the scope of human nature.

Archaeology was no exception to this general shamanic passion. For the new science of the past, shamans provided a name and form to the greater origin story of religion, amid the abstract spirituality expressed through art. They served as a convenient marker for the larger passage between the worlds of animals and that of modern humans mediated by evolution. As ancestral priests, artists, scientists, they could embody all the elaborate activities that might appear distinctively human, and yet do so in an appropriately simple and universal way. However, when prehistorians projected shamans into antiquity, they left aside the less comfortable details of the ethnographic record. The French Catholic priest-scientists, who appealed to creativity and art as aspects of the human spirit that exceeded material existence, described a more abstract figure of a magician, who was vaguely but certainly assumed to be male. As this template grew more refined, it reintroduced the shaman as a general anthropological type. Expanding on the connection between art and spirituality, it incorporated ethnographic examples far beyond Europe. The template then circled back to materialism in the form of neurobiology and transhistorical claims about the human brain.

Throughout this book I have followed the question of how a concept such as the shaman can move through varied times and places, repeatedly stabilizing only to dissolve again. Rather than seeking to define the shaman in any certain way, I emphasize the more fundamental problem of what we hope such a definition might achieve. Definitions work best, I suggest, when understood heuristically and treated as experimental tools, rather than as pious certainties. The search for historical shamans has proved a far more complicated story than I anticipated. Rather than yielding a stable definition, the preceding chapters combine to offer a

FIGURE C.1. South African rock art, Eastern Cape, 2010.
(Personal photo by the author.)

history of invention *and* reinvention. Instead of a singular category of
"the shaman," we have a set of interrelated historical examples from
which to choose, suggesting that there is no singular convenient or en-
compassing certainty to the form. Moments of discoveries and appro-
priations remain varied and historically situated.

Theories and concepts travel through meandering networks rather
than along straightforward channels. These networks are interesting
precisely because of their unpredictable historical and anthropological
geographies and pathways, and what they reveal about characters lurking in the shadows at the edges of our certainty. Working through historical accounts of Siberian explorations, people, and shamans, I have
come to recognize that travel does not involve merely a simple physical

motion across space, a change in context. Travel along different paths and times requires translation, an adjustment of vocabulary that speaks to new settings and enables understanding of different experiences in changed contexts. At times, it involves getting lost, becoming wayward, and finding a path into new circumstances.

Our current views of shamans are historical constructs just like any other, composed out of disparate pieces of what came before and chosen for a host of reasons, some now long forgotten. In recalling the significance of history, my central concern has never been to argue for a return to a pristine, true, or primordial shaman. Instead, I have sought to emphasize the process of selection and translation, the wide range of habits and practices, and the varied forms of research and investments. In the end, the shaman remains an elusive character, both person and metaphor: imagine a membrane between worlds, partly permeable and partly reflective, a mirror that sometimes permits a murky glimpse of another side.

Notes

INTRODUCTION

1. Klein, Guzmán, and Stanfield-Mazzi 2002, 392.

2. See, for example, Balzer 1990, 1999; Broz 2009; Grant 1995; Halemba 2006; Hamayon 1990, 2003; Humphrey 1996; Ssorin-Chaikov 2003; Vitebsky 2005; Willerslev 2007.

3. Balzer 2001, 140.

4. Lévi-Strauss 1963.

I. DISCOVERIES OF AN IMAGINARY PLACE

1. White 1992, 874.

2. Milne [1926] 1992, 135–36.

3. Diment and Slezkine 1993. Ethnographic and historical writing on Siberia has grown significantly in the last two decades. For rich and nuanced accounts, see Bassin 1999; Burbank, von Hangen, and Remnev 2007; Grant 1995; Kivelson 2006; Ssorin-Chaikov 2003; Sunderland 2004; Willerslev 2007.

4. McKinlay 1976, 161.

5. Kennan 1870, 24.

6. Kennan 1870, 19–20.

7. Cohen 2002, 61. For a broader discussion of issues of human origins (aside from mammoths) that are in the crevices of facts and imagination, see Cohen 1999.

8. Albanov [1917] 2000, 121.

9. Herodotus 2008, book 3, 106. For an analysis and a discussion, see Hartog 1988.

10. See, for example, Appleby 2001; Karp and Wolff 2001; Khodarkovsky 2002; Klug 1987; Wintle 2009.

11. Herodotus 2008, book 4, 45.1.

12. For a perceptive analytical reading of the maps and images from a classical perspective, see Small 2007.

13. At this point, the literature on maps as images and tools of colonial and imperial desires is rich and varied, but some regions have received far greater attention than others. Siberia has not been at the center of these conversations. Two earlier, still significant works are an edited volume by Godlewska and Smith (1994) and a study by Carter (1987). The cultural geographer Denis Cosgrove addressed the topic in his 2001 and 2008 works. For productive, nuanced discussions and historical perspectives, see Akerman 2009; Black 2003; Driver 2001; Edney 1997; Lestringant, Frank 1994. The French edited volume by Blais, Deprest, and Singaravélou (2011) devotes attention to French colonial mapping in North Africa as well as Spanish America and colonial maps of China.

14. Certeau 1984.

15. Small 2007, 326.

16. For wondrous illustrations and graphic detail, see Olaus 1996.

17. Ortelius 1964. For a discussion of Ortelius as a historical figure and the significance of his work, see Koeman 1964; Binding 2003; Broecke 2011.

18. Münster 1561. See also Fudge 2004.

19. For general points, see Cosgrove 2001, Wintle 2009. For a discussion specifically pertaining to Russia, see Mund 2003.

20. See Livingstone 2002.

21. The archaeologist Brian Fagan during a conversation on climate change and human mobility in prehistory on U.S. National Public Radio, February 7, 2008.

22. A well-known discussion of experimental science in a broader historical and political context is provided in Shapin 1985; see also Loewenson 1955.

23. Boyle 1665b, 47.

24. Behringer 2010. Also see the edited volume by Behringer, Lehmann, and Pfister (2005) for specific fascinating case studies of the cultural changes in Europe during the Little Ice Age.

25. Boyle 1665a, 49.

26. For a much more thorough discussion of Boyle's role in the history of experimental science, and his beliefs in alchemy and magic, see Hunter 2009.

27. Collins 1671, 10–11.

28. Collins 1671, 2.

29. Collins 1671, 2.

30. Pioneering work on the subject is Hodgen 1964. Only recently has the subject received more attention in the work of De Angelis 2008; Kenny 1998; Wolff and Cipolloni 2007.

31. Collins 1671, 64–65.

32. Collins 1671, 74–77.

33. See Appleby 2001; Berry and Crummey 1968; Sparwenfeld and Birgegård 2002; Teissier 2011; Strahlenberg [1736] 1970. For a different perspective of early Arabic travelers to regions of present day Kazakhstan, see Ibn Faḍlān 2012.

34. For a history of the search for the naval passage, see Granberg and Peresypkin 2006; Zeeberg 2005.

35. Grimmelshausén [1669] 1962, 437.

36. For a history of Ivan The Terrible and his rule, see Alshits 1988; Filjushkin 2008; Shambarov 2010. For a general history of the time period, see Forsyth 1992; Kappeler 2004; Khodarkovsky 2002; Lieven 2006.

37. Grimmelshausen [1669] 1962, 490, 442. John Parkinson explained in his *Theatrum botanicum: The Theater of plants or An herbal of a large extent* (1640):

Plantanimaleu Borametz Agnus Scythicus. The Scythian Lambe: This strange living plant as it is reported by divers good authors is called by the Natives Borametz quasi agnellus, by others either Planta Ruthenica agno similis, or Agnus Scythecus, or by some Planta animal; it groweth among the Tartares about Samarcanda and the parts thereabouts rising from a seede somewhat bigger and rounder then a Melon seede, with a stalke about five palmes high, without any leafe thereon, but onely bearing a certaine fruit on the toppe, in forme resembling a small lambe, whose coate or rinde is wolly like unto a Lambes skinne, the pulpe or meate underneath which is like the flesh of a Crevise or Lobster, having as it is sayd blood also in it, it hath the forme of an head, hanging downe, and feeding on the grasse round about it, untill it hath consumed it and then dyeth, or else will perish if the grasse round about it bee cut away of purpose: it hath foure legges also hanging downe: the Woolves much affect to feede on them. (chapter 67)

Joannes Jonstonus in 1657 provided an even more colourful description of the same animal/plant:

Scythian Lamb is a Plant that come from a seed like a Kernel, but not so long. The Tartars call it Borometz. It grows like a Lamb about three foot high, and is like a Lamb in his feet, claws, ears, the whole head, except the Horns. For Horns; it hath haire it is singular like a Horn, and a very thin Horn covers it, the inhabitants take it off, and use it for cloathing. It is of a wonderfull sweetnesse; Blood runs forth of the wound. As long as other herbs grow about it, so long it will live. It dies, when these are gone. Wolves desire it, but other beasts that feed on flesh, do not. The Bashfull-Tree draws back, if you but touch the leaves with your hand. They that are not used to it from their Childhood, if they eat it afterwards, it kills them: also it kills those that are used to it; but hurts not those if they continue it. The women of Cambaya· when they would avoid punishment feed of it; and dye without pain. The King of Province fed with this from his young yeares, grew so Venemous, that the very flies that but suckt his skin swelled and died with it" (131).

38. Bynum 1997.

39. For discussions of early travel, the discoveries of the marvelous and distinctions between monstrous animals and humans, see Campbell 1988; Daston and Katharine 1998; Fudge, Gilbert, and Wiseman 1999; Ostovich, Roebuck, and Silcox 2008. India occupies a dominant space in writing on travel and the wondrous; see Nayar 2008, but also earlier writing such as Wittkower 1942.

40. Daston 1998.

41. See historic writing on "the Scythian lamb" (as previously quoted).

42. See Daston and Park 1998; Daston and Kruger 2002; Impey and MacGregor 2001. Findlen 1994 focuses specifically on the rise of natural history museums.

43. Daston 1998, 49.

44. Tryon 1957, 1.

45. Darwin 1991.

46. Darwin, quoted in Browne 1989, 28.

47. Browne 1989, 604.

48. Laufer 1915.

49. For an extended argument, see Livingstone 2003; Naylor 2005.

2. STRANGE LANDSCAPES, FAMILIAR MAGIC

1. "On Experience," quoted in Mirollo 1999, 27.

2. A more detailed discussion will follow, but it is worth noting here that the earliest descriptions of the diplomat and mayor of Amsterdam Nicolaas Witsen were circulating by the beginning of the second decade of the eighteenth century in several languages. See, for example, Witsen 1996; Kirpichnikov and Witsen 1995. Numerous travelers repeated Witsen's descriptions almost verbatim; see, for example, Strahlenberg [1736] 1970; Engel 1777.

3. See Ankarloo and Clark 2002; Daston and Park 1998; Daston and Kruger 2002; Fudge, Gilbert, and Wiseman 1999; Ostovich, Roebuck, and Silcox 2008.

4. For a discussion of the eighteenth-century obsession with shamans in European art, see Flaherty 1992, 1988.

5. For a history of the idea of the golem, see Kieval 1997; from a literary perspective, see Mayer, *Golem: Die literarische Rezeption eines Stoffes* (1975).

6. See Campbell 1999; Dear 2005, 2006; Grafton 2005; Newman and Grafton 2001; Wittkower 1942.

7. Probably the earliest account is the sixteenth-century description by Herberstein (1851); see also Alexeev 1941; Collins 1671; Cross 1997; Ides 1706.

8. For recent writings on magic in Europe from a range of perspectives, see Ankarloo and Clark 2002; Grafton 2005; Kieckhefer 1998; Oldridge 2005.

9. For the earlier time period, see Campbell 1988; Hiatt 2008. For innovative cultural approaches, see Bailey, Diggelmann, and Phillips 2009; Kabir and Williams 2005. For anthropologists, the classic work arguably is Asad 1973.

10. The literature on magic and belief in early modern Europe is rich and worth exploring, with Ginzburg 1982 as one of the classics. For selected insightful writings, see the earlier work of Boas (1933); for more recent work, see, for example, Oldridge 2005; Wilson 2000.

11. See Borgolte and Schneidmüller 2010. Also see the insightful studies in the reader edited by Collins and Taylor 2006; as well as Lieberman 1999; Pagden 2002. On the eve of the official formation of the European Union in 1992, Paul Slack and Joanna Innes edited a special issue of the *Past and Present* "The Cultural and Political Construction of Europe," with studies that broadened the usual geographic range to include Central and Eastern Europe.

12. See Albera and Couroucli 2012.

13. The classic work that shifted the lens to the Mediterranean as a culturally shared space was Braudel 1949. See also Braudel 2001; Fusaro, Heywood, and Omri 2010; and the very accessible Backman 2009. For a different perspective that takes gender as its primary lens, see Beattie and Fenton 2011.

14. Political science may be one discipline that focuses on the present with the aim of offering political analyses and solutions while dealing with categories that have a much longer history. The twentieth century, whether World War II or the Balkan conflict, draws upon such categories as exemplars of eternal ethnic hatreds and clashes. See, for example, Jørgensen and Mouritsen 2008.

15. See the references in note 13.

16. Slack and Innes 1992.

17. For a new encyclopedia of comprehensive and nuanced knowledge about the region and the empire, see Woodhead 2012.

18. Yapp 1992.

19. See Classen 2002.

20. For an excellent overview of a cultural history of the peninsula, see entries in Corfis and Harris-Northall 2007. For a close reading of Spain's foundational myths, particularly with an eye toward the role of women in such stories, see Grieve 2009.

21. The classic works on the topic are Kamen 1985, 2005. For more detailed studies on specific aspects of the relationships in Iberia, see Gutas 2002; Nirenberg 2002; Shell 1991. For a literary analysis of writings about "the Moor," see Burshatin 1985.

22. Ginzburg 1976; Peters 2001.

23. Pietro Alfonsii, *Disciplina clericalis* (1106), quoted in Peters 1978, 63.

24. Kieckhefer 1998. Klingshirn (2003) offers a thorough and convincing analysis of the category "De Magis" in the writing of the seventh century Bishop of Seville, arguing that magic and magicians are too narrow to capture all "unauthorized knowledge" of the time.

25. Bailey 2001.

26. Brown 1972, 132. See also the classic work on the topic of Christianity and magic by Thomas (1971).

27. See the early work by Thorndike (1923), and more recently by Vickers (1984) and Wilson (2000). For a detailed discussion and definitions of the fifteenth-century understanding of magic and cabal and their differences, see Rousse-Lacordaire 2010.

28. Brown and Flores 2007.

29. See Subrahmanyam 1997.

30. For a detailed discussion of the events and their aftermath, see Kamen 2005.

31. See, for example, the multiple volumes edited by Ankarloo and Clark (1999–2002), but especially volume 3 (Jolly 2002).

32. Harrison 2006.

33. For example, Campbell 1999; Latour 1993; Osler 2000; Smith 2009.

34. MacDonald 2002.

35. MacDonald 2002, 655.

36. Bynum 1997, 3.

37. See entries in Impey and MacGregor 2001, and Smith and Findlen 2002.

38. For examples of histories of ethnographic and archaeological collections, see Larson and Petch 2007; Janacek 2008; MacGregor 2001; Parry 1995.

39. Gordin 2000.

40. For an excellent overview of the time period and Rudolf's interest in all things curious, see Marshall 2006, and the recent Czech collection from Purš (2011).

41. Idel 1990.

42. From *Galerie der Sippurim: Präger Sammlung Jüdischer Legenden* (1847), quoted in Kieval 1997, 1. For the full text, see Schmitz 1926.

43. Kieval 1997.

44. Johns 1999.

45. Yates 1975, 26.

46. Dear 2006.

47. See Grafton 2005; Smith 2009.

48. Osler 2000.

49. Schmidt 1998, 275.

3. PEOPLE IN A LAND BEFORE TIME

1. Herberstein [1530] 1851, 47; a microfilm of the original is available and was consulted at the Bavarian State Library in Munich, Germany. A Russian translation provides also a commentary by Russian historians (Herberstein 2008). For a careful reading of Herberstein's writings and their influence on subsequent travel reports, see Poe 2002.

2. Proctor and Schiebinger 2008, 8. See also Tuana and Sullivan 2006.

3. Tuana and Sullivan 2006, p. vii.

4. I make a distinction here between claims about Siberia (Tartary), and Muscovy as an imperial entity. Descriptions of Siberia are far more scant than the writings on Russia during this time period. The historian Marshall Poe (1995) has written extensively on Western sources describing Muscovy and their value in the absence of local/indigenous writing during the early period, especially the sixteenth and seventeenth centuries.

5. "O chelovecekh neznaemykh na vostochnoi strane i o iazycekh roznykh" [About unknown peoples in the East and their various languages]. Titov 1890.

6. Collins 1671, 2.

7. Collins 1671, 72.

8. Bell [1721] 1763, 147.

9. Kennan 1876, 96.

10. A lively discussion has emerged in the last decade in Russian literature about the earliest accounts of Siberia in Russian, rather than in German or Latin, and the degree to which foreign travelers relied on Russian sources to describe Siberia. See, for example, Pokrovskii 2006.

11. For details on Herberstein's life and career, see chapters in Kämpfer and Frätschner (2002) and entries in Pferschy (1989).

12. See the previous note.

13. See the previous entries, and also Poe 2003.

14. Herberstein [1530] 1851, 40.

15. This was a commonly repeated theme among Russian folklore scholars at the end of the nineteenth century and in the early twentieth century, and again among Soviet scholars in the postwar period. The goal may have been a suggestion of common folklore, a pagan and Christian custom that had existed from early times. See, for example, Alexeev 1941; Pypin 1891; Shunkov 1946; Titov 1890.

16. Miller 1750.

17. The theme of monsters has a long history in European narratives of cultural encounters in distant lands, starting with Pliny and Herodotus, and is tied to my earlier discussion of magic and wonder. For a richly illustrated discussion of the issue, see Wittkower 1942, 1977. Paola Ivanov (2002) has found the same discourse on cannibals and monsters as late as the nineteenth century in the writings about the Azande people in central Africa. Neil Whitehead (1995) offers an anthropological reading of historical texts about the Amerindians in the lower Oronoco valley. In his discussion of Ralegh's 1596 description of the Ewaipanoma (similar to Heberstein) as reported to him—"their eyes in their shoulders, and their mouths in the middle of their breasts, and . . . a long train of haire . . . backward between their shoulders" (56)—Whitehead convincingly suggests a wider traffic in marvels and wonders at the time of European travel and early ethnographic writing that should not immediately disqualify the entire text. Herberstein's volume, which was published by the same printing house as Ralegh's *The Discoverie of Guiana,* certainly strengthens the argument.

18. Herberstein [1530] 1851, 41. The same story in an even more embellished form circulated in a 1572 manuscript; see Titov 1890, 1–7.

19. Herberstein [1530] 1851, 49.

20. See Appleby 2001; Hooson 1968; Kivelson 2006. Also see the writings of Willard Sunderland (2004) and the entries in Burbank, von Hagen, and Remnev (2007). For a thorough discussion of early Russian maps, see Kurennaia 2007.

21. For more detail about the rule of Ivan the Terrible, see Filjushkin 2008. An excellent source on views of the ruler in Western Europe is Kappeler 1972; see also Shambarov 2010. For an early biography of Peter the Great, see Bancks 1740. For a historical discussion of the contributions of Peter the Great to geographical knowledge, see Baer [1872] 1969; and for more recent work, see Boeck 2009. For more on Russian expansionism, see Kappeler 2004; Khodarkovsky 2002; Lantzeff 1943; Lantzeff and Pierce 1973.

22. Sunderland 2007.

23. Maciej [1517] 2009. See also Poe 1995.

24. Kivelson 2006, 4.

25. Kivelson 2006. See also Kivelson 1999, 2008. For a Russian account of local mapping, particularly of routes along the rivers that tax collectors traveled, see Andreev 1960.

26. See Akerman 2009; Bassin 2006; Black 2003.

27. Tokarev 1966, 64.

28. See Alexeev 1941.

29. See Wilson 1970. Every library in Russia that I visited had this catalogue heading, with an extensive number of cards under the subject.

30. See, for example, Nozhnikova 2010. When I was working in the Akademgorodok library, I inquired about the fascination with foreign perceptions. The librarian, Tatiana Sergeevna, a helpful and cordial person who became quite frank in our discussions after a few weeks of my presence, was genuinely surprised by my question. "It is such a large subject." She proudly showed me the card catalogue and asked, "Don't you in your country collect everything that others write about you?"

31. Poe 2003; but also all chapters in Whittaker, Davis, and Kasinec 2003.

32. Titov 1890, 164 (translation from Russian by the author). Nerchinsk, mentioned in the text as the furthermost fort in Siberia, is only 400 miles east from Lake Baikal, and still a vast distance from the Pacific Ocean to the "edge of Siberia."

33. Lantzeff 1943; Lantzeff and Pierce 1973; for Russian sources, see Andreev 1960. For a veritable treasure trove of bibliographic references (in French), see Portal 1958.

34. Titov 1890, 78 (translation from Russian by the author).

35. Kivelson 1999; Poe 2003.

36. For a discussion of economic thought and the connection between land ownership, taxes, and social standing in Russia in the sixteenth and seventeenth centuries, see Raskov 2008. For a general discussion of attitudes toward land as a defining feature of a person, see Kivelson 2006.

37. See Khodarkovsky 1997; Slezkine 1994a. For a discussion of "aliens" in a later period, see Slocum 1998; Geraci and Khodarkovsky 2001.

38. For a detailed history of the Siberian fur trade, see Fisher 1943; Gibson 1969; Pavlov 1972, 1974.

39. April 4, 1558, a letter from the Tsar Ivan Vasilevich to Grigorii Stroganov granting financial, judicial, and trade privileges on uninhabited lands along the Kama river, east of Kazan, in Dmytryshyn, Crownhart-Vaughan and Vaughan 1985, 3–6 (italics added). Here, "uninhabited" is *Bezliudnyi*—without people.

40. See Lantzeff 1940; Skrynnikov 1986, 2008. The history of the Stroganov family is well documented; see, for instance, Metternich 2003; Mezenina 2007; Vvedenskii 1962. For a history of Stroganov's relationship to Ermak, see also Lantzeff and Pierce 1973; Gentes 2008.

41. The *iasak*—a tribute/tax system—has a fascinating and convoluted history. See Fisher 1944; Slezkine 1994a; Ssorin-Chaikov 2003; Witzenrath 2007.

42. May 30, 1574, A letter from Tsar Ivan Vasilevich to Iakov and Grigorii Stroganov granting twenty years' exemption from taxes and other obligations for their lands and their settlers on those lands in Takhcheia and along the Tobol river. Dmytryshyn, Crownhart-Vaughan, and Vaughan 1985, 9–12 (italics added).

43. Armstrong 1975; Lincoln 1994; Naumov and Collins 2006.

44. Dmytryshyn, Crownhart-Vaughan, and Vaughan, 1985, 23.

45. Some authors question the centrality of Ermak's historical role. See, for example, Kappeler 2004; Poe 2003.

46. A letter from the Tsar Boris Fedorovich to the Voevoda of Berezovo, Prince Ivan Baratinskii, concerning a legal action against one Stepan Purtiev and the Berezovo Ostiak, Shatrov Luguev, for selling women slaves. Dmytryshyn, Crownhart-Vaughan, and Vaughan 1985, 43.

47. The earliest colonial history of Russian expansion eastward remains a rich topic to be explored, particularly when it comes to gender politics. The majority of writing on Russian colonial interactions with the native peoples focuses on the eighteenth and nineteenth centuries. However, see entries in Breyfogle, Schrader, and Sunderland 2007; Witzenrath 2007.

48. Blackburn 1997, 83.

49. Khodarkovsky 2002, 22.

50. Hellie 1982.

51. Slezkine 1994a.

52. July 9, 1609, Voevoda of Tobolsk to the Voevoda of Tomsk, from Dmytryshyn, Crownhart-Vaughan, and Vaughan 1985, 68.

53. August 13, 1676, instructions from Voevoda of Iakutsk, Andrei Barneshlev, to the Cossack Vasilii Tarasov to collect iasak on the Pezhina river; Dmytryshyn, Crownhart-Vaughan, and Vaughan 1985, 418–28.

54. Slezkine 1994b.

55. A mountain region to the east of Lake Baikal, which under the Soviet regime was an autonomous region with Nerchinsk as the capitol.

56. Instructions from the Voevoda of Iakutsk, Dmitrii Frantsbekov, to the explorer Erofii Khabarov, regarding his expedition to the Land of Daurs, 1650; Dmytryshyn, Crownhart-Vaughan, and Vaughan 1985, 237–40.

57. Dmytryshyn, Crownhart-Vaughan, and Vaughan 1985, 237–40.

58. Lantzeff 1943, 96.

59. Slezkine 1994b, 170. For an illuminating case study from the eighteenth century, particularly the statistics on natives taken prisoner or killed, see Hartley 2008.

60. Tugolukov 1985, 42.

61. Tugolukov 1985, 42.

62. See Collins 2004.

63. Sunderland 1996, 807.

64. For a discussion of the relationship between the colonizers and the indigenous populations of Siberia, particularly in terms of early resistance and later subversion, see Werth 2000b.

65. Herberstein [1530] 1851, 224.

66. Purchas was an armchair traveler who had never visited Russia, but he was a prolific writer on the topic. See Purchas 1613, 4:365.

67. Olearius 1662, 3:133.

68. In Alexeev 1941, 123 (translated from Russian by the author).

69. Fletcher 1643, 75.

70. Fletcher 1643, 77.

71. Schimmel 2011. A more specific account related to the crossroad of Russian Orthodoxy, Tatar Muslim practices, and idolaters of the newly conquered regions is found in the work of Paul W. Werth. For a discussion related to "shaitan," see Werth 2000a.

72. Alexeev 1941, 295 (translated from Russian by the author). Alexeev also provides an extended discussion of the source and its possible origin (2006, 268–76).

73. Shirokogorov 1966; Tugolukov 1985, 42.

74. Titov 1890, 171–72.

4. THE INVENTION OF SIBERIAN ETHNOLOGY

1. Perry 1716, 78.
2. Catherine II, 1772, 54–55.
3. Vermeulen and Roldan 1995.
4. Vermeulen and Roldan, 39.
5. Perry 1716, 260.
6. See Lindenau 1983.
7. Perry 1716, 81.
8. Perry 1716, 64.
9. Perry 1716, 226.
10. Bell [1721] 1763, 33.
11. For an insightful discussion of chronological discrepancies between Russian and European history, see Raeff 1982.
12. For a discussion of the obsession with "size," see Sunderland 2007.
13. Custine [1839] 2001, viii.
14. Lomonosov 1794. See also Bassin 1991b.
15. Jones 2005.
16. Bassin 2006.
17. Tatishchev 1950.
18. Bassin 2006, 47.
19. Perry 1716, 92.
20. Bruyn 1737, 96.
21. Boeck 2009; Khodarkovsky 2002; Lantzeff 1943.
22. Ides 1706, 2; for an annotated edition in German, see Ides, Hundt, and Brand 1999.
23. Davis, Kasinec, and Whittaker 2003.
24. Ides 1706, 90.
25. Anemone 2000.
26. The "Ostiaks" of Ides' text—literally the "Easterners," a combination of a German and a Russian word—are now known to be the Khanty and the Mansi (or Vogul) people, two distinct indigenous groups living historically between the Urals and the river Ob, now the Khanty-Mansi Autonomous Region. Yet even the term Khanty is not a matter of self-identification but a word taken to identify a particular group of people with the earlier Siberian Khanat, a Muslim entity to the south and southeast of the Ural Mountains. For details on this particular indigenous group, see Jordan 2003. Similarly the "Tungus" in Ides's account, and in many that followed his descriptions, were the Eveny, the Evenki, and the Tungus treated as one people.

27. Ides 1706, 35–36.
28. Ides 1706, 29–30.

29. Ides 1706, 30–31.
30. Moréri 1701, 385.
31. Moloney 2005.
32. Ides 1706, 40. This particular "prince" appeared in numerous ethnographies, suggesting repetition and/or plagiarism of the encounter even by those who never visited Siberia.
33. Ides 1706, 41.
34. Schiebinger 2004a.
35. See Kan 2008 for a discussion of the development of the Museum of Anthropology.
36. Gordin 2000.
37. Gordin 2000.
38. Winter 1953.
39. Messerschmidt [1724] 1962–77; Heesen 1997, 2000.
40. Heesen 2000, 381.
41. Foucault 1970, 132–34.
42. Daston 1998.
43. Strahlenberg [1736] 1970, viii.
44. For an excellent broader discussion of new scientific institutions in this time period in Western Europe, see McClellan 1985.
45. Messerschmidt [1724] 1964, 2:34–35.
46. For a broader discussion of scientific studies of the northern regions, see Sörlin 2000.
47. Messerschmidt [1724] 1964, 2:88 (translation from German by the author).
48. Heesen 2002.
49. Messerschmidt [1724] 1968, 4:70–71.
50. Messerschmidt [1724] 1968, 4:65–68.
51. Messerschmidt [1724] 1968, 4:67.
52. Messerschmidt [1724] 1968, 4:67–68 (translation from German by the author).
53. Messerschmidt [1724] 1962, 1:59–60 (translation from German by the author).
54. Messerschmidt remarked upon the major differences between the indigenous languages, most of them mutually unintelligible. Noting words related to religious practice, among others, he recorded terms for god, the devil, and a priest. In "Láak-Ostiak," the word *Nopp* was god, *Loóse* was the devil, and *Ömepp* was mother, but no word for a priest or any religious leader seemed to have existed. The "Taugý-Samoied" had words for god—*Nmóa*, the devil—*Ngà*, a shaman—*Phéndjir*, and for mother—*Niáa*. In the Tungus language, his records note god as *Sewocký*, and *Tschawacký* was an idol or a schaitan; and near Irkutsk, a group he labels as Limpte Tungus note *Shamán* as a magician, an idol was *Sebhócky*, and ritual drum as *Unctogón*. Messerschmidt [1724] 1964, 2:67–121 (translation from German by the author).
55. See the earlier discussion of the Arabic origin of the word, identifying the devil in the Koran.
56. Bell [1721] 1763, 178.

57. Aalto 1996.
58. Messerschmidt [1724] 1962, 1:12–13.
59. Müller 1764, 59.
60. Müller 1732, 343–44.
61. Miller 2006, 721 (translation from Russian by the author).
62. Müller 1764, 4.
63. Miller 2009, 223.
64. Miller 2009, 214–15 (translation from Russian by the author).
65. Müller 1764, 17.
66. Müller 1764, 9. In a discussion of the sacred and devotional, we suddenly come across a rather unexpected claim about "filthy people." The text continues, and it becomes clear that the reference is not a metaphor for pollution but a statement of judgment. The persistent comments about filth among the natives is a common feature that united the diverse ethnic groups in the scientific documents of the day; even in a discussion of religion, it was added as a relevant side note. What was Müller suggesting when he pointed out that the Ostiaks have a religious specialist, a "Schaumann," and in the same sentence noted that they were "a very filthy people"?

Reading the eighteenth-century ethnographies of Siberia, one is struck by the frequency of claims of ever-present grime, and unwashed natives who seem to know nothing of personal hygiene. This was obviously a statement about difference of another order and should not be taken at face value. The eighteenth century in general—Russia in particular, and rural areas even more so—were not known for an abundance of running water or a great concern with cleanliness. Foul smell seemed to have bothered travelers to Russia as much as dirt, and they discussed at length the unpleasant feature of homes throughout the provinces of allowing smoke from the stove to enter the house so as to prevent heat loss. The visiting Germans complained about olfactory insults about as much as about the "filthy natives." Needless to say, "fragrance" may have been a feature of the court society but was certainly not common in the towns and even less so in rural areas. The detailed lists of traveling supplies for scientific expeditions did not include boxes of soap, and the personal journals with regular entries about health concerns, maladies, and treatments mentioned at most monthly bathing, if baths were available at all.

Elias (1978) has pointed out that manners related to bodily functions historically reflect social relationships more than they do health concerns, expressing respect, similarity, or difference in social standing. That is, washing oneself before receiving a visitor is a sign of deference, not a desire for cleanliness per se. The native "filth" would suggest a perceived civilizational difference and a lack of respect for the visiting foreigners than actual perceptible dirt. The ladder of civilization, as the German scientists saw it, led through a bath, and both the Russians and the Siberian natives were on a rung far below by European sensibilities.

67. Gmelin 1767, 32–33 (translation from French by the author).
68. Gmelin 1767, 39–40.
69. Krasheninnikov 1764, 1949.

70. For an extended discussion of the role that Russia played in the discussions of French eighteenth-century philosophers and Voltaire in particular, see Gorbatov 2006; Karp and Wolff 2001; Zaborov 2011. For broader discussions of anthropology and the eighteenth century, see Duchet 1978; Wolff and Cipolloni 2007.

71. Montesquieu and Davidson 1923.

72. Catherine II 1971, 216–17.

73. Catherine II 1772, 20.

74. Catherine II 1772, 70. The empress Catherine II published an "anonymous" response "*Antidote, ou Examen du mauvais livre superbement imprimé, intitulé Voyage en Sibérie*" (1770; English version 1772) to Abbé Chappe d'Auteroche (1768). The French astronomer had traveled to Siberia in 1761 to witness the transit of Venus. However, by his own account the travel was ordered by the French king and was an indirect attack on Catherine II and Russia as an aspiring new empire. Catherine II had her response published in no less than ten European languages, speaking to all the European royal courts but even more to the philosophers and scientists of the day. Equipped with detailed knowledge of the land, she chose to defend Russia as a European empire by explaining Siberia to her audiences. For a detailed discussion of the incident, see Levitt 1998.

5. SEX, GENDER, AND ENCOUNTERS WITH SPIRITS

1. Steller [1743] 2003, 203.

2. The literature on gender and shamans, particularly in modern day indigenous and postcolonial contexts, is at this point robust; see particularly Bacigalupo 2007; Glass-Coffin 1998; Laugrand 2008; Levin and Potapov 2005; Van Deusen 2001; also Marcos 2010. For a more controversial treatment of the "feminine" in shamanism, see Tedlock 2005.

3. For a useful overview of a broad range of approaches to shamanism, see entries in Harvey 2003, or Harvey and Wallis 2007.

4. See Czaplicka 1999; Krasheninnikov 1764, 1949; Steller [1743] 2003; Jochelson 1926, 1928, 1933.

5. Herberstein [1530] 1851, 41. See Figure 3.1. "Slata Baba" was claimed to have been a carved female idol of the Iuhra (Yugra or later Khanty and Mantsi) people who lived to the east of the River Ob.

6. Dahlmann 2006; Seniukova 2001.

7. Georgi 1780, 290.

8. Bogoras 1904b, 449.

9. Bogoras 1910, 182.

10. For a discussion of the narrative and explanatory work that gender does, especially in colonial contexts, see McClintock 1995; and Stoler 1995.

11. Bell [1721] 1763, 178–80.

12. Steller [1743] 2003, 209.

13. Krasheninnikov 1764, 206.

14. Krasheninnikov 1764, 230.

15. Bruyn 1759, 9.

16. Schiebinger 1990, 391.

17. Hughes 2002, 72.

18. For a discussion of Russian missionary work in Siberia, see Geraci and Khodarkovsky 2001; Znamenski 1999. A Western Siberian mission among the Khanty/Nenets people is described in Templing 2004. For an account of English missions, see Bawden 1985; Teissier 2011.

19. Steller [1743] 2003, 156.

20. Steller [1743] 2003, 227–28.

21. McClintock 1995.

22. Krasheninnikov 1764, 223.

23. Details of the journey are described in Black 1986; Büsching 1995; Miller 1996.

24. Hintzsche, Wieland, and Nickol 1996.

25. Tokarev 1966.

26. Kennan 1870, 214.

27. Kennan 1876, 107 (italics mine).

28. Steller [1743] 2003, viii.

29. Steller [1743] 2003, 218.

30. Steller [1743] 2003, 188.

31. Golder and Steller 1968, 46.

32. Steller [1743] 2003, 188.

33. Morgan 1997, 169.

34. The passionate interest in plant and human sexuality was common at the time, as Linneaus's classification system based on the sexual parts of a plant indicates. See Darwin [1789] 1991, and for more detail and numerous examples, see Schiebinger 2004b.

35. Steller [1743] 2003, 218–19.

36. The reference to Quakers as equal to sodomites is part of a larger discussion of private life and sexuality in early modern Protestant Germany. See Harrington 1995; Ozment 1999; Wiesner 2010. German Pietist and mainstream Lutherans were violently opposed to women's participation in leadership roles; this opposition and the attitudes toward sexuality in the Brethren movement produced a substantial amount of writing, including exhortations about beliefs and practices as well as complete fabrications about sexual orgies that were thought to be a regular aspect of Brethren religious services.

37. Steller [1743] 2003, 219.

38. Miller 2009, 151 (translation from Russian by the author).

39. Argentov 1857, 120 (translation from Russian by the author).

40. Krasheninnikov 1764, 216.

41. Morgan 1997.

42. Peucker 2006, 32.

43. In addition to the above reference, see also Fogleman 2003; Wiesner 2010.

44. See Hintzsche and Nickol 1996; Winter 1953.

45. Steller [1743] 2003, 222–23.

46. Steller [1743] 2003, 225–26.

47. See, for example, McClintock 1995; Levine 2004.
48. Steller [1743] 2003, 213.
49. Georgi 1780, 285–88.
50. Ortner 1974.
51. Gmelin 1770.
52. Steller [1743] 2003, 195.
53. Georgi 1780, 270, 296.

6. CHANGED MEN AND CHANGED WOMEN

1. Asad 1993, 13.
2. See, for example, Balzer 1996b. Gender issues have been far more prominent in the North American context; see Donald and Hurcombe 2000; Hollimon 2001. In reference to prehistory and rock art, Kelley Hays-Gilpin (2004) has offered a nuanced analysis.
3. Jochelson 1908, 13.
4. See Distant 1877; Tylor 1870.
5. Sewall 1882, 275.
6. See Foucault 1978; but also Stoler 1995.
7. Dixon 1908, 1.
8. Dixon 1908, 1–2.
9. While we find ethnographic accounts of the indigenous peoples in the New World from the early nineteenth century, the actual word "shaman" (or permutations on its spelling) does not appear until the end of the century. Ritual, religions, healing practices are all carefully noted, commented on, and described, but they enter the same framework as the Siberian shamans remarkably late. Abraham Rees in the first American edition of the *Universal Dictionary of Arts, Sciences, and Literature* identified a "schaman" as a solely Siberian phenomenon: "a denomination given in Siberia to the Samanes or Samaneans of India. Both the people and the priests of the Schaman religion are at present illiterate. . . . as to the word Schaman, Loubiere says it signifies a 'man living in the woods,' or a hermit, which is applicable enough to one who is addicted to life in contemplation." (Rees 1805, vol. 33: 145)

The earliest references to shamans in North America traveled through the Arctic North in search of connections between the Eskimo and the Siberian Chukchi. In 1866, Markham addressed the links between Siberian populations and the "Arctic Highlanders," and in the process described the Angekok of the Eskimo: "They believe in supernatural beings presiding over the elements, who are the familiar spirits of their *angekoks* or magicians; and the *angekoks* can converse with them, and thus prophesy the propects of the hunting season. . . . This *angekok* superstition is exactly the same as the Shamanism of the Siberian tribes" (Markham 1866, 133–34). Initially, all connections between North American and Siberian shamans were made very carefully, using distinct native terms, placing "shamans" unequivocally into their natural habitat in Asia. By the 1880s, such custom of translation and geographic specificity was abandoned and shamans went global. A Navajo shaman in a 1888 publication appeared without any qualification (Matthews 1888).

10. Bachofen [1861] 1969.

11. McLennan [1865] 1970.

12. Morgan [1877] 1964; Engels [1884] 1942.

13. Crawley 1895.

14. Pike 1869.

15. See Applebaum 2003; Gentes 2008. For a discussion of gender dynamic in such conditions, see Schrader 2007.

16. For a political history of the time period and Narodnaya Volya specifically, see Jochelson 1922; Monakhov 2009; Naimark 1983; Weeks 2011.

17. For a more detailed discussion of the lives and work of Bogoras, Shternberg, and Jochelson, see Grant 1999; Kan 2009; Krupnik 1996.

18. Bogoras 1904a, 1.

19. Russian exile has a long, varied, and colorful history (see the publications cited in note 15). At the end of the nineteenth century, it took the form of banishment into as distant a region as possible, with no possibility of return for at least ten years. Families of the exiles accompanied the prisoners, and they settled into assigned areas of Siberia. They were occasionally given permission to travel within a limited range inside the region.

20. Grant 1999, liv.

21. Bogoras 1904a, 35–36.

22. Bogoras 1904b, 624.

23. Bogoras 1904b, 547.

24. See Broido 1977; Hillyar and McDermid 2000; and Figner's autobiography (1991).

25. Dina Brodsky conducted interviews with women, took their photographs and measurements, and subsequently used the data in her own doctoral work on physical anthropology of the native peoples of Siberia at the University of Zurich where she obtained a medical degree in 1906.

26. For a classic, see Fernea 1969; Handler 2004.

27. The Special Collections at the American Museum of Natural History contain a selection of the personal correspondence and a substantial collection of black and white images. I thank all the staff of the photographic archives for their assistance with this aspect of my research during my 2009 visit.

28. For a discussion of the context of the images, see Kendall 1997; Krupnik and Fitzhugh 2001.

29. Shternberg 1933, xiii.

30. Zelenin 1999 (translation from Russian by the author).

31. Jochelson 1910, 61.

32. Jochelson 1908, 53.

33. Tylor 1870, 370.

34. For an extended and far more nuanced discussion, see entries in Francfort and Hamayon 2001; Hamayon 1990, 2006; Willerslev 2007.

35. Jochelson 1908, 53.

36. See Mikhailovskii and Wardrop 1895.

37. Erika Bourguignon (2004) offers an interesting perspective, suggesting that trance possession and hysteria may be an expression of powerlessness, acting out wishes denied.

38. Zelenin 1999, 731.

39. Bogoras 1901, 91.

40. For a history of the concept among northern peoples of Greenland and the role of Danish scientists in the early twentieth century, see Dick 1995.

41. Novakovsky 1924. A Polish geographer active at Clark University in Massachusetts, Novakovsky was one of the founders of American ecology (see Kingsland 2005).

42. Czaplicka remains a little known, tragic figure in the history of anthropology. A rare female student, she earned her degree at Oxford University under the same advisor as her fellow Polish anthropologist Bronislaw Malinowski. Despite extensive fieldwork experience, publication of her thesis, and support of her mentors, she failed to secure a steady academic position, and she committed suicide in 1921. See Czaplicka 1914, 1999; Collins and Urry 1997.

43. Czaplicka 1914, 197.

44. Loeb 1929, 61.

45. Layard 1930, 542.

46. Shterneberg 1936, 353 (translation from Russian by the author).

47. Layard 1930, 543.

48. Balzer 1990, 1995.

49. For a history of Russian ethnography in the twentieth century, see Hirsch 2005.

50. Dimitry Konstantinovich Zelenin was a prominent Russian linguist and ethnographer whose main interest, and subsequent contribution was a linguistic map of ethnic groups in postrevolutionary Russia.

51. Zelenin 1999, 790.

52. Zelenin 1999, 710.

53. A good beginning of this new, changed (mine)field is Gray, Vakhtin, and Schweitzer 2003. Ethnographies of the former Soviet Union are now plentiful, rich in ethnographic detail, and theoretically sophisticated. A selection would include Broz 2009; Grant 1995; Halemba 2006; Humphrey 2002; Pelkmans 2009; Rethmann 2001; Ssorin-Chaikov 2003; Willerslev 2007.

7. FRENCH CONNECTIONS AND THE SPIRITS OF PREHISTORY

Note: Parts of this chapter appeared in Silvia Tomášková, "From a Materialist Ethic to the Spirit of Prehistory," in *What Matters? Ethnographics of Value in a Not So Secular Age,* edited by Courtney Bender and Ann Taves, 34–60 (New York: Columbia University Press, 2012).

1. Jochelson 1924, 136.

2. See Steller, Schérer, and Miller 1774, 6. Nevertheless, Mircea Eliade as recently as 1961 put forth an interesting—if unsubstantiated—claim that Scythian shamans influenced Greek epics: "think of the important part played by the shamans in the creation of the epic songs of central Asia and of the influences that Scythian shamans have probably had on some Greek epics" (170).

3. The literature on the origins of art and religion is at this point substantial and takes a wide range of theoretical approaches from evolutionary biological to interpretive and social. See Bahn 2010; Bradley 2009; Conkey et al., 1997;

Cooke and Turner 1999; Lewis-Williams 2005; Murray and Schloss 2009; Whitley 2009.

4. For a history of French archaeology in its cultural and historical context, see Blanckaert 1996; Blanckaert, Porret, and Brandli 2006; Coye 1998; Hurel and Coye 2011; Ducros, Ducros, and Blanckaert 2000; Hurel 2007; Richard 2008.

5. For a nuanced case study of the scientific and Catholic French milieu in the early years of anthropology, see Defrance-Jublot 2005.

6. See Hecht 2003; Hurel and Noël 2011; Paul 1979.

7. Each and every one of these groups—scientists, amateurs, politicians, and religious practitioners—played an equally important role. They complemented each other through their battles, controversies, and collaborations, and their contribution cannot be overstated.

8. Cyon 1910, 265 (translated from French by the author). Elie de Cyon (Ilya Fadeyevich Tsion), a Russian doctor who settled in France in 1877 converted to Catholicism in 1908, was one of many vocal critics of prehistorians and natural scientists.

9. These two men stand for a larger group of passionate archaeologists, and are representative rather than necessarily leaders or sole defenders of the faith, as will be apparent from the discussion. For a sense of the basis of the "father of prehistory" appellation, see Broderick 1963.

10. See Chazan 1995.

11. A fascinating debate about the meaning of "anatomically modern" can be found in Corbey and Roebroeks 2001; Ingold 1995; Shea 2011.

12. For a biography, see Arnould 2011; Hurel 2011.

13. I do not suggest that the field of French prehistory in the twentieth century was singularly formed and shaped by Henri Breuil. Rather, he is the embodiment and representative of a group of prehistorians of the period. Count Henri Bégouën, Louis Capitan, Emile Carthaillac, and Edouard Piette were all members of his cohort and played an important role in the formation of the discipline and Breuil's views. A similarly important role was played Breuil's mentor, Abbé Jean Bouyssonie, and the controversial priest archaeologist Teilhard de Chardin. For a detailed discussion of these relationships, see Hurel 2011.

14. However, see Grimoult 2003, 2008.

15. Coon 1964, 647–48.

16. Broderick 1963, 141.

17. Blanckaert 2001; Coye 1998; Trigger 2006.

18. Sommer (2006) illustrates the battle between the Catholic establishment and the evolutionists in the French press over the image of the Neanderthal from La Chapelle-aux-Saints.

19. The topic of amateurs and experts in late nineteenth-century science and in archeology in particular is a rich one and has been explored only very recently. See, for example, Defrance-Jublot 2005. In the North American context, the topic has been addressed by Snead 2001.

20. See Grimoult 2003; Hecht 2003; McMillan 1985; Zeldin 1970.

21. Mortillet 1849.

22. The complex history of French archaeology and the nineteenth-century intellectual milieu in which it emerged is discussed largely in French (see note 4) and is unfortunately largely unavailable in English translation.

23. Reinach 1899, 75; for an analysis of de Mortillet's role in publishing his political views through anthropological journals, see Richard 1989, 234.

24. Grayson 1983; Richard 2008.

25. Richard 1992.

26. Hecht 2003, 64.

27. Lefèvre 1879, 459.

28. For a detailed discussion of the issue, see Coye 1998, 136–49.

29. The fierce opposition to prehistoric burials was not unique to the late nineteenth century nor restricted to de Mortillet's companions. In the late 1980s, a lively debate erupted over the possibility of Neanderthal burials, again linking the capacity of empathy in burial rites to spiritual awareness as a sign of "modern behavior." The discussion still continues in major anthropological journals, only now it is the Neanderthals who are claimed to be devoid of religious sentiment unlike the "behaviorally modern" Paleolithic humans. See Belfer-Cohen and Hovers 1992; Gargett et al., 1989; Kooijmans et al., 1989; Mithen 2001; Shea 2011.

30. Richards 2002.

31. Clémance Royer, quoted in Fraisse 1985, 127 (translation from French by the author).

32. Mortillet 1910, 311 (translation from French by the author).

33. Mortillet 1910, 336 (translation from French by the author).

34. Boule 1922, 154.

35. Bisson and Bolduc 1994.

36. For a detailed discussion of the history of acceptance of prehistoric art in France, see Moro-Abadía and González Morales 2003, 2005, 2007.

37. With an appeal to the power of scientific fact, Cartailhac wrote: "It was absolutely new and strange. We must bow to the reality of a fact. . . . The world is now without mystery . . . our science, like others, wrote a story that will never be complete, but whose value increases continuously" (1902, 350).

38. See Breuil 1909; Capitan and Peyrony 1910; Hurel 2003.

39. Guébhard 1911. For a wider context and more detail on the struggle over the leadership and staffing of the Institute, see Hurel 2011.

40. Arnaud Hurel (2011) provides a nuanced and detailed discussion of the issue.

41. The term "history of the human spirit" *Geistesgeschichte,* popular in early-twentieth-century art history, has been used since Herder (1774), especially by influential German thinkers, to suggest undercurrents of ideas, an intellectual history that is different from natural history. See Kleinbauer 1970, Kelley 1996.

42. Salomon Reinach came from a family of prominent French Jewish intellectuals, and was the brother of archaeologist Theodore and politician Joseph, the latter best known for his active role in the defense of Alfred Dreyfus.

43. Reinach 1903.

44. Damme 2010.

45. Reinach 1903, 265 (italics in the original; translation from French by the author).

46. For a history of the use of the concept, see Bahn and Vertut 1997; Conkey 2000; White 2003.

47. Reinach 1903, 264 (italics in the original; translation from French by the author).

48. Reinach 1905. The vigorous response that disputed his claim suggests the degree to which this was a controversial issue at the time. See Gaffarel and Deonna 1913; Leuba 1913; Luquet 1913.

49. Here I draw on two excellent studies: Marchand 1996, 2009.

50. Reinach 1903, 259 (translation from French by the author).

51. Reinach 1903, 261 (translation from French by the author).

52. I conducted a thorough search of English, French, and German journal articles, and noted a break from the use of the term "Hyperborean" around World War II.

53. Bégouën 1920, 303 (translation from French by the author).

54. Bégouën 1920, 310 (translation from French by the author).

55. Bégouën 1927, 407 (italics in the original; translation from French by the author).

56. For a much more detailed and critical analysis of Eliade's work and his background, see Dubuisson 2006; Ellwood 1999; Rennie 2007.

57. Starting in 1946, Eliade produced a large volume of literature reviews from multiple languages, culminating in his most famous and most cited work translated into numerous languages in 1951 (see Eliade 1946, 1951, 1987).

58. For critical approaches from a range of disciplines to the study and variation of "shamanism" around the world, see Flaherty 1992; Kehoe 2000; Sidky 2008, 2010; Thomas and Humphrey 1994. For an excellent historical overview, see Znamenski 2007.

CONCLUSION

1. For a comprehensive history of South African rock art research, see Deacon 2007; Lewis-Williams 2002; Mitchell and Smith 2009.

2. See Bahn 2010; Conkey 1987; Halverson et al., 1987; Robb 1998. For a nuanced example of a structuralist approach in French Paleolithic art, see Leroi-Gourhan 1982.

3. The archive consists of some 12,000 handwritten pages of narratives and personal histories containing folklore, grammar, and ethnographic information collected in the 1870s by the German linguist Wilhelm Heinrich Immanuel Bleek, his sister-in-law Lucy Lloyd, and later his daughter Dorothea Bleek. For a detailed discussion of the archives, see Bank 2006; Deacon and Dowson 1996; Hewitt 1986; Wessels 2010. For an artistic interpretation of the same materials, see Skotnes 2007.

4. Weintroub 2009.

5. Deacon 1988.

6. Mitchell and Benjamin 2009; Vinnicombe 1976.

7. Vinnicombe 1976, 194.

8. Biesele 1978, 1993; Marshall 1976, 1999.

9. Lewis-Williams 2002, 51.

10. Lewis-Williams 2002, 70.

11. Lewis-Williams 1987, 171.

12. Lewis-Williams 2002, 107.

13. Lewis-Williams and Dowson 1988, 204.

14. See, for example, Gero and Conkey 1991; Hodder 1986.

15. An example of one of the early questioning statements about theory and Western science can be found in Shanks 1987.

16. See Renfrew 1994, 3–13.

17. Whitley 1992.

18. Lewis-Williams 2002, 137–40.

19. Lewis-Williams 2002, 141–42.

20. Lewis-Williams and Dowson 1988, 201.

21. Lewis-Williams 2005.

22. See entries in Francfort and Hamayon 2001; Klein et al. 2002; Lorblanchet and Bahn 2006; Nordbladh 2005.

23. See the publications cited in the previous note, and Hamayon 1993.

24. See Bank 2006; Penn 2005; Solomon 2011; Wessels 2009, 2010.

25. For an extended recent discussion of the history of the issue from the perspective of medical anthropology and a detailed bibliography, see Rees 2010.

26. Dowson 2007, 51.

27. Jochelson 1924, 185–186.

28. For exceptions, see Hays-Gilpin 2004; Kehoe 2000.

29. See Clottes and Lewis-Williams 1998; Lewis-Williams 2004; Whitley 2009; Winkelman 2010.

30. Gingrich 2005.

Bibliographic Note

Literature for the topic explored in this book spreads across many countries, languages, centuries, and theoretical divides. Reading in multiple languages is not common these days when English has become the *lingua franca*. Yet there are many sources that have not been translated for reasons of small audience, or temporal and geographic distance from current centers of knowledge. Rather than list individual sources, I will offer more general research suggestions based on my experience in this project that may be useful to readers.

Research in Russia has become much easier in the post-soviet period but it still is bureaucratically complicated and much depends on personal relations that subsequently open doors. While working in Novosibirsk, a number of academics derisively talked about western "academic tourists", scholars who visit to conduct research but do not show "true commitment" to the region or the people. Many archives have resources that are not officially recorded and one may stumble upon them only with the assistance of a kind librarian. Repeated visits, vast amounts of patience, and determination, in addition to human kindness and understanding, are the key research methods necessary for work in most parts of Russia. On the other hand publication of many older materials, or new treatment of older topics, has blossomed and Russian texts are now widely available in libraries in the west. The availability of Russian materials is unprecedented, even if most of it is not translated into other languages. Furthermore, numerous centers of Slavic research, linguistic as well as historical, have been infused with new energy (and finances) particularly in Germany, France and Holland. Consequently most historical topics can be researched from various angles in Russian, German, French, and Dutch opening an interesting interpretive window. Munich, and the Bavarian State Library, the Göttingen Library, the Max Planck Institute in Halle, the Scott's Polar Institute at Cambridge University, the University of Aberdeen, and Groningen University all have vibrant

Siberian research divisions with active scholars in history, ethnology and current issues facing the indigenous people of the region.

The Bibliothèque National in France and the Göttinger Digitalisierungszentrums in Germany have been on the forefront of libraries in digitizing efforts. At this point a vast number of historical texts in a range of languages are available in digital form, even if knowledge of French and German is necessary to navigate the pages of the digital archives. French research on the history of the social sciences and the humanities is a lively field with an impressive line of publications. Yet similarly to the Russian literature, most of it remains untranslated. At least a reading knowledge of French is necessary to discover the vibrant debates in the social sciences. History of archaeology is a very lively field in France. The Museum of Archaeology in Saint-Germain-en-Lay has a library and archives that are truly unparalleled. I spent weeks reading the personal correspondence of major, and many minor or unknown, figures of early twentieth century archaeology. None of these materials are available in a digital form and similarly to the Russian research, only a personal visit reveals all there is.

In the United States some of the personal correspondence of the Russian members of the Jesup North Pacific Expedition—Bogoras, Jochelson, and Shternberg—is held in the Special Collections at the American Museum of Natural History. Depending on the correspondent, some of it is in Russian, in German and in English; some of it is heart breaking.

The references from the text are numerous and I hope prove useful as a resource in their multilingual composition. I consequently opted not to translate each title, if it is not available in English. The only modification I made is that the Russian titles are transcribed/transliterated rather than written in Cyrillic.

References

Aalto, Pentti
    1996   "John Bell's (1691–1780) Notes from His Journeys in Siberia and Mongolia." *International Journal of Central Asian Studies* 1: 1–15.

Akerman, James R., ed.
    2009   *The Imperial Map: Cartography and the Mastery of Empire.* Chicago: University of Chicago Press.

Albanov, Valerian
    (1917) 2000   *In the Land of White Death: An Epic Story of Survival in the Siberian Arctic.* New York: Random House.

Albera, Dionigi, and Maria Couroucli, eds.
    2012   *Sharing Sacred Spaces in the Mediterranean: Christians, Muslims, and Jews at Shrines and Sanctuaries.* Bloomington: Indiana University Press.

Alexeev, Mikhail Pavlovich
    2006   *Sibir v Izvestiiakh Zapadno-Evropeiskikh Puteshestvennikov i Pisatelei XIII–XVII Vv: Vvedenie, Teksty i Kommentarii.* Novosibirsk, Russia: Nauka.

Alshits, Daniil N.
    1988   *Nachalo Samoderzhaviia v Rossii: Gosudarstvo Ivana Groznogo.* Leningrad: Nauka.

Andreev, Alexander I.
    1960   *Ocherki po Istochnikovedeniu Sibiri.* Leningrad: Akademia Nauk.

Anemone, Anthony
    2000   "The Monsters of Peter the Great: The Culture of the St. Petersburg Kunstkamera in the Eighteenth Century." *Slavic and East European Journal* 44 (4): 583–602.

Ankarloo, Bengt, and Stuart Clark, eds.
    1999–2002   *Witchcraft and Magic in Europe.* 6 vols. Philadelphia: University of Pennsylvania Press.

2002   *Witchcraft and Magic in Europe: The Middle Ages*. Vol. 2 of *Witchcraft and Magic in Europe*. Philadelphia: University of Pennsylvania Press.

Applebaum, Anne

2003   *Gulag: A History*. New York: Doubleday.

Appleby, John H.

2001   "Mapping Russia: Farquharson, Delisle and the Royal Society." *Notes and Records of the Royal Society of London* 55 (2): 191–204.

Argentov, Andrei

1857   *Description of the Arrival of Nikolaev Chaunskii*. Zapiski Vostochno-Sibirskovo Otdela Imperatorskovo Russkovo Geograficheskovo Obshchestva. Vol. 3. St. Petersburg: IRGO.

Armstrong, Terence E., ed.

1975   *Yermak's Campaign in Siberia: A Selection of Documents*. London: Hakluyt Society.

Arnould, Jacques

2011   *L'Abbé Breuil: Le pape de la préhistoire*. Tours, France: CLD.

Asad, Talal

1973   *Anthropology and the Colonial Encounter*. Atlantic Highlands, N.J.: Humanities Press.

1993   *Genealogies of Religion: Discipline and Reasons of Power in Christianity and Islam*. Baltimore: Johns Hopkins University Press.

Bachofen, Johann Jakob

(1861) 1969   *Das Mutterrecht: Eine Untersuchung über die Gynaikokratie der alten Welt nach ihrer religiösen und rechtlichen Natur*. Brussels: Culture et civilisation.

Bacigalupo, Ana Mariella

2007   *Shamans of the Foye Tree: Gender, Power, and Healing among Chilean Mapuche*. Austin: University of Texas Press.

Backman, Clifford R.

2009   *The Worlds of Medieval Europe*. New York: Oxford University Press.

Baer, Karl Ernst von

(1872) 1969   *Peter's des Großen Verdienste um die Erweiterung der geographischen Kenntnisse*. Osnaburg, Germany: Biblio Verlag.

Bahn, Paul G.

2010   *Prehistoric Rock Art: Polemics and Progress*. New York: Cambridge University Press.

Bahn, Paul G., and Jean Vertut

1997   *Journey through the Ice Age*. Berkeley: University of California Press.

Bailey, Lisa Kaaren, Lindsay Diggelmann, and Kim M. Phillips, eds.

2009   *Old Worlds, New Worlds: European Cultural Encounters, C.1000–C.1750*. Turnhout, Belgium: Brepols.

Bailey, Michael D.

2001   "From Sorcery to Witchcraft: Clerical Conceptions of Magic in the Later Middle Ages." *Speculum* 76 (4): 960–90.

Balzer, Marjorie Mandelstam, ed.

1990   *Shamanism: Soviet Studies of Traditional Religion in Siberia and Central Asia*. Armonk, N.Y.: M. E. Sharpe.

1995   *Culture Incarnate: Native Anthropology from Russia.* Armonk, N.Y.: M. E. Sharpe.

Balzer, Marjorie Mandelstam

1996a   "Flights of the Sacred: Symbolism and Theory in Siberian Shamanism." *American Anthropologist* 98 (2): 305–18.

1996b   "Sacred Genders in Siberia." In *Gender Reversals and Gender Cultures: Anthropological and Historical Perspectives,* edited by Sabrina P. Ramet, 164–82. London: Routledge.

1999   *The Tenacity of Ethnicity: A Siberian Saga in Global Perspective.* Princeton, N.J.: Princeton University Press.

2001   "Healing Failed Faith? Contemporary Siberian Shamanism." *Anthropology and Humanism* 26 (2): 134–49.

Bancks, John

1740   *A New History of the Life and Reign of the Czar Peter the Great.* London: J. Hodges.

Bank, Andrew

2006   *Bushmen in a Victorian World: The Remarkable Story of the Bleek-Lloyd Collection of Bushmen Folklore.* Cape Town, South Africa: Double Storey.

Bassin, Mark

1991a   "Inventing Siberia: Visions of the Russian East in the Early Nineteenth Century." *American Historical Review* 96 (3): 763–94.

1991b   "Russia between Europe and Asia: The Ideological Construction of Geographical Space." *Slavic Review* 50 (1): 1–17.

1999   *Imperial Visions: Nationalist Imagination and Geographical Expansion in the Russian Far East, 1840–1865.* New York: Cambridge University Press.

2006   "Geographies of Imperial Identity." In *Imperial Russia, 1689–1917.* Vol. 2 of *The Cambridge History of Russia.* Edited by Dominic Lieven, 45–63. Cambridge: Cambridge University Press.

Bawden, Charles R.

1985   *Shamans, Lamas, and Evangelicals: the English Missionaries in Siberia.* London: Routledge & Kegan Paul.

Beattie, Cordelia, and Kirsten A. Fenton, eds.

2011   *Intersections of Gender, Religion and Ethnicity in the Middle Ages.* Basingstoke, U.K.: Palgrave Macmillan.

Bégouën, Henri (compte de)

1920   "Un dessin relevé dans la caverne des Trois-Frères, à Montesquieu-Avants (Ariège)." *Comptes Rendus des Séances de l'Académie des Inscriptions et Belles-Lettres,* 4: 303–10.

1927   *L'art préhistorique est d'origine magique.* Coimbra, Portugal: Coimbra Editora.

Behringer, Wolfgang

2010   *A Cultural History of Climate.* Cambridge: Polity.

Behringer, Wolfgang, Hartmut Lehmann, and Christian Pfister, eds.

2005   *Kulturelle Konsequenzen der "Kleinen Eiszeit."* Göttingen, Germany: Vandenhoeck & Ruprecht.

Belfer-Cohen, Anna, and Erella Hovers
  1992 "In the Eye of the Beholder: Mousterian and Natufian Burials in the Levant." *Current Anthropology* 33 (4): 463–71.
Bell, John
  (1721) 1763 *Travels from St. Petersburg in Russia, to Diverse Parts of Asia.* Glasgow: Robert and Andrew Foulis.
Berry, Lloyd E., and Robert O. Crummey, eds.
  1968 *Rude and Barbarous Kingdom. Russia in the Accounts of Sixteenth-Century English Voyagers.* Madison: University of Wisconsin Press.
Biesele, Megan
  1978 *The Bushmen: San Hunters and Herders of Southern Africa.* Cape Town, South Africa: Human & Rousseau.
  1993 *Women Like Meat: The Folklore and Foraging Ideology of the Kalahari Ju/'Hoan.* Bloomington, Ind.: Witwatersrand University Press.
Binding, Paul
  2003 *Imagined Corners: Exploring the World's First Atlas.* London: Headline.
Bisson, Michael, and Pierre Bolduc
  1994 "Previously Undescribed Figurines from the Grimaldi Caves." *Current Anthropology* 35:458–68.
Black, Jeremy
  2003 *Visions of the World: A History of Maps.* London: Mitchell Beazley.
Black, Joseph L.
  1986 *G.-F. Müller and the Imperial Russian Academy.* Kingston, Ont.: McGill-Queen's University Press.
Blackburn, Robin
  1997 "The Old World Background to European Colonial Slavery." *William and Mary Quarterly* 54 (1): 65–102.
Blais, Hélène, Florence Deprest, and Pierre Singaravélou, eds.
  2011 *Territoires impériaux: Une histoire spatiale du fait colonial.* Paris: Publications de la Sorbonne.
Blanckaert, Claude
  1996 *Le terrain des sciences humaines: Instructions et enquêtes, XVIIIE–XXE siècle.* Paris: L'Harmattan.
Blanckaert, Claude, ed.
  2001 *Les politiques de l'anthropologie: Discours et pratiques en France (1860–1940).* Paris: L'Harmattan.
Blanckaert, Claude, Michel Porret, and Fabrice Brandli, eds.
  2006 *L'encyclopédie méthodique (1782–1832): Des lumières au positivisme.* Geneva: Droz.
Boas, George
  1933 *The Happy Beast in French Thought of the Seventeenth Century: Contributions to the History of Primitivism.* Baltimore: Johns Hopkins University Press.
Boeck, Brian J.
  2009 *Imperial Boundaries: Cossack Communities and Empire-Building in the Age of Peter the Great.* Cambridge: Cambridge University Press.

Bogoras, Waldemar

1901 "The Chukchi of Northeastern Asia." *American Anthropologist* 3 (1): 80–108.

1904a *The Chukchee: Material Culture.* Vol. 1 of *Memoirs of the American Museum of Natural History.* Leiden, Germany/New York: E. J. Brill/G. E. Stechert.

1904b *The Chukchee: Religion.* Vol. 2 of *Memoirs of the American Museum of Natural History.* Leiden, Germany/New York: E. J. Brill/G. E. Stechert.

1910 *Chukchee Mythology.* Vol. 8 of *Memoirs of the American Museum of Natural History.* Leiden, Germany/New York: E. J. Brill/G. E. Stechert.

Borgolte, Michael, and Bernd Schneidmüller, eds.

2010 *Hybride Kulturen im Mittelalterlichen Europa.* Vorträge und Workshops einer internationalen frühlingsschule. Berlin: Akademie Verlag.

Boule, Marcellin

1922 "L'oeuvre anthropologique du Prince Albert Ier de Monaco et les récents progrès de la paléontologie humaine en France." *Journal of the Royal Anthropological Institute of Great Britain and Ireland* 52: 151–63.

Bourguignon, Erika

2004 "Suffering and Healing, Subordination and Power: Women and Possession Trance." *Ethos* 32 (4): 557–74.

Boyle, Robert

1665a "A further Account of Mr. Boyle's Experimental History of Cold." *Philosophical Transactions of the Royal Society* 1 (3): 47–52.

1665b *New experiments and observations touching cold, or, an experimental history of cold begun: to which are added an examen of antiperistasis and an examen of Mr. Hobs's doctrine about cold.* Edited by Christopher Merret. London: John Crook.

Bradley, Richard

2009 *Image and Audience: Rethinking Prehistoric Art.* Oxford: Oxford University Press.

Braudel, Fernand

1949 *La Méditerranée et le monde méditerranéen a l'époque de Philippe II.* Paris: Colin.

2001 *Memory and the Mediterranean.* New York: Knopf.

Breuil, Henri

1909 L'évolution d'arts quartenaire. *Revue Archéologique* 13: 378–411.

Breyfogle, Nicholas B., Abby Schrader, and Willard Sunderland, eds.

2007 *Peopling the Russian Periphery: Borderland Colonization in Eurasian History.* New York: Routledge.

Broderick, Alan Houghton

1963 *Father of Prehistory: The Abbé Henri Breuil: His Life and Times.* New York: Morrow.

Broecke, van den Marcel

2011 *Ortelius Atlas Maps: An Illustrated Guide.* Houten, the Netherlands: Hes & de Graaf.

Broido, Vera
  1977. *Apostles into Terrorists: Women and the Revolutionary Movement in the Russia of Alexander II.* New York: Viking Press.
Brown, Peter, ed.
  1972 *Religion and Society in the Age of St. Augustine.* New York: Harper and Brown.
Brown, Stephen F., and Juan Carlos Flores, eds.
  2007 *Historical Dictionary of Medieval Philosophy and Theology.* Lanham, Md.: Scarecrow Press.
Browne, Janet
  1989 "Botany for Gentlemen: Erasmus Darwin and 'The Loves of the Plants'," *Isis* 80 (4): 592–621.
Broz, Ludek
  2009 "Substance, Conduct, and History: 'Altaian-ness' in the Twenty-First Century." *Sibirica* 8 (2): 43–70.
Bruyn, Cornelius de
  1737 *Voyages de Corneille le Brun par la Moscovie, en Perse, et aux Indes Orientales.* London.
  1759 *A new and more correct translation than has hitherto appeared in public of Mr. Cornelius Le Brun's travels into Moscovy, Persia, and divers parts of the East-Indies.* London: J. Warcus.
Burbank, Jane, Mark von Hagen, and Alex Remnev, eds.
  2007 *Russian Empire: Space, People, Power, 1700–1930.* Bloomington: Indiana University Press.
Burshatin, Israel
  1985 "The Moor in the Text: Metaphor, Emblem, and Silence." *Critical Inquiry* 12 (1): 98–118.
Büsching, Anton Friedrich
  1995 *Geographie, Geschichte und Bildungswesen in Rußland und Deutschland im 18. Jahrhundert: Briefwechsel Anton Friedrich Büsching—Gerhard Friedrich Müller, 1751 bis 1783.* Edited by Peter Hoffmann. Berlin: Akademie Verlag.
Bynum, Caroline
  1997 "Wonder." *American Historical Review* 102 (1): 1–26.
Campbell, Mary B.
  1988 *The Witness and the Other World: Exotic European Travel Writing, 400–1600.* Ithaca, N.Y.: Cornell University Press.
  1999 *Wonder and Science: Imagining Worlds in Early Modern Europe.* Ithaca, N.Y.: Cornell University Press.
Capitan, Louis, Henri Breuil, and Denis Peyrony
  1910 *La caverne de Font-de-Gaume aux Eyzies (Dordogne).* Monaco: S.A.S. le Prince Albert Ier de Monaco.
Cartailhac, Emile
  1902 "La grotte d'Altamira, Espagne: Mea culpa d'un sceptique." *L'Anthropologie* 13: 348–54.
Carter, Paul
  1987 *The Road to Botany Bay: An Essay in Special History.* Boston: Faber & Faber.

Catherine II, Empress of Russia
   1772   *The antidote. Or an enquiry into the merits of a book, entitled A jour-
       ney into Siberia, made in MDCCLXI . . . and published by the abbé
       Chappe d'Auteroche, by a lover of truth.* London: S. Leacroft.
   1971   *Documents of Catherine the Great: The Correspondence with Vol-
       taire and the Instruction of 1767 in the English Text of 1768.* New
       York: Russell & Russell.
Certeau, Michel de
   1984   *The Practice of Everyday Life.* Berkeley: University of California
       Press.
Chazan, Michael
   1995   "Conceptions of Time and the Development of Paleolithic Chronol-
       ogy." *American Anthropologist* 97 (3): 457–67.
Classen, Albrecht, ed.
   2002   *Meeting the Foreign in the Middle Age.* New York: Routledge.
Clottes, Jean, and J. David Lewis-Williams
   1998   *The Shamans of Prehistory: Trance and Magic in the Painted Caves.*
       New York: Abrams.
Cohen, Claudine
   1999   *L'homme des origines: Savoirs et fictions en préhistoire.* Paris: Édi-
       tions du seuil.
   2002   *The Fate of the Mammoth: Fossils, Myths, and History.* Chicago:
       Chicago University Press.
Collins, David N.
   2004   "Sexual Imbalance in Frontier Communities: Siberia and New France."
       Sibirica 4 (2): 162–85.
Collins, David N., and James Urry
   1997   "A Flame Too Intense for Mortal Body to Support." *Anthropology
       Today* 13 (6): 18–20.
Collins, James B., and Karen L. Taylor, eds.
   2006   *Early Modern Europe: Issues and Interpretations.* Malden, Mass.:
       Blackwell.
Collins, Samuel
   1671   *The Present State of Russia: In a Letter to a Friend at London.* Lon-
       don: J. Winter for D. Newman.
Conkey, Margaret W.
   1987.   "New Approaches in the Search for Meaning: A Review of Research
       in 'Paleolithic art.'" *Journal of Field Archaeology* 14 (4): 413–30.
   2000   "A Spanish Resistance? Social Archaeology and the Study of Paleo-
       lithic Art in Spain." *Journal of Anthropological Research* 56 (1):
       77–93.
Conkey, Margaret W., Olga Soffer, Debora Stratman, and Nina Jablonski,
eds.
   1997   *Beyond Art: Pleistocene Image and Symbol.* San Francisco, Calif.:
       California Academy of Sciences.
Cooke, Brett, and Frederick Turner, eds.
   1999   *Biopoetics: Evolutionary Explorations in the Arts.* Lexington, Ky.:
       ICUS.

Coon, Carleton
  1964   Review of *Father of Prehistory, the Abbé Henri Breuil: His Life and Times,* by Alan Houghton Broderick." *American Anthropologist* 66: 647–48.
Corbey, Raymond, and Wil Roebroeks, eds.
  2001   *Studying Human Origins: Disciplinary History and Epistemology.* Amsterdam: Amsterdam University Press.
Corfis, Ivy A., and Ray Harris-Northall, eds.
  2007.   *Medieval Iberia: Changing Societies and Cultures in Contact and Transition.* Rochester, N.Y.: Tamesis.
Cosgrove, Denis
  2001   *Apollo's Eye: A Cartographic Genealogy of the Earth in the Western Imagination.* Baltimore: Johns Hopkins University Press.
  2008   *Geography and Vision: Seeing, Imagining and Representing the World.* New York: I. B. Tauris.
Coye, Noël
  1998   *La préhistoire en parole et en acte méthodes et enjeux de la pratique archéologique, 1830–1950.* Paris: L'Harmattan.
Crawley, Ernest Alfred
  1895   "Sexual Taboo: A Study in the Relations of the Sexes." *Journal of the Anthropological Institute of Great Britain and Ireland* 24: 116–25.
Cross, Anthony Glenn
  1997   *By the Banks of the Neva: Chapters from the Lives and Careers of the British in Eighteenth-Century Russia.* New York: Cambridge University Press.
Custine, Astolphe (marquis de)
  (1839) 2001   *Journey for Our Time: The Journals of the Marquis de Custine.* London: Phoenix Press.
Cyon, Elie de
  1910   *Dieu et science: Essais de psychologie des sciences.* Paris: F. Alcan.
Czaplicka, Marie Antoinette
  1914   *Aboriginal Siberia, a Study in Social Anthropology.* Oxford, Clarendon Press.
  1999   *The Collected Works of M. A. Czaplicka.* Edited by David N. Collins. Richmond, Surrey, U.K.: Curzon Press.
Dahlmann, Dittmar
  2006   *Die Kenntnis Rußlands im Deutschsprachigen Raum im 18. Jahrhundert: Wissenschaft und Publizistik Über Das Russische Reich.* Göttingen, Germany: V&R Unipress.
Damme, Wilfried van
  2010   "Ernst Grosse and the 'Ethnological Method' in Art Theory." *Philosophy and Literature* 34 (2): 302–12.
Darwin, Erasmus
  (1789) 1991   *The Loves of the Plants.* Oxford: Woodstock Books.
Daston, Lorraine
  1998   "What Can Be a Scientific Object? Reflections on Monsters and Meteors." *Bulletin of the American Academy of Arts and Sciences* 52 (2): 35–50.

Daston, Lorraine, and Katharine Park
  1998 *Wonders and the Order of Nature, 1150–1750.* New York: Zone Books.
Daston, Lorraine, and Klaus Kruger
  2002 *Curiositas: Welterfahrung und Ästhetische Neugierde in Mittelalter und Früher Neuzeit.* Göttingen, Germany: Wallstein.
Davis, Robert H., Edward Kasinec, and Cynthia H. Whittaker, eds.
  2003 *Russia Engages the World, 1453–1825.* Cambridge, Mass.: Harvard University Press.
Deacon, Jeanette
  1988 "The Power of a Place in Understanding Southern San Rock Engravings." *World Archaeology* 20 (1): 129–40.
Deacon, Jeanette, ed.
  2007 *African Rock Art: The Future of Africa's Past.* Proceedings of the 2004 International Rock Art Conference. Nairobi: Trust for African Rock Art.
Deacon, Jeanette, and Thomas Dowson
  1996 *Voices from the Past: /Xam Bushmen and the Bleek and Lloyd Collection.* Johannesburg: Witwatersrand University Press.
De Angelis, Simone
  2008 *Anthropologien: Genese und Konfiguration einer "Wissenschaft vom Menschen" in der Frühen Neuzeit.* Berlin: Walter De Gruyter.
Dear, Peter
  2005 "What Is the History of Science the History of? Early Modern Roots of the Ideology of Modern Science." *Isis* 96: 390–406.
  2006 *The Intelligibility of Nature: How Science Makes Sense of the World.* Chicago: University of Chicago Press.
Defrance-Jublot, Fanny
  2005 "Question laïque et légitimité scientifique en préhistoire, la revue 'L'Anthropologie' (1890–1910)." *Vingtième Siècle: Revue d'Histoire* 87: 73–84.
Dick, Lyle
  1995 "'Pibloktoq' (Arctic Hysteria): A Construction of European-Inuit Relations?" *Arctic Anthropology* 32 (2): 1–42.
Diment, Galya, and Yuri Slezkine
  1993 *Between Heaven and Hell: The Myth of Siberia in Russian Culture.* New York: St. Martin's Press.
Distant, W. L.
  1877 On the Term "Religion" as Used in Anthropology. *Journal of the Anthropological Institute of Great Britain and Ireland* 6: 60–70.
Dixon, Roland
  1908 "Some Aspects of the American Shaman." *Journal of American Folklore* 21 (80): 1–12.
Dmytryshyn, Basil, E. A. P. Crownhart-Vaughan, and Thomas Vaughan, eds.
  1985 *Russia's Conquest of Siberia, 1558–1700: A Documentary Record.* Portland, Ore.: Western Imprints, Press of the Oregon Historical Society.

Donald, Moira, and Linda Hurcombe, eds.

2000 *Representations of Gender from Prehistory to the Present.* New York: St. Martin's Press.

Dowson, Thomas

2007 "Debating Shamanism in Southern African Rock Art: Time to Move on . . ." *South African Archaeological Bulletin* 62 (185): 49–61.

Driver, Felix

2001 *Geography Militant: Cultures of Exploration and Empire.* Malden, Mass.: Blackwell.

Dubuisson, Daniel

2006 *Twentieth Century Mythologies: Dumézil, Levi-Strauss, Eliade.* London: Equinox.

Duchet, Michèle

1978 *Anthropologie et histoire au Siècle des Lumières: Buffon, Voltaire, Rousseau, Helvétius, Diderot.* Paris: Flammarion.

Ducros, Albert, Jaqueline Ducros, and Claude Blanckaert

2000 *L'homme préhistorique: Images et imaginaire.* Paris: L'Harmattan.

Duret, Claude

1605 *Histoire admirable des plantes et herbes esmerueillables & miraculeuses en nature: Mesmes d'aucunes qui sont vrays Zoophytes, ou Plant-animales, Plantes & Animaux tout ensemble, pour auoir vie vegetatiue sensitiue & animale : auec leurs portraicts au naturel, selon les histoires, descriptions, voyages, & nauigations des anciens & modernes. . . .* Paris: Nicolas Buon.

Edney, Matthew H.

1997 *Mapping an Empire: The Geographical Construction of British India, 1765–1843.* Chicago: University of Chicago Press.

Eliade, Mircea

1946 "Le problème du chamanisme." *Revue de l'Histoire des Religions* 131 (1–3): 5–52.

1951 *Le chamanisme et les techniques archaïques de l'extase.* Paris: Payot.

1961 "Recent Works on Shamanism: A Review Article." *History of Religions* 1 (1): 152–86.

1987 *The Sacred and the Profane: The Nature of Religion.* San Diego, Calif.: Harcourt Brace Jovanovich.

Ellwood, Robert S.

1999 *The Politics of Myth: A Study of C. G. Jung, Mircea Eliade, and Joseph Campbell.* Albany: State University of New York Press.

Engel, Samuel

1777 *Geographische und kritische Nachrichten und Anmerkungen über die Lage der nördlichen Gegenden von Asien und America.* Mitau, Latvia: Jacob Friedrich Hinz.

Engels, Friedrich

(1884) 1942 *The Origin of the Family, Private Property and the State: In the Light of the Researches of Lewis H. Morgan.* New York: International Publishers.

Fernea, Elizabeth Warnock
1969 *Guests of the Sheik: An Ethnography of an Iraqi Village.* Garden City, N.Y.: Anchor books.

Figner, Vera
1991 *Memoirs of a Revolutionist.* DeKalb, Ill.: Northern Illinois University Press.

Filjushkin, Alexander
2008. *Ivan the Terrible: A Military History.* London: Frontline Books.

Findlen, Paula
1994 *Possessing Nature: Museums, Collecting, and Scientific Culture in Early Modern Italy.* Berkeley: University of California Press.

Fisher, Raymond H.
1943 *The Russian Fur Trade, 1550–1700.* Berkeley: University of California Press.
1944. "Mangazeia: A Boomtown of Seventeenth Century Siberia." *Russian Review* 4 (1): 89–99.

Flaherty, Gloria
1988 "The Performing Artist as the Shaman of Higher Civilization." *Modern Language Notes* 103 (3): 519–39.
1992 *Shamanism and the Eighteenth Century.* Princeton, N.J.: Princeton University Press.

Fletcher, Giles
1643 *The History of Russia, or, the Government of the Emperour of Muscovia: with the manners & fashions of the People of that Countrey.* London.

Fogleman, Aaron Spencer
2003 "Jesus Is Female: The Moravian Challenge in the German Communities of British North America." *William and Mary Quarterly* 60 (2): 295–332.

Forsyth, James
1992 *A History of the Peoples of Siberia: Russia's North Asian Colony, 1581–1990.* New York: Cambridge University Press.

Foucault, Michel
1970 *The Order of Things: An Archaeology of the Human Sciences.* Trans. Alan Sheridan. New York: Vintage.
1978 *An Introduction.* Vol. 1 of *The History of Sexuality.* Trans. Robert Hurley. New York: Pantheon Books.

Fraisse, Geneviève
1985 *Clémence Royer, philosophe et femme de sciences.* Paris: La découverte.

Francfort, Henri Paul, and Roberte N. Hamayon, eds.
2001 *The Concept of Shamanism: Uses and Abuses.* Budapest: Akadémiai Kiadó.

Fudge, Erica
2004 *Renaissance Beasts: of Animals, Humans, and Other Wonderful Creatures.* Urbana: University of Illinois Press.

Fudge, Erica, Ruth Gilbert, and Susan Wiseman, eds.
  1999 *At the Borders of the Human: Beasts, Bodies and Natural Philosophy in the Early Modern Period.* New York: St. Martin's Press.
Fusaro, Maria, Colin Heywood, and Mohamed Salah Omri, eds.
  2010 *Trade and Cultural Exchange in the Early Modern Mediterranean: Braudel's Maritime Legacy.* New York: Tauris Academic Studies.
Gaffarel, Jacques, and Waldemar Deonna
  1913 "Un précurseur de la théorie actuelle des origines de l'art." *Isis* 1 (4): 655–60.
Gargett, Robert H., Harvey M. Bricker, Geoffrey Clark, John Lindly, Catherine Farizy, Claude Masset, David W. Frayer, et al.
  1989 "Grave Shortcomings: The Evidence for Neanderthal Burial." *Current Anthropology* 30 (2): 157–90.
Gentes, Andrew Armand
  2008 *Exile to Siberia, 1590–1822.* New York: Palgrave Macmillan.
Georgi, Johann Gottlieb
  1780 *Russia: Or, a Compleat Historical Account of all the Nations Which Compose that Empire.* London: J. Nichols, T. Cadell, H. Payne, and N. Conant.
Geraci, Robert P., and Michael Khodarkovsky, eds.
  2001 *Of Religion and Empire: Missions, Conversion, and Tolerance in Tsarist Russia.* Ithaca, N.Y.: Cornell University Press.
Gero, Joan, and Margaret W. Conkey, eds.
  1991 *Engendering Archaeology.* Oxford: Blackwell.
Gibson, James
  1969 *Feeding the Russian Fur Trade: Provisionment of the Okhotsk Seaboard and the Kamchatka Peninsula, 1639–1856.* Madison: University of Wisconsin Press.
Gingrich, Andre
  2005 "The German-Speaking Countries," In *One Discipline, Four Ways: British, German, French, and American Anthropology.* Edited by Frederik Barth, 61–156. Chicago: University of Chicago Press.
Ginzburg, Carlo
  1976. "High and Low: The Theme of Forbidden Knowledge in Sixteenth and Seventeenth Centuries." *Past and Present* 73: 28–41.
  1982 *The Cheese and the Worms: The Cosmos of a Sixteenth-Century Miller.* New York: Penguin Books.
Glass-Coffin, Bonnie
  1998 *The Gift of Life: Female Spirituality and Healing in Northern Peru.* Albuquerque: University of New Mexico Press.
Gmelin, Johann Georg
  1767 *Voyage en Sibérie, contenant la description des meurs & usages des peuples de ce pays, le cours des rivières considérables, la situation de chaines de montagnes, des grandes forêts, des mines, avec tous les faits d'histoire naturelle qui sont particuliers à cette contrée.* Paris: Desaint.

Gmelin, Samuel Gottlieb
1770   *Samuel Georg Gmelins reise durch Rußland zur Untersuchung der drey Naturreiche.* Edited by Peter Simon Pallas. St. Petersburg: Gedruckt bey der Kayserl, Academie der Wissenschaften.

Godlewska, Anne, and Neil Smith, eds.
1994   *Geography and Empire.* Oxford: Blackwell.

Golder, F. Alfred, and Georg Wilhelm Steller
1968   *Bering's Voyages: An Account of the Efforts of the Russians to Determine the Relation of Asia and America.* New York: Octagon Books.

Gorbatov, Inna
2006   *Catherine the Great and the French Philosophers of the Enlightenment: Montesquieu, Voltaire, Rousseau, Diderot and Grimm.* Palo Alto, Calif.: Academica Press.

Gordin, Michael D
2000   "The Importation of Being Earnest: The Early St. Petersburg Academy of Sciences." *Isis* 91 (1): 1–31.
2005   *Magic and Technology in Early Modern Europe.* Washington, D.C.: Smithsonian Institution Libraries.

Granberg, Aleksandr Grigorievich, and Vsevolod Iliich Peresypkin, eds.
2006   *Problemy Severnogo Morskogo Puti.* Moscow: Nauka.

Grant, Bruce
1995   *In the Soviet House of Culture: A Century of Perestroikas.* Princeton, N.J.: Princeton University Press.
1999   "Foreword." In Lev I. Shternberg, *The Social Organization of the Gilyak.* Edited and trans. by Bruce Grant, xxiii–lvi. Seattle: University of Washington Press.

Gray, Patty A., Nikolai Vakhtin, and Peter Schweitzer
2003   "Who Owns Siberian Ethnography? A Critical Assessment of a Reinternationalized Field." *Sibirica* 3 (2): 194–216.

Grayson, Donald
1983   *The Establishment of Human Antiquity.* New York: Academic Press.

Grieve, Patricia E.
2009   *The Eve of Spain: Myths of Origins in the History of Christian, Muslim, and Jewish Conflict.* Baltimore: Johns Hopkins University Press.

Grimmelshausen, Hans Jakob Christoph von
(1669) 1962   *The Adventurous Simplicissimus, Being the Description of the Life of a Strange Vagabond Named Melchior Sternfels Von Fuchshaim.* Trans. A. T. S. Goodrick. Lincoln: University of Nebraska Press.

Grimoult, Cédric
2003   *Histoire de l'historie des sciences: Historiographie de l'évolutionnisme dans le monde francophone.* Geneva: Droz.
2008   *Sciences et politique en France: De Descartes a la révolte des chercheurs.* Paris: Elipses.

Guébhard, Adrien
  1911 "L'église et la préhistoire." *La Grande Revue* 44 (July 25): 353–62.
Gutas, Dimitri
  2002 "Certainty, Doubt, Error: Comments on the Epistemological Founda-
         tions of Medieval Arabic Science." *Early Science and Medicine* 7 (3):
         276–89.
Halemba, Agnieszka
  2006 *The Telengits of Southern Siberia: Landscape, Religion and Knowl-
         edge in Motion.* London: Routledge.
Halverson, John, Levon H. Abrahamian, Kathleen M. Adams, Paul G. Bahn,
Lydia T. Black, Whitney Davis, and Robin Frost
  1987 "Art for Art's Sake in the Paleolithic." *Current Anthropology* 28 (1):
         63–89.
Hamayon, Roberte N.
  1990 *La chasse a l'âme: Esquisse d'une théorie du chamanisme sibérien.*
         Nanterre, France: Société d'ethnologie.
  1993 "Are 'Trance,' 'Ecstasy,' and Similar Concepts Appropriate in the
         Study of Shamanism?" *Shaman: An International Journal for Sha-
         manistic Research* 1 (2): 3–25.
  2003 *Chamanismes.* (*Revue Diogène,* no. 396.) Paris: P.U.F.
  2006 "L'idée de 'contact direct avec des esprits' et ses contraintes d'après
         l'exemple de sociétés sibériennes." *Afrique et Histoire* 2 (6): 13–39.
Handler, Richard, ed.
  2004 *Significant Others: Interpersonal and Professional Commitments in
         Anthropology.* Madison: University of Wisconsin Press.
Harrington, Joel Francis
  1995 *Reordering Marriage and Society in Reformation Germany.* Cam-
         bridge: Cambridge University Press.
Harrison, Peter
  2006 "'Science' and 'Religion': Constructing the Boundaries." *Journal of
         Religion* 86 (1): 81–106.
Hartley, Janet
  2008 "Gizhiga: Military Presence and Social Encounters in Russia's Wild
         East." *Slavonic and East European Review* 86 (4): 665–84.
Hartog, Francois
  1988 *The Mirror of Herodotus: The Representation of the Other in the
         Writing of History.* Berkeley: University of California Press.
Harvey, Graham, ed.
  2003 *Shamanism: A Reader.* London: Routledge.
Harvey, Graham, and Robert J. Wallis, eds.
  2007 *Historical Dictionary of Shamanism.* Lanham, Md.: Scarecrow Press.
Hays-Gilpin, Kelley
  2004 *Ambiguous Images: Gender and Rock Art.* Walnut Creek, Calif.:
         AltaMira Press.
Hecht, Jennifer Michael
  2003 *The End of the Soul: Scientific Modernity, Atheism, and Anthropol-
         ogy in France.* New York: Columbia University Press.

Heesen, Anke te
 1997   *Der Weltkasten. Die Geschichte einer Bildenzyklopädie aus dem 18. Jahrhundert.* Göttingen, Germany: Wallstein Verlag.
 2000   "Boxes in Nature." *Studies in History and Philosophy of Science* 31 (3): 381–403.
 2002   *The World in a Box: The Story of an Eighteenth-Century Picture Encyclopedia.* Chicago: University of Chicago Press.
Hellie, Richard
 1982   *Slavery in Russia, 1450–1725.* Chicago: University of Chicago Press.
Herberstein, Sigmund von
 (1530) 1851   *Notes upon Russia: Being a Translation of the Earliest Account of That Country.* Edited by Richard Henry Major. London: Hakluyt Society.
 2008   *Zapiski o Moskovii: v Dvukh Tomakh.* Edited by Anna Leonidovna Khoroshkevich. Moscow: Pamiatniki istoricheskoi mysli.
Herodotus
 2008   *The Histories.* Trans. Robin Waterfield. New York: Oxford University Press.
Hewitt, Roger
 1986.   *Structure, Meaning and Ritual in the Narratives of the Southern San.* Hamburg: H. Buske.
Hiatt, Alfred
 2008   *Terra Incognita: Mapping the Antipodes before 1600.* Chicago: University of Chicago Press.
Hillyar, Anna, and Jane McDermid
 2000   *Revolutionary Women in Russia, 1870–1917: A Study in Collective Biography.* Manchester: Manchester University Press.
Hintzsche, Wieland, and Thomas Nickol, eds.
 1996   *Die Große Nordische Expedition: Georg Wilhelm Steller (1709–1746), ein Lutheraner Erforscht Sibirien und Alaska.* Gotha, Germany: Justus Perthes Verlag.
Hirsch, Francine
 2005   *Empire of Nations: Ethnographic Knowledge and the Making of the Soviet Union.* Ithaca, N.Y.: Cornell University Press.
Hodder, Ian
 1986   *Reading the Past: Current Approaches to Interpretation in Archaeology.* Cambridge: Cambridge University Press.
Hodgen, Margaret T.
 1964   *Early Anthropology in the Sixteenth and Seventeenth Centuries.* Philadelphia: University of Pennsylvania Press.
Hollimon, Sandra E.
 2001   The Gendered Peopling of North America: Addressing the Antiquity of Systems of Multiple Genders." In *The Archaeology of Shamanism.* Edited by Neil Price, 123–34. London: Routledge.
Hooson, David J. M.
 1968   "The Development of Geography in Pre-Soviet Russia." *Annals of the Association of American Geographers* 58 (2): 250–72.

Hughes, Lindsey

    2002   *Peter the Great: A Biography*. New Haven, Conn.: Yale University Press.

Humphrey, Caroline

    1996   *Shamans and Elders: Experience, Knowledge and Power among the Daur Mongols*. Oxford: Clarendon Press.

    2002   *The Unmaking of Soviet Life: Everyday Economies after Socialism*. Ithaca, N.Y.: Cornell University Press.

Hunter, Michael C. W.

    2009   *Boyle: Between God and Science*. New Haven, Conn.: Yale University Press.

Hurel, Arnaud

    2003   "Un prêtre, un savant dans la marche vers l'institutionnalisation de la préhistoire. L'abbé Henri Breuil (1877–1961)." *La Revue pour l'Histoire du CNRS* 8: 2–13.

    2007   *La France préhistorienne de 1789 à 1941*. Paris: CNRS.

    2011   *L'abbé Breuil: un préhistorien dans le siècle*. Paris: CNRS.

Hurel, Arnaud, and Noël Coye, eds.

    2011   *Dans l'épaisseur du temps: Archéologues et géologues inventent la préhistoire*. Paris: Muséum national d'histoire naturelle.

Ibn Fadlan, Ahmad

    2012   *Ibn Fadlan and the Land of Darkness: Arab Travellers in the Far North*. Edited by Paul Lunde and Caroline Stone. London: Penguin.

Idel, Moshe

    1990   *Golem: Jewish Magical and Mystical Traditions on the Artificial Anthropoid*. Albany: State University of New York Press.

Ides, Evert Ysbrants

    1706   *Three Years Travels from Moscow Over-Land to China: Thro' Great Ustiga, Siriania, Permia, Sibiria, Daour, Great Tartary, & to Peking*. London: W. Freeman, J. Walthoe, T. Newborough, J. Nicholson, and R. Parker.

Ides, Evert Ysbrants, Michael Hundt, and Adam Brand

    1999   *Beschreibung der Dreijährigen Chinesischen Reise: die Russische Gesandtschaft von Moskau nach Peking 1692 bis 1695 in den Darstellungen von Eberhard Isbrand Ides und Adam Brand*. Quellen und Studien zur Geschichte des östlichen Europa, Bd. 53. Stuttgart: Steiner.

Impey, Oliver, and Arthur MacGregor, eds.

    2001   *The Origins of Museums: The Cabinet of Curiosities in Sixteenth- and Seventeenth-Century Europe*. London: House of Stratus.

Ingold, Tim

    1995   "People Like Us: The Concept of Anatomically Modern Human." *Cultural Dynamics* 7: 187–214.

Ivanov, Paola

    2002   "Cannibals, Warriors, Conquerors, and Colonizers: Western Perceptions and Azande Historiography." *History in Africa* 29: 89–217.

Janacek, Bruce
   2008   "A Virtuoso's History: Antiquarianism and the Transmission of Knowledge in the Alchemical Studies of Elias Ashmole." *Journal of the History of Ideas* 69 (3): 395–417.
Jochelson, Waldemar
   1908   *The Koryak: Religion and Myths*. Vol. 6 of the *Memoirs of the American Museum of Natural History*. Leiden, Germany/New York: E. J. Brill/G. E. Stechert.
   1910   *The Yukaghir and the Yukaghirized Tungus*. Vol. 9, part 1 of the *Memoirs of the American Museum of Natural History*. Leiden, Germany/New York: E. J. Brill/G. E. Stechert.
   1922   *Pervye dni Narodnoi Voli*. Peterburg: Muzei revoliutsii.
   1924   *The Yukaghir and the Yukaghirized Tungus*. Vol. 9, part 2 of the *Memoirs of the American Museum of Natural History*. Leiden, Germany/New York: E. J. Brill/G. E. Stechert.
   1926   *The Yukaghir and the Yukaghirized Tungus*. Vol. 9, part 3, of the *Memoirs of the American Museum of Natural History*. Leiden, Germany/New York: E. J. Brill/G. E. Stechert.
   1928   *Peoples of Asiatic Russia*. New York: American Museum of Natural History.
   1933   *The Yakut*. Vol. 33 of the Anthropological Papers of the American Museum of Natural History. New York: American Museum of Natural History.
Johns, Adrian
   1999   "Identity, Practice, and Trust in Early Modern Natural Philosophy." *Historical Journal* 42 (4): 1125–45.
Jolly, Karen
   2002   "Witchcraft and Magic in Europe: The Middle Ages." In *Witchcraft and Magic in Europe: The Middle Ages*. Edited by Bengt Ankarloo and Stuart Clark, 1–6. Philadelphia: University of Pennsylvania Press.
Jones, Adrian
   2005   "A Russian Bourgeois' Arctic Enlightenment." *Historical Journal* 48 (3): 623–40.
Jonstonus, Joannes
   1657   *An History of the Wonderful Things of Nature: Set Forth in Ten Severall Classes*. Edited by Andreas Libavius and John Rowland, M.D. London: John Streater.
Jordan, Peter
   2003   *Material Culture and Sacred Landscape: The Anthropology of the Siberian Khanty*. Walnut Creek, Calif.: AltaMira Press.
Jørgensen, Knud Erik, and Per Mouritsen, eds.
   2008   *Constituting Communities: Political Solutions to Cultural Conflict*. New York: Palgrave Macmillan.
Kabir, Ananya Jahanara, and Deanne Williams, eds.
   2005   *Postcolonial Approaches to the European Middle Ages: Translating Cultures*. New York: Cambridge University Press.

Kamen, Henry

    1985   *Inquisition and Society in Spain in the Sixteenth and Seventeenth Centuries*. London: Weidenfeld and Nicolson.

    2005   *Spain, 1469–1714: A Society of Conflict*. Harlow, U.K.: Pearson/Longman.

Kämpfer, Frank, and Reinhardt Frätschner, eds.

    2002   *450 Jahre Sigismund von Herbersteins Rerum Moscoviticarum Commentarii: 1549–1999*. Wiesbaden, Germany: Harrassowitz.

Kan, Sergei

    2008   "Evolutionism and Historical Particularism at the St. Petersburg Museum of Anthropology and Ethnography." *Museum Anthropology* 31 (1): 28–46.

    2009   *Lev Shternberg: Anthropologist, Russian Socialist, Jewish Activist*. Lincoln: University of Nebraska Press.

Kappeler, Andreas

    1972   *Ivan Groznyj im Spiegel der Ausländischen Druckschriften Seiner Zeit. ein Beitrag zur Geschichte des Westlichen Rußlandbildes*. Bern, Switzerland: H. Lang.

    2004   *Die Geschichte Rußlands im 16. und 17. Jahrhundert aus der Perspektive Seiner Regionen*. Wiesbaden, Germany: Harrassowitz.

Karp, S. Ilya, and Larry Wolff

    2001   *Le mirage russe au XVIIIe siècle*. Publications du centre international d'étude du XVIIIe siècle. Vol. 10. Ferney-Voltaire, France: Centre international d'étude du XVIIIe siècle.

Kehoe, Alice Beck

    2000   *Shamans and Religion: An Anthropological Exploration in Critical Thinking*. Prospect Heights, Ill.: Waveland Press.

Kelley, Donald R.

    1996   "The Old Cultural History." *History of the Human Sciences* 9 (3): 101–126.

Kendall, Laurel, ed.

    1997   *Drawing Shadows to Stone: The Photography of the Jesup North Pacific Expedition, 1897–1902*. New York: American Museum of Natural History/University of Washington Press.

Kennan, George

    1870   *Tent Life in Siberia, A New Account of an Old Undertaking. Adventures among the Koraks and Other Tribes in Kamchatka and Northern Asia*. New York: G. P. Putnam.

    1876   "A Dog-Sledge Journey in Kamtschatka and North-Eastern Siberia." *Journal of the American Geographical Society of New York* 8: 96–130.

Kenny, Neil

    1998   *Curiosity in Early Modern Europe: Word Histories*. Wiesbaden, Germany: Harrassowitz.

Khodarkovsky, Michael

    1997   "'Ignoble Savages and Unfaithful Subjects': Constructing Non-Christian Identities in Early Modern Russia." In *Russia's Orient: Imperial Borderlands and Peoples, 1700–1917*. Edited by Daniel R.

Brower and Edward J. Lazzerini, 9–26. Bloomington: Indiana University Press.

2002   *Russia's Steppe Frontier: The Making of a Colonial Empire, 1500–1800*. Bloomington: Indiana University Press.

Kieckhefer, Richard
1998   *Forbidden Rites: A Necromancer's Manual of the Fifteenth Century*. University Park, Pa.: Pennsylvania State University Press.

Kieval, Hillel
1997   "Pursuing the Golem of Prague: Jewish Culture and the Invention of Tradition." *Modern Judaism* 17 (1): 1–23.

Kingsland, Sharon E.
2005   *The Evolution of American Ecology, 1890–2000*. Baltimore: Johns Hopkins University Press.

Kirpichnikov, Anatolii Nikolaevich, and Nicolaas Witsen
1995   *Rossia XVII Veka v Risunkakh i Opisaniakh Gollandskovo Puteshestvennika Nikolaasa Vitsena*. St. Petersburg: Slavia.

Kivelson, Valerie A.
1999   "Cartography, Autocracy and State Powerlessness: The Uses of Maps in Early Modern Russia. *Imago Mundi* 51: 83–105.

2006   *Cartographies of Tsardom: The Land and Its Meanings in Seventeenth-Century Russia*. Ithaca, N.Y.: Cornell University Press.

2008   "'Between All Parts of the Universe': Russian Cosmographies and Imperial Strategies in Early Modern Siberia and Ukraine." *Imago Mundi* 60 (2): 166–81.

Klein, Cecelia F., Eulogio Guzmán, Elisa C. Mandell, and Maya Stanfield-Mazzi
2002   "The Role of Shamanism in Mesoamerican Art: A Reassessment." *Current Anthropology* 43 (3): 383–419.

Kleinbauer, Eugene W.
1970   "Geistesgeschichte and Art History." *Art Journal* 30 (2):148–153.

Klingshirn, William E.
2003   "Isidore of Seville's Taxonomy of Magicians and Diviners." *Traditio* 58: 59–90.

Klug, Ekkehard
1987   "Das 'asiatische' Rußland: über die Entstehung eines europäischen Vorurteils." *Historische Zeitschrift* 245 (2): 265–89.

Koeman, Cornelis
1964   *The History of Abraham Ortelius and His Theatrum Orbis Terrarum*. Lausanne, Switzerland: Sequoia.

Kooijmans, L. P. Louwe, Yuri Smirnov, Ralph S. Solecki, Paola Villa, Thomas Weber, and Robert H. Gargett
1989   "On the Evidence for Neanderthal Burial." *Current Anthropology* 30 (3): 322–30.

Krasheninnikov, Stepan Petrovich
1764   *Of the Nation of the Koreki, The History of Kamtschatka, and the Kurilski Islands, with the Countries Adjacent*. Gloucester, U.K.: R. Raikes, T. Jefferys.

1949   *Opisanie Zemli Kamchatki, s Prilozheniem Raportov, Doneseni i Drugikh Neopublikovannykh Materialov*. Moscow: Izdatelstvo Glavsevmorputi.

Krupnik, Igor
1996   "The 'Bogoraz Enigma': Bounds of Culture and Formats of Anthropologists." In *Grasping the Changing World: Anthropological Concepts in the Postmodern Era*. Edited by Václav Hübinger, 35–52. London: Routledge.

Krupnik, Igor, and William W. Fitzhugh, eds.
2001   *Gateways: Exploring the Legacy of the Jesup North Pacific Expedition, 1897–1902*. Washington, D.C.: Arctic Studies Center, National Museum of Natural History, Smithsonian Institution.

Kurennaia, Irina G.
2007   *Zagadka Nikolaia Vitsena: k Istorii Kartografii Vostochnogo Zabaikalia i ego Stolitsy*. Chita, Russia: Chitinskaia Regionalnaia Organizatsiia Rossiiskogo Obshchestva Istorikov-arkhivistov.

Lantzeff, George V.
1940   "Beginnings of the Siberian Colonial Administration." *Pacific Historical Review*, 9 (1): 47–52.
1943   *Siberia in the Seventeenth Century: A Study of the Colonial Administration*. Berkeley: University of California Press.

Lantzeff, George V., and Richard A. Pierce
1973   *Eastward to Empire. Exploration and Conquest on the Russian Open Frontier to 1750*. Montreal: McGill-Queen's University Press.

Larson, Frances, and Alison Petch, eds.
2007   *Knowing Things: Exploring the Collections at the Pitt Rivers Museum, 1884–1945*. Oxford: Oxford University Press.

Latour, Bruno
1993.   *We Have Never Been Modern*. Cambridge, Mass.: Harvard University Press.

Laufer, Berthold
1915   "The Story of the Pinna and the Syrian Lamb." *Journal of American Folklore* 28 (108): 103–28.

Laugrand, Frédéric
2008   *The Sea Woman: Sedna in Inuit Shamanism and Art in the Eastern Arctic*. Fairbanks: University of Alaska Press.

Layard, John W.
1930   Shamanism: An Analysis Based on Comparison with the Flying Tricksters of Malekula. *Journal of the Royal Anthropological Institute of Great Britain and Ireland* 60: 525–50.

Lefèvre, André
1879   *Philosophy Historical, and Critical*. London: Chapman and Hall.

Leroi-Gourhan, André
1982   *The Dawn of European Art: an Introduction to Paleolithic Cave Painting*. Cambridge: Cambridge University Press.

Lestringant, Frank

1994 *Mapping the Renaissance World: The Geographical Imagination in the Age of Discovery.* Cambridge: Polity Press.

Leuba, Jean-Louis.

1913 La conception de la religion et de la magie, discussion des théories de Durkheim et d'Hubert et Mauss. *Revue Philosophique de la France et de l'Étranger* 76: 337–57.

Levin, Maksim Grigorevich, and Potapov, Leonid Pavlovich

2005 *Zhenshchina i Vozrozhdenie Shamanizma: Postsovetskoe Prostranstvo na Rubezhe Tysiacheletii.* Moscow: Institut etnologii i antropologii.

Levine, Phillippa, ed.

2004 *Gender and Empire.* New York: Oxford University Press.

Lévi-Strauss, Claude

1963 "The Sorcerer and His Magic." In *Structural Anthropology,* 167–85. New York: Basic Books.

Levitt, Marcus C.

1998 "An Antidote to Nervous Juice: Catherine the Great's Debate with Chappe d'Auteroche over Russian Culture." *Eighteenth-Century Studies* 32 (1): 49–63.

Lewis-Williams, David J.

1987 "A Dream of Eland: An Unexplored Component of San Shamanism and Rock Art." *World Archaeology* 19: 165–77.

2002 *A Cosmos in Stone: Interpreting Religion and Society through Rock Art.* Walnut Creek, Calif.: AltaMira Press.

2004 "Consciousness, Intelligence, and Art: A View of the West European Middle to Upper Paleolithic Transition." In *New Perspectives on Prehistoric Art.* Edited by Berghaus, Günter, 11–30. Westport, Conn.: Praeger.

2005 *Inside the Neolithic Mind: Consciousness, Cosmos and the Realm of the Gods.* London: Thames & Hudson.

Lewis-Williams, David J., and Thomas A. Dowson

1988 "The Signs of All Times: Entoptic Phenomena in Upper Paleolithic Art." *Current Anthropology* 29 (2): 201–45.

Lieberman, Victor B., ed.

1999 *Beyond Binary Histories: Re-imagining Eurasia to c.1830.* Ann Arbor: University of Michigan Press.

Lieven, Dominic

2006 *The Cambridge History of Russia.* New York: Cambridge University Press.

Lincoln, W. Bruce

1994 *The Conquest of a Continent: Siberia and the Russians.* New York: Random House.

Lindenau, Ia. I.

1983 *Opisanie Narodov Sibiri: Pervaia Polovina XVIII Veka: Istoriko-Etnograficheskie Materialy o Narodakh Sibiri i Severo-Vostoka.* Magadan, Russia: Magadanskoe knizhnoe izdatelstvo.

Livingstone, David N.

2002 "Race, Space and Moral Climatology: Notes toward a Genealogy." *Journal of Historical Geography* 28 (2): 159–80.

2003 *Putting Science in Its Place: Geographies of Scientific Knowledge.* Chicago: University of Chicago Press.

Loeb, Edwin Meyer

1929 "Shaman and Seer." *American Anthropologist* 31 (1): 60–84.

Loewenson, Leo

1955 "The Works of Robert Boyle and 'The Present State of Russia' by Samuel Collins (1671)." *Slavonic and East European Review* 33 (81): 470–85.

Lomonosov, Mikhail Vasilievich

1794 *Polnoe sobranie sochinenii Mikhaila Vasilievicha Lomonosova.* St. Petersburg: Imperatorskaia Akademia Nauk.

Lorblanchet, Michel, and Paul G. Bahn

2006 *Chamanismes et arts préhistoriques: vision critique.* Paris: Errance.

Luquet, Georges-Henri

1913 "Le problème des origines de l'art et l'art paléolithique." *Revue Philosophique de la France et de l'Étranger* 75: 471–85.

MacDonald, Deanna

2002 "Collecting a New World: The Ethnographic Collections of Margaret of Austria." *Sixteenth Century Journal* 33 (3): 649–63.

MacGregor, Arthur

2001 *The Ashmolean Museum: A Brief History of the Museum and Its Collections.* Oxford: Ashmolean Museum.

Maciej, z Miechowa

(1517) 2009 *Traktat o dvukh Sarmatiiakh/Tractatus de duabus Sarmatiis.* Edited by Sergei Andreevich Kozin. Ryazan, Russia: Aleksandriia.

Marchand, Suzanne L.

1996 *Down from Olympus: Archaeology and Philhellenism in Germany, 1750–1970.* Princeton, N.J.: Princeton University Press.

2009 *German Orientalism in the Age of Empire: Religion, Race, and Scholarship.* Washington, D.C./Cambridge: German Historical Institute/ Cambridge University Press.

Marcos, Sylvia, ed.

2010 *Women and Indigenous Religions.* Santa Barbara, Calif.: Praeger.

Markham, C. R.

1866 "The Arctic Highlanders." *Transactions of the Ethnological Society of London* 4: 125–37.

Marshall, Lorna

1976 *The !Kung of Nyae Nyae.* Cambridge, Mass.: Harvard University Press.

1999 *Nyae Nyae !Kung Beliefs and Rites.* Cambridge, Mass.: Peabody Museum of Archaeology and Ethnology, Harvard University.

Marshall, Peter H.

2006 *The Theatre of the World: Alchemy, Astrology and Magic in Renaissance Prague.* London: Harvell Secker.

Matthews, Washington
    1888   "The Prayer of a Navajo Shaman." *American Anthropologist* 1 (2): 148–71.

Mayer, Sigrid
    1975   *Golem: Die Literarische Rezeption eines Stoffes.* Frankfurt am Main, Germany: P. Lang.

McClellan, James E.
    1985   *Science Reorganized: Scientific Societies in the Eighteenth Century.* New York: Columbia University Press.

McClintock, Anne
    1995   *Imperial Leather: Race, Gender, and Sexuality in the Colonial Contest.* New York: Routledge.

McKinlay, William Laird
    1976   *The Last Voyage of the Karluk: A Survivor's Memoir of Arctic Disaster.* New York: St. Martin's Press.

McLennan, John Ferguson
    (1865) 1970   *Primitive Marriage: An Inquiry into the Origin of the Form of Capture in Marriage Ceremonies.* Chicago: University of Chicago Press.

McMillan, James F.
    1985   *Dreyfus to de Gaulle: Politics and Society in France, 1898–1969.* London: E. Arnold.

Messerschmidt, Daniel Gottlieb
    (1724) 1962–77   *Forschungsreise durch Sibirien, 1720–1727.* Vols. 1–5. Berlin: Akademie Verlag.

Metternich, Tatiana
    2003   *Stroganovy: Istoriia Roda.* St. Petersburg: Aleteiia.

Mezenina, Tatiana Gennadevna, ed.
    2007   *Rod Stroganovykh: Kulturno-Istoricheskie Ocherki.* Ekaterinburg: Izdatelstvo "Sokrat".

Mikhailovskii, V. M., and Oliver Wardrop
    1895   "Shamanism in Siberia and European Russia, Being the Second Part of 'Shamanstvo'." *Journal of the Anthropological Institute of Great Britain and Ireland* 24: 62–100.

Miller (Müller), Gerhard Friedrich
    1750   *Opisanie Sibirskovo Carstva i Vsech Proizsedshikh v Nem Del, ot Nachala a Osoblivo ot Pokorenija Ego.* St. Petersburg.

    1996   *Akademik G. F. Miller—Pervyi Issledovatel Moskvy i Moskovskoi Provintsii.* Moscow: Ianus.

    2006   *Izbrannye Trudy.* Moscow: Ianus-K: Moskovskie uchebniki.

    2009   *Opisanie Sibirskikh Narodov.* Moscow: Pamiatniki istoricheskoi mysli.

Milne, Alan Alexander
    (1926) 1992   *Winnie-the-Pooh.* New York: Puffin Books.

Mirollo, James
    1999   "The Aesthetics of the Marvelous: The Wondrous Work of Art in a Wondrous World." In *Wonders, Marvels, and Monsters in Early*

Modern Culture. Edited by Peter Platt, 24–46. Cranbury, N.J.: University of Delaware Press.

Mitchell, Peter, and Benjamin Smith
2009 *The Eland's People: New Perspectives in the Rock Art of the Moloti-Drakensberg Bushmen: Essays in Memory of Patricia Vinnicombe.* Johannesburg: Wits University Press.

Mithen, Steven
2001 "The Evolution of Imagination: An Archaeological Perspective." *SubStance* 30: 28–54.

Moloney, Pat
2005 "Savages in the Scottish Enlightenment's History of Desire." *Journal of the History of Sexuality* 14 (3): 237–65.

Monakhov, Dmitrii
2009 *Bomba Dlia Tsaria: Okhota na Aleksandra II.* Moscow: Profizdat.

Montesquieu, Charles de Secondat, and John Davidson
1923 *Persian Letters.* London: G. Routledge & Sons.

Moréri, Louis
1701 *The Great Historical, Geographical, Genealogical and Poetical Dictionary. Being a Curious Miscellany of Sacred and Prophane History.* Edited by Jeremy Collier. London: Henry Rhodes.

Morgan, Jennifer L.
1997 "'Some Could Suckle over Their Shoulder': Male Travelers, Female Bodies, and the Gendering of Racial Ideology, 1500–1770." *William and Mary Quarterly,* 3rd ser., 54 (1): 167–92.

Morgan, Lewis Henry
(1877) 1964 *Ancient Society.* Cambridge: Belknap Press/Harvard University Press.

Moro-Abadía, Oscar, and Manuel R. González Morales
2003 "L'art bourgeois de la fin du XIXe siècle face à l'art mobilier paléolithique." *L'Anthropologie* 107 (10): 455–70.
2005 "L'analogie et la représentation de l'art primitif à la fin du XIXe siècle." *L'Anthropologie* 109 (11): 703–21.
2007 "L'art paléolithique est-il un 'art'?: Réflexions autour d'une question d'actualité." *L'Anthropologie* 111 (10): 687–704.

Mortillet, Gabriel de
1849 *Politique et socialisme a la portée de tous.* Paris: E. Désoyé.
1910 *Le préhistoire: origine et antiquité de l'homme.* Paris: Schleicher.

Müller (Miller), Gerhard Friedrich
1732 *Sammlung Russischer Geschichte.* St. Petersburg.
1764 *Voyages from Asia to America, for Completing the Discoveries of the North West Coast of America. To which is Prefixed, a Summary of the Voyages Made by the Russians on the Frozen Sea, in Search of a North East Passage.* London: T. Jefferys.

Mund, Stéphane
2003 *Orbis russiarum: Genèse et développement de la représentation du monde "russe" en occident a la renaissance.* Geneva: Droz.

Münster, Sebastian

1561 *Cosmographei, oder, Beschreibung aller Länder, Herrschafften, Fürnemsten Stetten, Geschichten Gebreüche Hantierungen, etc.* Basel, Switzerland: Henrichum Petri.

Murray, Michael J., and Jeffrey Schloss, eds.

2009 *The Believing Primate: Scientific, Philosophical, and Theological Reflections on the Origin of Religion.* Oxford: Oxford University Press.

Naimark, Norman M.

1983 *Terrorists and Social Democrats: The Russian Revolutionary Movement under Alexander II.* Cambridge, Mass.: Harvard University Press.

Naumov, Igor Vladimirovich, and David Norman Collins, ed.

2006 *The History of Siberia.* London: Routledge.

Nayar, Pramod K.

2008 *English Writing and India, 1600–1920: Colonizing Aesthetics.* New York: Routledge.

Naylor, Simon

2005 "Introduction: Historical Geographies of Science—Places, Contexts, Cartographies." *British Journal for the History of Science* 38 (1): 1–12.

Newman, William R., and Anthony Grafton

2001 *Secrets of Nature: Astrology and Alchemy in Early Modern Europe. Transformations.* Cambridge, Mass.: The MIT Press.

Nirenberg, David

2002 Conversion, Sex, and Segregation: Jews and Christians in Medieval Spain. *American Historical Review* 107 (4): 1065–93.

Nordbladh, Jarl

2005 "Review: San Rock Art, Ethnography and Neuropsychology: Lewis-Williams's Interpretative Approach." *Journal of Southern African Studies* 31 (1): 239–42.

Novakovsky, Stanislaus

1924 "Arctic or Siberian Hysteria as a Reflex of the Geographic Environment." *Ecology* 5 (2): 113–27.

Nozhnikova, Zoia

2010 *Zagadochnaia Moskoviia: Rossiia Glazami Inostrantsev.* Moscow: Astrel.

Olaus, Magnus

1996 *Historia De Gentibus Septentrionalibus: Romæ 1555 (Description of the northern peoples: Rome 1555).* Edited by Peter Fisher, Peter Foote, John Granlund, and Humphrey Higgens. London: Hakluyt Society.

Oldridge, Darren

2005 *Strange Histories: The Trial of the Pig, the Walking Dead, and Other Matters of Fact from the Medieval and Renaissance Worlds.* New York: Routledge.

Olearius, Adam
  1662   *The Voyages and Travels of the Ambassadors Sent by Frederick Duke of Holstein, to the Great Duke of Muscovy, and the King of Persia.* 7 vols. London: Thomas Dring and John Starkey.
Ortelius, Abraham
  1964   *Theatrum Orbis Terrarum: Antwerp, 1570.* Edited by Humphrey Llwyd and Raleigh Ashlin Skelton. Amsterdam: World Publishing.
Ortner, Sherry
  1974   "Is Female to Male as Nature Is to Culture?" In *Women, Culture, and Society.* Edited by Michele Rosaldo and Louise Lamphere, 67–88. Stanford, Calif.: Stanford University Press.
Osler, Margaret J.
  2000   *Rethinking the Scientific Revolution.* Cambridge: Cambridge University Press.
Ostovich, Helen, Graham Roebuck, and Mary V. Silcox, eds.
  2008   *The Mysterious and the Foreign in Early Modern England.* Newark: University of Delaware Press.
Ozment, Steven E.
  1999   *Flesh and Spirit: Private Life in Early Modern Germany.* New York: Viking.
Pagden, Anthony, ed.
  2002   *The Idea of Europe: from Antiquity to the European Union.* New York: Cambridge University Press.
Parkinson, John
  1640   *Theatrum botanicum: The Theater of plants or An herbal of a large extent.* Edited by William Marshall. London: Cotes.
Parry, Graham
  1995   *The Trophies of Time: English Antiquarians of the Seventeenth Century.* Oxford: Oxford University Press.
Paul, Harry W.
  1979   *The Edge of Contingency: French Catholic Reaction to Scientific Change from Darwin to Duhem.* Gainesville: University Presses of Florida.
Pavlov, Pavel Nikolaevich
  1972   *Pushnoi Promysel v Sibiri v XVII Veke.* Krasnoyarsk: Krasnoyarskii Gosudarstvennyi Pedagogičeskii Institut.
  1974   *Promyslovaia Kolonizatsiia Sibiri v XVII Veke.* Krasnoyarsk: Krasnoyarskii Gosudarstvennyi Pedagogičeskii Institut.
Pelkmans, Mathijs, ed.
  2009   *Conversion after Socialism: Disruptions, Modernisms and Technologies of Faith in the Former Soviet Union.* New York: Berghahn Books.
Penn, Nigel
  2005   *The Forgotten Frontier: Colonist and Khoisan on the Cape's Northern Frontier in the 18th Century.* Athens: Ohio University Press.
Perry, John
  1716   *The State of Russia under the Present Czar.* London: B. Tooke.

Peters, Edward
1978   *The Magician, the Witch, and the Law.* Philadelphia: University of Pennsylvania Press.
2001   "The Desire to Know the Secrets of the World." *Journal of the History of Ideas* 62 (4): 593–610.

Peucker, Paul
2006   "'Inspired by Flames of Love": Homosexuality, Mysticism, and Moravian Brothers around 1750." *Journal of the History of Sexuality* 15 (1): 30–64.

Pferschy, Gerhard, ed.
1989   *Siegmund von Herberstein: Kaiserlicher Gesandter und Begründer der Rußlandkunde und die Europäische Diplomatie.* Graz, Austria: Akademische Druck u. Verlagsanstalt.

Pike, Luke Owen
1869   "On the Claims of Women to Political Power." *Journal of the Anthropological Society of London* 7: 47–61.

Poe, Marshall
1995   *Foreign Descriptions of Muscovy: An Analytic Bibliography of Primary and Secondary Sources.* Columbus, OH: Slavica Publishers.
2002   "Sigismund von Herberstein and the Origin of the European Image of Muscovite Government." In *450 Jahre Sigismund von Herbersteins Rerum Moscoviticarum Commentarii: 1549–1999.* Edited by Frank Kämpfer and Reinhardt Frätschner, 131–72. Wiesbaden, Germany: Harrassowitz Verlag.

Poe, Marshall, ed.
2003   *Early Exploration of Russia.* London: Routledge.

Pokrovskii, Nikolai Nikolaevich
2006   *Obshchestvennoe Soznanie Naseleniia Rossii po Otechestvennym Narrativnym Istochnikam: Sbornik Nauchnykh Trudov.* Novosibirsk: SO RAN.

Portal, Roger
1958   "La Russes en Sibérie au XVII siècle." *Revue d'Histoire Moderne et Contemporaine* 5 (1): 5–38.

Proctor, Robert, and Londa L. Schiebinger, eds.
2008   *Agnotology: The Making and Unmaking of Ignorance.* Stanford, Calif.: Stanford University Press.

Purchas, Samuel
1613   *Purchas his Pilgrimage, or, Relations of the World and the Religions Obserued in all Ages and Places Discouered, from the Creation vnto this present. In foure partes.* London: William Stansby for Henrie Fetherstone.

Purš, Ivo, ed.
2011   *Alchymie a Rudolf II: Hledání Tajemství Přírody ve Střední Evrope v 16. a 17. Století.* Prague: Artefactum.

Pypin, Aleksander Nikolaevich
1891   *Istoria Russkoi Etnografii.* St. Petersburg: Tip. M. M. Stasliulevicha.

Raeff, Marc
    1982   "Seventeenth-Century Europe in Eighteenth-Century Russia?" *Slavic Review* 41 (4): 611–19.
Raskov, Danila
    2008   "Economic Thought in Muscovy: Ownership, Money and Trade." In *Economics in Russia: Studies in Intellectual History.* Edited by Vincent Barnett and Joachym Zweynert, 7–23. Burlington, Vt.: Ashgate.
Rees, Abraham
    1805   *Universal Dictionary of Arts, Sciences, and Literature.* Philadelphia: Samuel F. Bradford and Murray, Fairman and Co.
Rees, Tobias
    2010   "Being Neurologically Human Today: Life and Science and Adult Cerebral Plasticity (an Ethical Analysis)." *American Ethnologist* 37 (1): 150–66.
Reinach, Salomon
    1899   "Gabriel de Mortillet." *Revue Historique* 1: 67–95.
    1903   "L'art et la magie. Les peintures et des gravures de l'âge du renne." *L'Anthropologie* 14: 257–66.
    1905   *Cultes, Mythes et Religions.* Paris: E. Leroux.
Renfrew, Colin
    1994   "Towards a cognitive archaeology." In *The Ancient Mind: Elements of Cognitive Archaeology.* Edited by Colin Renfrew and Ezra B. W. Zubrow, 3–13. Cambridge: Cambridge University Press.
Rennie, Bryan S.
    2007   *The International Eliade.* Albany: State University of New York Press.
Rethmann, Petra
    2001   *Tundra Passages: History and Gender in the Russian Far East.* University Park: Pennsylvania State University Press.
Richard, Natalie
    1989   "La revue 'L'Homme' de Gabriel de Mortillet—anthropologie et politique au début de la troisième République." *Bulletin et Mémoire: Société d'Anthropologie de Paris* 1: 231–55.
    1992   *L'invention de la préhistoire: Anthologie.* Paris: Presses Pocket.
    2008   *Inventer la préhistoire: Débuts de l'archéologie préhistorique.* Paris: Vuibert.
Richards, Robert J.
    2002   *The Romantic Conception of Life: Science and Philosophy in the Age of Goethe.* Chicago: University of Chicago Press.
Robb, John E.
    1998   "The Archaeology of Symbols." *Annual Review of Anthropology* 27: 329–46.
Rousse-Lacordaire, J.
    2010   *Une controverse sur la magie et la kabbale a la Renaissance.* Geneva: Droz.
Schiebinger, Londa L.
    1990   "The Anatomy of Difference: Race and Sex in Eighteenth-Century Science." *Eighteenth-Century Studies* 23 (4): 387–405.

2004a "Feminist History of Colonial Science." *Hypatia*, 19 (1): 233–54.
2004b *Nature's Body: Gender in the Making of Modern Science.* New Brunswick, N.J.: Rutgers University Press.

Schimmel, Annemarie
2011 *Mystical Dimensions of Islam.* Edited by Carl W. Ernst. Chapel Hill: University of North Carolina Press.

Schmidt, Leigh Eric
1998 "From Demon Possession to Magic Show: Ventriloquism, Religion, and the Enlightenment." *Church History* 67 (2): 275.

Schmitz, Siegfried, ed.
1926 *Sippurim: Präger Sammlung Jüdischer Legenden.* Wien, Germany: R. Löwit.

Schrader, Abby M.
2007 "Unruly Felons and Civilizing Wives: Cultivating Marriage in the Siberian Exile System, 1822–1860." *Slavic Review* 66 (2): 230–56.

Seniukova, N. L., ed.
2001 *Otkrytie Sibiri: Nemetskie Issledovateli Sibiri XVIII–XIX vv.* Tomsk, Russia: Tomskii Oblastnoi Kraevedcheskii Muzei.

Sewall, May Wright
1882 "The Idea of the Home." *Journal of Speculative Philosophy* 16 (3): 274–85.

Shambarov, Valerii
2010 *Rozhdenie Tsarstva: Mifa i Pravda ob Ivane Groznom.* Moscow: Eksmo, Algoritm.

Shanks, Michael
1987 *Re-constructing Archaeology: Theory and Practice.* Cambridge: Cambridge University Press.

Shapin, Steven
1985 *Leviathan and the Air-Pump: Hobbes, Boyle, and the Experimental Life.* Cambridge: Cambridge University Press.

Shea, John J.
2011 "Homo Sapiens Is as Homo Sapiens Was, Behavioral Variability versus 'Behavioral Modernity' in Paleolithic Archaeology." *Current Anthropology* 52 (1): 1–35.

Shell, Marc
1991 "*Marranos* (Pigs), or from Coexistence to Toleration." *Critical Inquiry*, 17 (2): 306–35.

Shirokogorov, Sergei Mikhailovich
1966 *Social Organization of the Northern Tungus, with Introductory Chapters Concerning Geographical Distribution and History of These Groups.* Oosterhout, the Netherlands: Anthropological Publications.

Shternberg, Lev Iakovlevich
1933 *Giliaki, Orochi, Goldy, Negidaltsy, Ainy. Stati i Materialy.* Kharabovsk: Dalgiz.
1936 *Pervobytnaia Religia v Svete Etnografii: Issledovania, Statii, Lektsii.* Leningrad: Izdatelstvo Insituta Narodov Severa.

Shunkov, Viktor Ivanovich
  1946 *Ocherki po Istorii Kolonizatsii Sibiri v XVII–Nachale XVIII Vekov.*
        Moscow: Akademia nauk SSSR.
Sidky, Homayun
  2010 "On the Antiquity of Shamanism and Its Role in Human Religiosity."
        Method and Theory in the Study of Religion 22: 68–92.
  2008 *Haunted by the Archaic Shaman: Himalayan Jhākris and the Dis-
        course on Shamanism.* Lanham, MD: Lexington Books.
Skotnes, Pippa
  2007 *Claim to the Country: The Archive of Lucy Lloyd and Wilhelm Bleek.*
        Athens: Ohio University Press.
Skrynnikov, Ruslan G.
  1986 *Sibirskaia Ekspeditsiia Ermaka.* Novosibirsk, Russia: Nauka.
  2008 *Ermak.* Moscow: Molodaia Gvardiia.
Slack, Paul, and Joanna Innes
  1992 "The Cultural and Political Construction of Europe: Foreword." *Past
        and Present* 137: 3–7.
Slezkine, Yuri
  1994a *Arctic Mirrors: Russia and the Small Peoples of the North.* Ithaca,
         N.Y.: Cornell University Press.
  1994b "Naturalists versus Nations: Eighteenth-Century Russian Scholars
         Confront Ethnic Diversity." *Representations* 47: 170–95.
Slocum, John W.
  1998 "Who, and When, Were the Inorodtsy? The Evolution of the Cate-
        gory of 'Aliens' in Imperial Russia." *Russian Review* 57 (2):
        173–90.
Small, Margaret
  2007 "From Jellied Seas to Open Waterways: Redefining the North-
        ern Limit of the Knowable World." *Renaissance Studies* 21 (3):
        315–39.
Smith, Pamela H.
  2009 "Science on the Move: Recent Trends in the History of Early Modern
        Science." *Renaissance Quarterly* 62 (2): 345–75.
Smith, Pamela H., and Paula Findlen, eds.
  2002 *Merchants and Marvels: Commerce, Science, and Art in Early Mod-
        ern Europe.* New York: Routledge.
Snead, James
  2001 *Ruins and Rivals: The Making of Southwest Archaeology.* Tucson:
        University of Arizona Press.
Solomon, Anne
  2011 "Writing San Histories: The /Xam and 'Shamanism' Revisited." *Jour-
        nal of Southern African Studies* 37 (1): 99–117.
Sommer, Marianne
  2006 "Mirror, Mirror on the Wall: Neanderthal as Image and 'Distortion'
        in Early 20th-Century French Science and Press." *Social Studies of Sci-
        ence* 36: 207–40.

Sörlin, Sverker
2000   "Ordering the World for Europe: Science as Intelligence and Informa-
        tion as Seen from the Northern Periphery." *Osiris,* 2nd ser., 15: 51–69.
Sparwenfeld, Johan Gabriel, and Ulla Birgegård
2002   *J. G. Sparwenfeld's Diary of a Journey to Russia, 1684–87.* Stock-
        holm: Kungl. Vitterhets Historien och Antikvitets Akademien.
Ssorin-Chaikov, Nikolai
2003   *The Social Life of the State in Subarctic Siberia.* Stanford, Calif.:
        Stanford University Press.
Steller, Georg Wilhelm
(1743) 2003   *Steller's History of Kamchatka: Collected Information Con-
        cerning the History of Kamchatka, Its Peoples, Their Manners,
        Names, Lifestyle, and Various Customary Practices.* Edited by
        Marvin W. Falk, trans. by Margritt Engel and Karen Willmore.
        Fairbanks: University of Alaska Press.
Steller, Georg Wilhelm, Jean-Benoît Schérer, and Gerard Fridrikh Miller
1774   *Georg Wilhelm Stellers Beschreibung von dem Lande Kamtschatka,
        Dessen Einwohnern, Deren Sitten, Nahmen, Lebensart und Verschie-
        denen Gewohnheiten.* Frankfurt und Leipzig: J. G. Fleischer.
Stoler, Ann Laura
1995   *Race and the Education of Desire: Foucault's History of Sexuality and
        the Colonial Order of Things.* Durham, N.C.: Duke University Press.
Strahlenberg, Phillip Johann Tabbert von
1736   *An Histori-Geographical Description of the North and Eastern Part
        of Europe and Asia. But More Particularly of Russia, Siberia, and
        Great Tartary.* London.
(1736) 1970   *Russia, Siberia, and Great Tartary.* New York: Arno Press.
Subrahmanyam, Sanjay
1997   "Connected Histories: Notes towards a Reconfiguration of Early
        Modern Eurasia." *Modern Asian Studies* 31: 735–62.
Sunderland, Willard
1996   "Russians into Iakuts? 'Going native' and Problems of Russian Na-
        tional Identity in the Siberian North, 1870s–1914." *Slavic Review* 55
        (4): 806–25.
2004   *Taming the Wild Field: Colonization and Empire on the Russian
        Steppe.* Ithaca, N.Y.: Cornell University Press.
2007   "Imperial Space: Territorial Thought and Practice in the Eighteenth
        Century." In *Russian Empire: Space, People, Power, 1700–1930.* Ed-
        ited by Jane Burbank, Mark von Hagen, and Alex Remnev, 33–66.
        Bloomington: Indiana University Press.
Tatishchev, Vasilii N.
1950   *Izbrannye Trudy po Geografii Rossii.* Moscow: Gossudarstvennoe Iz-
        datelstvo Geograficheskoi Literatury.
Tedlock, Barbara
2005   *The Woman in the Shaman's Body: Reclaiming the Feminine in Reli-
        gion and Medicine.* New York: Bantam Books.

Teissier, Beatrice
 2011 *Russian Frontiers: Eighteenth-Century British Travellers in the Caspian, Caucasus and Central Asia.* Oxford, England: Signal Books.
Templing, V., ed.
 2004 *Iz Istorii Obdorskoi Missii.* Tyumen, Russia: Mandr i Ka.
Thomas, Keith
 1971 *Religion and the Decline of Magic.* New York: Scribner.
Thomas, Nicholas, and Caroline Humphrey, eds.
 1994 *Shamanism, History, and the State.* Ann Arbor: University of Michigan Press.
Thorndike, Lynn
 1923 *A History of Magic and Experimental Science.* New York: Macmillan.
Titov, Andrei Alexandrovich
 1890 *Sibir v XVII Veke: Sbornik Starinnykh Russkikh Statei o Sibiri i Prilezhashchikh k nei Zemliakh.* Edited by Gennadii Vasilievich Iudin. Moscow: Tip. L. i A. Snegirevykh.
Tokarev, Sergei Aleksandrovich
 1966 *Istoria Russkoi Etnografii. Dooktiabrskii Period.* Moscow: Nauka.
Trigger, Bruce
 2006 *A History of Archaeological Thought.* 2nd ed. Cambridge: Cambridge University Press.
Tryon, Alice
 1957 "The Vegetable Lamb of Tartary." *American Fern Journal* 47 (1): 1–7.
Tuana, Nancy, and Shannon Sullivan
 2006 "Introduction: Feminist Epistemologies of Ignorance." *Hypatia* 21 (3): vii–ix.
Tugolukov, Vladillen Aleksandrovich
 1985 *Tungusy (Evenki i Eveny) Srednei i Zapadnoi Sibiri.* Moscow: Nauka.
Tylor, Edward B.
 1870 "The Philosophy of Religion among the Lower Races of Mankind." *Journal of the Ethnological Society of London* 2 (4): 369–81.
Van Deusen, Kira
 2001 *The Flying Tiger: Women Shamans and Storytellers of the Amur.* Montreal: McGill-Queen's University Press.
Vermeulen, Hans F., and Arturo Alvarez Roldan, eds.
 1995 *Fieldwork and Footnotes: Studies in the History of European Anthropology.* London: Routledge.
Vickers, Brian, ed.
 1984 *Occult and Scientific Mentalities in the Renaissance.* New York: Cambridge University Press.
Vinnicombe, Patricia
 1976 *People of the Eland: Rock Paintings of the Drakensberg Bushmen as a Reflection of Their Life and Thought.* Pietermaritzburg, South Africa: University of Natal Press.

Vitebsky, Piers
  2005   *Reindeer People: Living with Animals and Spirits in Siberia.* London: HarperCollins.
Vvedenskii, Alexander A.
  1962   *Dom Stroganovykh v XVI–XVII Vekakh.* Moscow: Izdatelstvo Sotsialno-ekonomicheskoi literatury.
Weeks, Theodore R.
  2011   *Across the Revolutionary Divide: Russia and the USSR, 1861–1945.* Malden, Mass.: Wiley-Blackwell.
Weintroub, Jill
  2009   "Sisters at the Rockface—the Van der Riet Twins and Dorothea Bleek's Rock Art Research and Publishing, 1932–1940." *African Studies* 68 (3): 402–28.
Werth, Paul W.
  2000a "From 'Pagan' Muslims to 'Baptized' Communists: Religious Conversion and Ethnic Particularity in Russia's Eastern Provinces." *Comparative Studies in Society and History* 42 (3): 497–523.
  2000b "From Resistance to Subversion: Imperial Power, Indigenous Opposition, and Their Entanglement." *Kritika* 1 (1): 21–43.
Wessels, Michael
  2009   "Reading the Hartebeest: A Critical Appraisal of Roger Hewitt's Interpretation of the /Xam Narratives." *Research in African Literatures* 40 (2): 82–108.
  2010   *Bushman Letters: Interpreting /Xam Narrative.* Johannesburg: Witwatersrand University Press.
White, Randall
  2003   *Prehistoric Art: The Symbolic Journey of Humankind.* New York: Harry N. Abrams.
White, Richard
  1992   "Discovering Nature in North America." *Journal of American History* 79 (3): 874–91.
Whitehead, Neil L.
  1995   "The Historical Anthropology of Text: The Interpretation of Ralegh's *Discoverie of Guiana.*" *Current Anthropology* 36 (1): 53–74.
Whitley, David
  1992   "Prehistory and Post-Positivist Science: A Prolegomenon to Cognitive Archaeology." *Archaeological Method and Theory* 4: 57–100.
  2009   *Cave Paintings and the Human Spirit: The Origin of Creativity and Belief.* Amherst, N.Y.: Prometheus Books.
Whittaker, Cynthia H., Robert H. Davis, and E. Kasinec, eds.
  2003   *Russia Engages the World, 1453–1825.* Cambridge, Mass.: Harvard University Press.
Wiesner, Merry E.
  2010   *Christianity and Sexuality in the Early Modern World: Regulating Desire, Reforming Practice.* New York: Routledge.

Willerslev, Rane

2007   *Soul Hunters: Hunting, Animism, and Personhood among the Siberian Yukaghirs.* Berkeley: University of California Press.

Wilson, Francesca

1970   *Muscovy Russia through Foreign Eyes, 1553–1900.* New York: Praeger.

Wilson, Stephen

2000   *The Magical Universe: Everyday Ritual and Magic in Premodern Europe.* London: Hambledon and London.

Winkelman, Michael

2010   *Shamanism: A Biopsychosocial Paradigm of Consciousness and Healing.* Santa Barbara, Calif.: Praeger.

Winter, Eduard

1953   *Halle Als Ausgangspunkt der Deutschen Rußland Künde im 18. Jahrhundert.* Berlin: Akademie Verlag.

Wintle, Michael J.

2009   *The Image of Europe: Visualizing Europe in Cartography and Iconography throughout the Ages.* New York: Cambridge University Press.

Witsen, Nicolaas

1996   *Puteshestvie v Moskoviu, 1664–1665: Dnevnik.* Edited by V. G. Trisman. St. Petersburg: Simpozium.

Wittkower, Rudolf

1942   "Marvels of the East: A Study in the History of Monsters." *Journal of the Warburg and Courtauld Institutes* 5: 159–97.

1977   *Allegory and the Migration of Symbols.* London: Thames and Hudson.

Witzenrath, Christoph

2007   *Cossacks and the Russian Empire, 1598–1725: Manipulation, Rebellion and Expansion into Siberia.* London: Routledge.

Wolff, Larry, and Marco Cipolloni

2007   *The Anthropology of the Enlightenment.* Stanford, Calif.: Stanford University Press.

Woodhead, Christine, ed.

2012   *The Ottoman World.* New York: Routledge.

Yapp, M. E.

1992   "Europe in the Turkish Mirror." *Past and Present* 137: 134–55.

Yates, Frances Amelia

1975   *The Rosicrucian Enlightenment.* St. Albans, U.K.: Paladin.

Zaborov, Petr Romanovich

2011   *Voltaire dans la culture russe.* Ferney-Voltaire, France: Centre international d'étude du XVIIIe siècle.

Zeeberg, Jaap Jan

2005   *Into the Ice Sea: Barents' Wintering on Novaya Zemlya. A Renaissance Voyage of Discovery.* Amsterdam: Rozenberg.

Zeldin, Theodore, ed.

1970   *Conflicts in French Society: Anticlericalism, Education and Morals in the Nineteenth Century: Essays.* London: Allen and Unwin.

Zelenin, Dimitry Konstantinovich

1999 *Izbrannye Trudy. Stati po Dukhovnoi Kulture, 1917–1934.* Moscow: Izdatelstvovo Indrik.

Znamenski, Andrei A.

1999 *Shamanism and Christianity: Native Encounters with Russian Orthodox Missions in Siberia and Alaska, 1820–1917.* Westport, Conn.: Greenwood Press.

2007 *The Beauty of the Primitive: Shamanism and the Western Imagination.* Oxford: Oxford University Press.

Index

Page numbers followed by an italic *fig.* indicate images.

vegetable lamb (Barometz), 31–36,
205n37
Vermeulen, Hans F., 80
Vinnicombe, Patricia, 191
Vogul people, 64–67
Völker-Beschreibung, 80
Voltaire, 112

Whitehead, Neil, 209n17
Winnie-the-Pooh (Milne), 16–17
Witsen, Nicolaas, 88, 97*fig.*, 206n2
women. *See* female shamans; gender;
sexuality
wonder, 32–36, 47

writers' perspectives. *See* projections of
writers' views

Yakimova, Anna, 149–51
Yakut people, 71; changed women shamans
of, 152–54; houses of, 147*fig.*; hysteria
among, 157–58; Jochelson's writing on,
147*fig.*, 152, 157; photos of, 152*fig.*;
two categories of shamans of, 151–53
Yates, Frances, 51
Yukagir people. *See* Yakut people

Zelenin, Dimitrii, 160, 219n50
zoology, 101